DECKS

DECKS

How to Design and Build the Perfect Deck for Your Home

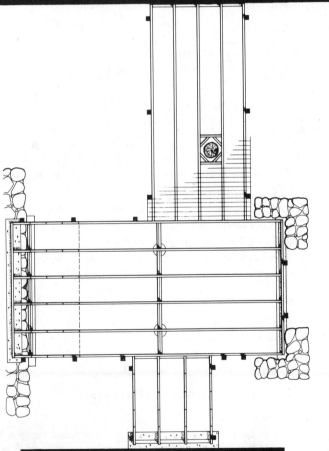

TIM SNYDER
Coauthor, *The New Yankee Workshop*

Rodale Press, Emmaus, Pennsylvania

Copyright ©1991 by Tim Snyder

Printed in the United States of America on acid-free ⊗, recycled ♻ paper

Senior Managing Editor: Margaret Lydic Balitas
Editor: David Schiff
Copy Editor: Sally L. Schaffer
Editorial/Administrative Assistant: Stacy A. Brobst

Cover Design: Linda Brightbill
Book Design: Acey Lee
Book Layout: Lisa Carpenter
Cover Photography: Donna H. Chiarelli
Drawings: Vince Babak

Black and White Photography:
Tim and Barbara Snyder, except for the following: Photo 4-1, J. Michael Kanouff; Photos 4-2, 4-8, and 4-12, Carmine Presti; Photos 1-6, 1-8, and 1-11, courtesy of the California Redwood Association; Photos 7-14 and 7-15, Jeff Snyder; Photos 9-1 and 9-4, Carl Weese; Photos, page 224, 10-3, 10-4, and 10-5, courtesy of TerraDek; Photo, page 194, Muffy Kibbey; Photo, page 204, David Schiff; Photo, page 214, courtesy of Kop-Coat, Inc.

Project Designers and Builders:
Deck with Aboveground Pool: design and construction by Blue Ridge Construction.
Second-Story Deck: design and construction by Julian Hodges.
Raised-Ranch Deck: design by Vince Babak.
Deck Trellis: design by Paul Douglas; construction by Phillip Welter.
Steep-Site Deck: design by Louis Alley; construction by Ralph Tondre.

If you have any questions or comments concerning this book, please write:

Rodale Press
Book Reader Service
33 East Minor Street
Emmaus, PA 18098

Library of Congress Cataloging-in-Publication Data

Snyder, Tim.
    Decks : how to design and build the perfect deck for your home /
Tim Snyder.
        p.   cm.
    Includes bibliographical references and index.
    ISBN 0–87857–949–4 hardcover
    ISBN 0–87857–955–9 paperback
    1. Decks (Architecture, Domestic)—Design and construction—
—Amateurs' manuals.   I. Title.
TH4970.S68   1991
690'.89--dc20   90–25479
                                                                                CIP

Distributed in the book trade by St. Martin's Press

        6 8 10 9 7   hardcover
               10 9   paperback

To my father, Bill Snyder, who taught me that any job worth doing is worth doing well; and to Cecil Goodfellow, my grandfather, who patiently put tools in a child's hands in hopes that he might someday become a carpenter.

CONTENTS

ACKNOWLEDGMENTS

One thing you learn early as a carpenter is that good work doesn't come easily. It's not difficult to throw a project together, aiming for speed and expediency. But to do an exemplary job, you need to design and plan carefully, select the best materials you can afford, and then use good tools and sound techniques through each phase of construction.

Good books also take plenty of work to produce. For their cooperation and support, I'd like to acknowledge the California Redwood Association, the Southern Forest Products Association, the Stanley Tool Corporation, Black & Decker, and the Simpson Strong-Tie Company. I'm also grateful to Allen Enterprises and to my friends at the Nazareth Hardware Store here in Pennsylvania. Special thanks go to Tom Richmond, Eli Sutton, Paul Spring, Bill Feist, and Jack Mosher for sharing their knowledge and enthusiasm.

Book designer Acey Lee and editor David Schiff teamed up to give form and focus to my collection of text, photos, and drawings. Vince Babak, the artist, proved to be a great friend as well as an exceptional talent as he brought my sketches to life.

CHAPTER *1*

DESIGNING YOUR DECK

It's not difficult to understand why decks have become so popular. Building a deck is one of the least expensive ways to expand your living space. Instead of the concrete foundation walls, sheathing, insulation, drywall, and roof shingles that go into an addition, a deck requires little more than dimension lumber—posts, beams, joists, decking, and railings. There's a catch, of course. Decks are *outdoor rooms*. Rather than shelter us from the outdoor environment, decks are meant to enhance our enjoyment of being outside.

Several factors separate decks that are merely ordinary or adequate from decks that are outstanding: good design, sound construction, well-crafted details, and smart maintenance. This book is organized to cover every aspect of deck design, construction, and care. Working through the book, you'll learn about different types of wood that can be used in deck construction. Corrosion-resistant fasteners are covered, as well as special hardware that can speed the work of deck joinery and strengthen the joints themselves. There are quite a few different foundation details for decks, so you'll need

to evaluate the options shown in chapter 5. You'll also learn about different types of railings and stairways and about choosing decking boards. Electrical wiring and deck maintenance are other important factors in the equation that yields extraordinary decks.

This chapter is about planning a deck. Long before lumber arrives at the site and sawdust starts to accumulate, careful planning must occur to ensure a deck's success. In this chapter, we'll explore the broad range of possibilities that exist in designing a deck. We'll also discuss how to prepare plan, elevation, and detail drawings. One of the benefits of good planning is that mistakes and difficulties can turn up on the drawing board instead of on the site. This saves time, money, and aggravation.

LOOKING AT DECKS

One of the best ways to get deck design ideas is to look at as many different decks as possible. Many neighborhoods and new developments offer good deck-viewing opportunities, and this is a nice excuse for a drive or a bike trip. You can add to your design file by clipping photos of interesting decks that appear in magazines. And throughout this book, you'll see all kinds of decks in a wide variety of sizes and shapes. Deck design is remarkably open-ended. As long as you comply with local building codes, there's little to limit a deck's size, shape, and style.

Decks can do a lot of things. A deck built off the living room serves as overflow space when entertaining guests. It can also be a quiet place to read or sunbathe. When built off a children's playroom or den, a deck becomes a play area that's flatter and cleaner than the yard. A deck can even take the place of an absent or unusable backyard. Houses built on steep sites are good candidates for decks. So are beach houses that are surrounded by sand instead of grass.

Adding a barbecue grill and picnic table to a deck makes it an outdoor eating area. Hot tubs or spas usually require decks around them for safety, convenience, and privacy. A deck can be built to cover or replace an existing terrace or walkway, or it can be built to establish new paths and gathering areas. Decks can function well as transitional elements, linking the house with part or all of the yard, expanding an entry, or providing access to a pool, spa, or gazebo. They can also be small and self-contained, such as a balcony-style deck that might be built off an upstairs apartment.

CONSIDERING THE LANDSCAPE

Integration is a key word in deck design. It's not enough for a deck to match the house that it serves. The deck should also be a part of the surrounding landscape. It's a common mistake to put a high degree of craftsmanship into a deck, while disregarding the need to plant new grass or shrubs, put down gravel, or relocate a garden area in response to the new structure. A deck is part house and part landscape; it bridges the gap between the man-made environment and the natural environment. So when designing a deck, it's critical to integrate the deck with an overall landscape plan. A few common landscape treatments are discussed below.

When a deck is built at or near grade level, there are several ways to handle the transition between deck and lawn. The simplest way is to let the lawn run right up against the deck. This means that care should be taken to protect the grass during construction. Alternatively, it's possible to cre-

Photo 1–1: Good landscaping will make a significant difference in any deck design. Washed gravel makes an excellent ground cover beneath elevated decks like this one. Bushes, planted in a bed of wood chips, will enhance the deck's appearance as they mature. Design and construction by Allen Enterprises

ate a garden border along all or part of the deck perimeter. Bark chips make a nice ground cover for a perimeter garden, but they need to be confined within a border (bricks, landscape timbers, or vinyl edging) that separates the lawn from the garden. To protect the garden (especially if there are children around) you may need to incorporate a perimeter railing in the deck design.

Gravel can be very helpful in finishing off the areas underneath and around a deck. When a deck is elevated above the ground, the area beneath the deck will usually look much better if it's covered by several inches of washed gravel. White granite gravel, smooth beach stone, or colored gravel can be used, depending on taste and availability. Unlike bare earth or grass, the gravel cover won't show the linear drainage pattern between decking boards.

To prevent vegetation from growing underneath a deck, you can spray this area with an herbicide. Another option is to install a polyethylene sheet beneath the gravel layer. Trim the sheet carefully where the gravel meets the lawn. For appearance and ease of maintenance, use vinyl edging or some other edge treatment to separate the graveled area from the lawn.

If there's sufficient headroom beneath an elevated deck, you might consider using it as a storage area for firewood, garden tools, recycling containers, or other items. When the area beneath the deck is more like a crawl space, lattice panels can be installed between foundation posts to hide this under-deck area from view.

Another way to hide an under-deck area is to plant shrubs or low-growing bushes at the edge of a deck. Holly, privet, yew, juniper, barberry,

Scotch heather, boxwood, and coto- neaster are just a few of the shrubs that can be used alone or in combinations to enhance a deck with color, texture, and form. To find out what species will do best in your geographical area, con- sult a knowledgeable nursery owner or your state agricultural extension service.

SUN, SHADE, AND SHELTER

Still another way to integrate a deck with the landscape is to build the deck partially or fully around a tree. Trees with trunk diameters under about 1½ feet aren't difficult to frame completely around, but it's important to build in room for decking boards to be trimmed as the tree grows (See

Photo 1–2: Privacy and shade were priorities in the design of this deck. The trellis creates a dense grid of shade. Its three support beams are attached to the house wall and suspended from it with three cables. The solid board fence provides maximum privacy.

Photo 1–3: Metal railings provide safety while obstructing the view as little as possible. On this shore property, trees were selectively thinned as part of the landscape plan, balancing the desire for dramatic vistas against the need for shade and privacy.

"Entry Deck to Stone House" on page 204).

If your deck site lacks shade, you might consider incorporating a trellis in the deck design. With its layering of overlapping boards, a trellis provides visual interest as well as shade. You can control the shading effect of a trellis by using different size members or different spacings between members. Training honeysuckle, clematis, or another vine across a trellis adds shade as well as fragrance. To create a private corner of shade on the deck, consider combining a trellis with a privacy screen. For movable shade, try an umbrella mounted in a table that has a weighted base.

Awnings offer another option for shading a deck. There are retractable awnings available, and these are popular in regions where bright, sunny days aren't a year-round phenomenon. These awnings shouldn't be used where high winds occur frequently. A permanent awning might be a good choice in sunny regions, but the expense of erecting a permanent support structure for an awning approaches the cost of framing a conventional roof over all or part of the deck.

THE HOUSE CONNECTION

If your deck will be attached to the house, the connection between house and deck is an important design factor. In some situations, deck access already exists in the form of an exterior door. But to make the most of a deck addition, you may want to transform a nondescript single door into a set of sliding glass doors or hinged double doors with glass panels (sometimes called French doors).

If no access exists, it's possible to remove an existing window and expand the window opening to accom-modate a door. This is usually an economical option, since the window opening will already have a header that might be used for the doorway. If there aren't any windows to transform into doors, then a new doorway will need to be added from scratch.

Whatever the existing conditions, the important thing is to integrate the planned deck with the house. To make the deck a true outdoor room, you need to blur the distinction between interior and exterior space. Sliding glass doors, double doors with large expanses of insulated glass, or even glass-paneled single doors help in this regard.

PRIVACY, EXTERIOR ACCESS, AND TRAFFIC FLOW

The privacy of a deck and deck access from outside the house are related considerations. Some decks are meant to be open and easily accessible, while others require limited access and more privacy. On larger decks or multi-level decks, one section (or level) may need to be private, while the other remains open.

Steps, stairways, railings, and privacy screens are elements that can be used to adjust both access and privacy in a deck design (see chapter 7 for more specific details on railings and stairways). For example, a deck built off a second-story bedroom can probably do without an exterior stairway to ground level. On the other hand, an elevated deck off the living room will probably need a stairway to connect it with the yard. Unlike the stairways that are built inside a house, a deck's stairway can be as wide as you'd like to make it. On decks built close to ground level, it's even possible to eliminate a conventional stairway in favor of a broad cascade of steps that form all or part of the deck perimeter. Steps like this function easily as a seating area or as a place to display potted plants. For wheelchair access, a ramp will need to be built instead of a stairway or in addition to one.

The location of stairways or steps on a deck is important, since it will affect traffic flow on and around the deck. When planning the deck, you should map out major routes between the deck, house, backyard, driveway, and other frequent destinations. Also note areas (such as a clothesline or propane tank) from which you'd like to divert attention. Depending on stairway or step location, the house-to-yard route can involve just a few steps on the deck. Or you can lengthen deck

travel by placing the stairway farther away from the exterior door that opens onto the deck. Planned locations for picnic tables, built-in benches, and barbecue grills should be kept clear of traffic routes (see Drawing 1-1 below).

On stairways and elevated decks, railings are required safety features. On ground-level decks, railings can be used to limit access and control deck traffic. In situations where a deck will be located close to the street or to another house, it might be a good idea to use a privacy screen instead of a railing. Remember, however, that screens will also restrict your view beyond the deck. By adjusting the height and density of the screen, you can achieve the right balance of privacy and view.

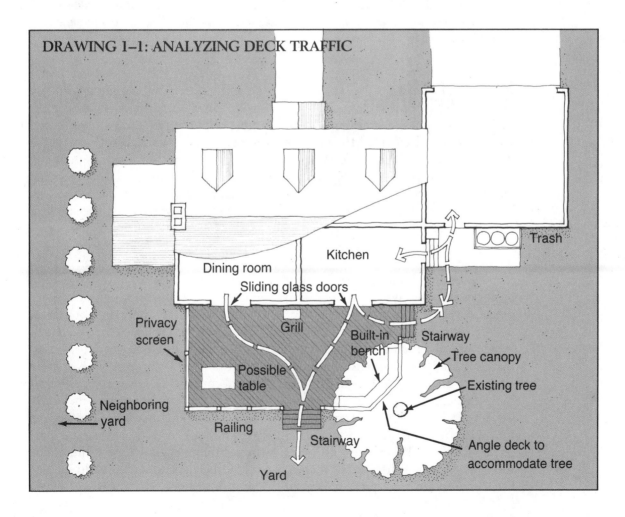

DRAWING 1–1: ANALYZING DECK TRAFFIC

Trash

Kitchen

Dining room

Sliding glass doors

Privacy screen

Grill

Built-in bench

Stairway

Tree canopy

Possible table

Existing tree

Neighboring yard

Railing

Stairway

Angle deck to accommodate tree

Yard

Photo 1–4: A built-in bench takes the place of a railing on the lower level of this multi-level deck. A hot tub occupies its own level in the background, and stairs lead up to a second-story deck. Design by Eli Sutton

MAKING IT LEGAL: THE BUILDING PERMIT

In most areas, a building permit will be required in order to start the construction of a deck. In addition to filling out the proper forms at your building department, you'll need to submit a scale drawing of the deck, showing the deck's location on the property, along with other pertinent details.

To secure a building permit, your deck design will have to comply with the building code regulations that apply in your area. Locally established setback requirements will determine the allowable distance between property lines and the finished deck. The building department should also have information about local soil conditions that will affect the type of foundation required for a deck. For example, if the frost line is established at 34 inches, then poured-concrete piers will need to extend at least 34 inches below grade. In some areas, concrete piers must be poured in tubular fiber forms; in other locations, the hole can act as the form or precast concrete pads can be used. Where unusual soil or seismic conditions are present (as in the San Francisco Bay area), even the smallest deck may have to be designed or at least approved by an engineer.

Before you start to design a deck, be sure to check with your building inspector to find out about specific regulations that apply in your area. Your inspector will also be able to tell you which building code is used locally. These comprehensive code books contain standards relating to all aspects of construction, including decks. The four main building codes used in the United States are the Uniform Building Code (UBC), the Building Officials and Code Administrators International (BOCA) Basic

Building Code, the Council of American Building Officials (CABO) One and Two-Family Dwelling Code, and the Southern Building Code (SBC). For addresses to obtain copies of these building codes, see Sources on page 238.

FULL-SCALE DESIGN: STAKEOUT

A close examination of the building site is crucial when designing a deck. A 25-foot tape measure, some wooden stakes, a ball of string, and a hammer are the tools you'll need to stake out the location and size of the deck. To approximate the perimeter of the deck, drive a stake into the ground at all corner locations; then run string between adjacent stakes. Even for an elevated deck, this full-scale layout will provide important details about the deck's *footprint*—the area covered by the deck.

A preliminary stakeout should provide quite a bit of helpful information that you can take back to the drawing board. First of all, you can note the location of trees and bushes that will have to be accommodated in the deck design, transplanted, or (as a last resort) cut down. The planned deck may cover or pass over permanent features like masonry patios, walkways, and basement windows, and you'll need to note the size, location, and elevation of those features. Find out if the planned deck will be located over underground utility lines or over part of the septic system. If so, you may be limited with regard to post and pier locations, and excavation will have to be done carefully. If a more accurate stakeout is required, use the 3-4-5 triangle method (see Drawing 4-1 on page 37) to relocate stakes for square corners.

Changes in level are also important to determine if the site is sloped or if an elevated or multilevel deck is planned. Rather than use a transit or builder's level at this stage, a line level can be positioned on a tightly stretched string to help establish different elevations. When planning the deck's size, shape, and elevation, remember to consider sight lines from inside the house as well as from the deck. There may be a particular view that you want to preserve rather than block.

Photo 1–5: Benches, planters, and a simple railing form the border of this deck, which is built around a small pool and spa. To create visual interest, decking boards run at different angles at each deck level and bench location.

AT THE DRAWING BOARD

Once you've noted important details about the site, it's time to make a scale drawing that shows a plan view of the deck location and its surroundings. Graph paper, available at stationery and office supply stores, is good for making scale drawings. The most versatile type of paper will show a large grid of 1-inch squares superimposed over a grid of smaller squares that measure eight or ten to the inch. With this type of graph paper, it's possible to make drawings at quite a few different scales. Depending on the size of your project, you can let two, four, six, eight, or ten squares equal 1 foot.

As an alternative to graph paper, you can make scale drawings on plain paper, using an architect's scale and a couple of triangles. Architects, designers, and woodworkers use these tools

Photo 1–6: Trees, stone outcroppings, and the natural slope of the property are landscape features that can be integrated in a deck design. In this design, an angled retaining wall covered with redwood boards nestles the deck into a hillside. A built-in bench fills a niche in the wall. The deck platform skirts a tree, further unifying the deck with its surroundings. Design by Eli Sutton

Photo 1–7: The flexibility of deck construction facilitates barrier-free designs. This entry deck incorporates a ramp for wheelchair access as well as a stairway. Ramp slopes should rise no more than 1 foot for every 12 feet of run. They should be at least 42 inches wide.

to make scale drawings of different projects. The architect's scale has three sides that actually contain ten different scales as well as a 12-inch rule. The smallest scale is ³⁄₃₂ inch equals 1 foot; the largest scale is 3 inches equals 1 foot. To draw up an overall plan of the site where the deck will be installed, you'll probably find it easiest to use a scale of ¼ inch to the foot, ⅜ inch to the foot, or ½ inch to the foot.

Drafting triangles, usually made from clear plastic, enable you to accurately draw straight lines, corners, and a limited number of angles. Most designers use a 30-60-90-degree triangle and a 45-45-90-degree triangle. You'll need a protractor to measure off other angles and a compass to trace arcs and circles. Two other tools to consider if you do much drawing are a T-square and a drafting board. With this setup, you can mark parallel lines quickly and easily, using the T-square alone or in combination with one or more triangles. Finally, you'll need a good mechanical pencil (one that takes a 0.05 lead) and a soft eraser. With these tools, you should be able to produce drawings that are good enough to present to a building inspector.

Make sure your site plan includes all the existing features that will influence the size and shape of your deck—the exterior wall of the house, exterior doors that will be on or near the deck; walkways, clotheslines, hedges, flower beds, rock outcroppings, and trees. Mark the location and approximate diameter of each tree on the plan, and also the spread of branches that define the tree canopy overhead. The site plan should also note existing conditions like solar orientation and views

Photo 1–8: This backyard transformation owes its success to a well-integrated deck and landscape design. Deck levels step down between pine trees, following the natural slope of the land. Railroad ties retain a broad border of bark chips and shrubs, separating the deck from the lawn. Planters and built-in benches provide comfort and color at different corners of the deck.

that are desirable or undesirable. Double-check your drawing by examining the site again.

Once the site plan is complete, it's a good idea to make a half dozen photocopies of the plan so that you can experiment with different deck designs. Work in pencil so that changes will be easy to make. As you try out different deck dimensions and configurations, be sure to allow room for items that will be more or less permanently at home on the deck: lounge chairs, tables, a barbecue grill, benches, and so on.

If your deck will be elevated above grade, you'll have to decide whether the joists will cantilever beyond a beam or be supported by perimeter posts. The plan view of a deck should show where foundation piers and posts are located, as well as beams, ledgers, joists, and other framing members. You'll also need to determine what kind of railing to use and how stairways will be built. You'll find information on these and other construction details in chapters 4 through 7.

To work out joinery details at corners and in other places where different members meet or intersect, it's a good idea to make one or more detail drawings, working at a larger scale (¾ inch equals 1 foot, or even 1½ inch equals 1 foot). This will enable you to see how joints can overlap, how angles can be cut, and how fasteners can be used to optimize strength and appearance. Here, you may want to make elevation drawings to augment your plan drawings. Elevations depict what is seen using a horizontal line of sight.

Apart from satisfying your building inspector and enabling you to fine-tune your deck design, drawings have an additional benefit. When they're complete, you can determine exactly how many joists, beams, posts, decking boards, and other materials will be required to build the deck. (To decide on what type of wood to use, have a look at chapter 2.)

Photo 1–9: A deck can offer several benefits when integrated into the design of a backyard pool. A raised deck such as this one can give a built-in appearance to an aboveground pool while offering the convenience and comfort of decking that comes close to the water's edge. At the same time, the deck railing attractively satisfies the safety requirement for a fence enclosing the pool.

Photo 1–10: Brick walks or patios can be good companions for decks. In the foreground, a frame made from pressure-treated lumber holds bricks that are installed dry over a bed of tamped-down sand.

Photo 1–11: Changing levels is a good way to delineate different deck activities. It also facilitates a graceful transition to grade level on sloping sites such as this one. Here, the outdoor eating area overlooks a lower sunbathing level. The spa occupies its own intermediate level at the opposite end of the deck. Note how the placement of stairways lengthens the pathway between house and yard, directing through traffic away from spa and sunbathing areas.

CHAPTER 2

WOOD FOR BUILDING DECKS

Wood used to build decks has to answer many requirements. It should be available in many dimensions, from 1-inch-thick decking boards to 2 × 10 joists and 6 × 6 posts. It should be easy to work and reasonably priced. But above all, the wood needs to weather years of exposure without losing its strength, stability, or appearance. Sun, rain, mold, and wood-boring insects can make life difficult for decks. So it's crucial to choose and use your wood with care. Fortunately, there are types of wood that lend themselves particularly well to deck projects. With sound construction details, wisely chosen wood, and a minimum of maintenance, the decks you build can last for many years. Let's start with a look at woods that are naturally resistant to decay and insect attack.

REDWOOD

Sequoia sempervirens, commonly known as redwood, is native to the moist, foggy coast of the Pacific Northwest. Redwood trees are legendary for their size and for the quality of lumber they provide. Today, strict logging

regulations protect virgin stands of redwood and towering specimen trees. In the meantime, research and reforestation programs have made redwood one of the fastest growing commercial conifers in the United States.

With its straight grain and tawny color, redwood has been used for all kinds of outdoor building, from patio furniture and planters to water towers, bridges, exterior siding, and, of course, decks. The reddish color identifies heartwood, the denser inner wood of the tree. When sawn or milled, this wood produces a detectable fragrance, releasing the same extractive compounds that wood-boring insects find so unappetizing. Apart from its decay resistance, heartwood is prized for its stability (shrinkage of 4.5 percent or less) and workability. Good grades of redwood can be milled and sanded to produce an extremely smooth surface that accepts paint or stain easily. Redwood's lighter-colored sapwood isn't nearly as dense, stable, or decay resistant as the heartwood.

There are quite a few grades of redwood. *Clear All Heart* is the premium grade, distinctive for its clear, knot-free appearance. Because of its expense, this top grade of redwood is used sparingly in deck construction—for railings and trim pieces that need to be supersmooth and knot-free. Redwood graded as *Construction Heart* (Con-Heart for short) is well-suited to deck construction. Milled from heartwood only, Con-Heart is less expensive than *Clear All Heart* because a limited number of knots are permitted. Grades of redwood containing sapwood include *Clear, B Grade, Construction Common*, and *Merchantable*. While not recommended for decking or deck framing, these economical grades do well for outdoor furniture, trellises, fence boards, and planters.

Redwood can be ordered in standard dimension lumber sizes. Custom orders for long or large dimension timbers are also possible but require extra time. You can choose between kiln-dried (KD) and unseasoned stock. More expensive KD lumber usually isn't necessary for framing members. But where tight joinery is important—for railings, skirt boards, and trim—the extra stability of KD boards will make a difference over time.

Redwood doesn't last as long as pressure-treated lumber under

---

GRADES OF REDWOOD

GRADES CONTAINING ONLY HEARTWOOD

Clear all heart

Select heart

Construction heart

Merchantable heart

GRADES THAT MAY CONTAIN SAPWOOD

Clear

B grade

Select

Construction common

ground-contact conditions. So when redwood posts are used in a deck, it's best if they rest several inches above grade on poured-concrete piers.

WESTERN RED CEDAR

Like redwood, western red cedar is native to the Pacific Northwest, but its range extends beyond coastal areas. Red cedar is more decay resistant than eastern cedar varieties. Western red cedar trees are also significantly larger, so they can yield a reasonable selection of dimension lumber. Cedar's fragrant, dark-colored heartwood is extremely stable and decay resistant. Cedar works easily and takes paint or stain well.

Softness and lack of strength are cedar's chief limitations. It's not a good choice for framing members because thicker stock and closer spacing are required to match the load-bearing capacities of redwood, yellow pine, Douglas fir, and other dimension lumber species. Cost is another consideration. There's a high demand for cedar shingles, clapboards, and other forms of exterior siding. This drives up the price of cedar planks in *two-by* form for decking and structural members.

CYPRESS

Bald cypress (also called southern cypress) is the southerner's answer to redwood. Native to swamps and lowland areas throughout the Southeast, bald cypress is exceptionally resistant to decay and insect attack. Typically a light tan when first cut, cypress is similar to redwood in hardness and strength but not as stable. To avoid shrinkage, warping, and general wood movement, cypress lumber for decks should be dried to a moisture content of 14 percent or less before it is used.

The wood is moderately easy to work, with a slightly waxy feel and an odor reminiscent of its swampy home.

Cypress lumber isn't usually stocked by lumberyards outside its native region but it can be custom-ordered. In the southern United States, local sawmills can be a very economical source of cypress for building decks.

OTHER DECAY-RESISTANT WOODS

Among trees native to North America, quite a few lesser-known species have decay-resistant qualities that rival those of redwood, cedar, and cypress. Osage orange, black locust, sassafras, black walnut, Pacific yew, and white oak are also excellent outdoor woods. The trouble is, these species aren't used by large lumber companies to manufacture dimension lumber. Availability is limited, unless you have access to a local sawmill that can mill logs to your specifications.

PRESSURE-TREATED WOOD

Taking a cue from naturally occurring preservative compounds, man has developed a broad range of chemical treatments that discourage decay and insect infestation in wood. Pressure treatment provides the longest, most effective insurance against wood degradation under severe exposure conditions.

Pressure-treated wood (it often is simply called treated wood) is used all over the world in many different ways. Pressure-treated telephone poles have become a part of our rural landscape. Docks, bridges, and marinas are built using pressure-treated wood pilings that are driven deep into the riverbed or ocean floor. Pressure-treated plywood and dimension lumber are used in place of masonry to build permanent wood foundations. And, of course, decks also benefit from the durability and widespread availability of pressure-treated lumber.

Treated wood's long-term resistance to decay and insect attack is attributable to two factors: the saturation achieved during the treatment process and the effectiveness of the preservative used. Compared to dip treatment or application by brush or spray, pressure treatment provides far superior penetration of the preservative into the wood.

There are several methods of pressure treatment, each designed to maximize the saturation of wood with preservatives in a given length of time. Pressure treatment takes place in a huge cylindrical container called a retort, with a door on one end that can be sealed airtight while a load of lumber is treated. Pumps, valves, storage tanks, boilers, and sophisticated control equipment are other components in the pressure-treatment process.

In *full-cell* pressure treatment, wood in the retort is subjected to vacuum conditions. Once air and moisture have been evacuated from the wood, preservative is added. Then pressure inside the retort is gradually increased to force more preservative into the wood. For maximum retention levels, wood can be treated to *refusal*, or until it can no longer absorb preservative.

In the *empty-cell* process, preservative is forced into the wood under pressure without first drawing a vacuum inside the retort. There are variations on both full-cell and empty-cell methods, designed to cope with different preservatives and different types of wood. It's even possible to treat frozen or green wood by sealing the retort and heating the wood prior to treatment.

Not all wood preservatives are suitable for use in pressure treatment. For more on wood finishes that can be applied by other means, see chapter 9. The preservatives used in pressure treatment include creosote, pentachlorophenol, copper-8-quinolinolate, ammoniacal copper arsenite, sodium borate, and chromated copper arsenate.

There are many factors that determine the suitability of a wood preservative. All of the preservatives mentioned above have limitations, but some are more suitable than others for treating lumber that will be used to build decks. Creosote leaves an oily residue on wood that won't accept paint and is also a skin irritant and fire hazard. Pentachlorophenol (penta for short) is severely toxic, not just to humans and animals but to plants as well. Relatively clear, it can *bloom* on the wood surface following pressure treatment, creating a hazardous concentration of penta crystals that can leach into the ground.

Copper-8-quinolinolate is an oil-borne preservative that is odorless and fairly safe for humans to handle. It's the only preservative permitted by the Food and Drug Administration for use on wood that will be in contact with food. But pressure treatment with copper-8-quinolinolate won't provide wood with sufficient decay resistance for ground contact.

Today, chromated copper arsenate (CCA) is the most widely used compound for pressure treating wood in the United States. The greenish cast on CCA-treated dimension lumber, plywood, lattice panels, and other wood products is a familiar sight at lumber yards across the country. Though toxic, CCA has demonstrated extremely high retention levels following pressure treatment. In other words, CCA is very resistant to leaching, so the compound stays in the wood where it belongs. Cutting and handling CCA-treated wood can be hazardous if you don't follow some basic precautions. For specific safety guidelines, see "Safety Precautions When Handling Treated Wood" below.

SAFETY PRECAUTIONS WHEN HANDLING TREATED WOOD

There are some important safety precautions to observe when using pressure-treated wood. First, remember that chromated copper arsenate-treated lumber is meant for outdoor use. It shouldn't be used inside where it will be frequently handled or come into contact with food. Treated wood borders or posts can be used in garden areas where vegetables will be grown, but don't grow vegetables or fruit in planters or boxes constructed with treated wood.

Whenever you've handled treated wood, always wash your hands thoroughly before eating. Clothes that come into contact with the wood should be washed promptly and separately from other laundry. If you've been cutting treated wood or otherwise have been exposed to its sawdust, take a shower at the end of the day.

If you're sawing or machining treated wood, wear a dust mask. Inexpensive disposable dust masks offer good protection. Always try to work outdoors if you have to cut treated wood.

Sawdust and wood scraps should never be burned for any reason, since this can produce toxic gases and ashes. Wood scraps can be buried, but not in an area that you plan to use as a garden. Or they can be taken to a sanitary landfill.

Photo 2–1: A dust mask is a must, and gloves are a good idea when cutting and handling treated wood. Eye protection is important for any wood cutting.

Types and Grades
of Pressure-Treated Lumber

Treated lumber comes in a full range of dimensions, from 2 × 4 studs to 2 × 12 joists. You can order 4 × 4, 4 × 6, and 6 × 6 posts, as well as 8 × 8 landscape timbers. Remember that these dimensions are nominal, just as they are for untreated dimension lumber: A 2 × 4 measures 1½ inches thick by 3½ inches wide. Pressure-treated railings, balusters, and trellis panels are also stock items at most lumberyards.

Southern yellow pine is the predominant wood species used for pressure treatment. (In some western sections of the United States and Canada, native softwoods such as Douglas fir, ponderosa pine, and Engelman spruce replace southern pine as the wood favored for pressure treatment.) In addition to being relatively inexpensive and plentiful, yellow pine has excellent characteristics for pressure treatment. Yellow pine logs yield a high proportion of sapwood. The sapwood has poor decay resistance in its untreated state, but it can absorb and retain preservatives better than other common softwoods.

The retention level achieved during pressure treatment determines the recommended uses for treated wood. Retention levels are set by the American Wood Preservers Association. Licensed treatment plants are inspected and overseen by the American Wood Preservers Bureau (AWPB). Pressure-treated lumber should be stamped with the AWPB seal. As the table shows, wood treated to a retention level of 0.25 pound of preservative per cubic foot is suitable for outdoor use above ground level. Posts, stair stringers, and other lumber that will be in contact with the ground should have a 0.40 retention rating. Higher retention levels are available for special construction purposes such as wood foundations (0.60) and marine pilings (2.50).

RETENTION LEVELS AND RECOMMENDED USES FOR PRESSURE-TREATED WOOD

Retention (lbs./cubic ft.)	Recommended Use
0.25	Aboveground exposure
0.40	Ground contact
0.60	Permanent wood foundation
0.80	Marine use: freshwater contact
2.50	Marine use: saltwater contact

Like untreated dimension lumber, pressure-treated wood is graded according to structural and visual defects. Wood graded as *Select* or *No. 1* will be relatively free of knots and other imperfections. Consistency in appearance and clear grain make these premium grades ideal where looks are important. For structural members that won't be visible in the completed deck, *No. 2* lumber is a good choice. At some lumberyards, treated wood will be grouped under a broad grade designated as *No. 2 and better*. If this is the case, you may have to go through your lumber order piece by piece to pick out a sufficient number of clear, straight boards. Grades below No. 2 aren't recommended for deck construction.

Because CCA is a water-borne preservative, CCA-treated lumber leaves the retort soaking wet. The wood often is still wet when delivered to the building site. As it dries out, treated lumber will shrink slightly in thickness and width. The drying process can also cause boards to twist, cup, and warp. This is especially true with lower grades of wood where knots and uneven grain are present. It's possible for some boards to deform so much that they're unusable.

One way to limit warp and twist is to build the deck while the wood is still wet, fastening members together before they have a chance to deform. (See chapter 3 for information on fasteners.) If the wood will dry out before you complete the deck, *stickering* boards is a good way to limit twisting and warping by promoting even drying (see "Storing Lumber on Site" on the opposite page).

Another way to ensure straight lumber is to order treated wood that is kiln dried after treatment (KDAT). More expensive than regular treated wood, KDAT stock is far more stable, even if the wood gets soaked with rain before you have a chance to use it.

BORATE-TREATED WOOD

Disodium octaborate tetrahydrate (borate for short) has been used extensively as a wood preservative in Australia and New Zealand. Now available on a limited basis in the United States and Canada, borate-treated wood is becoming a viable alternative to wood treated with chromated copper arsenate (CCA). The U.S. Borax and Chemical Corporation now distributes borate under the brand name of *Tim-bor* wood preservative. There are some important differences between borate and CCA treatment. First, borate treatment is done predominantly by dip-diffusion. Instead of the pressurized retorts used in the pressure-treatment process, dip-diffusion relies on open tanks or troughs to hold the borate preservative and the wood being treated. The wood is submerged for a short period of time in a hot concentrated solution of water and disodium octaborate tetrahydrate. A period of air drying follows dip treatment. Depending on the wood species and the size of the timber, it usually takes one to three weeks for the preservative to diffuse completely through the wood. To enhance this process, freshly treated lumber is kept in closely packed bundles for several days.

Borate has a high toxicity to carpenter ants, termites, and other wood-boring insects. But unlike CCA, it's not poisonous to mammals. This makes it a reasonable choice for people who have reservations about using CCA-treated lumber. Borate treatment imparts neither color nor odor to the wood, and paint or stain can be

STORING LUMBER ON SITE

If the wood for your building project isn't going to be used right away, it's good practice to *sticker* the wood and even cover it if heavy rain is in the forecast. Stickering is the traditional way to air dry lumber after it's been cut from the log. You won't find lumber companies storing or transporting their wood this way because it's too expensive and it takes up extra space. But even pressure-treated lumber can benefit from this technique. Properly stickered, each board can absorb and release moisture evenly on all sides. When wood is merely stacked, moisture absorption will be uneven, causing the board to cup. An extra benefit in stickering your lumber is that it gives you an opportunity to examine each piece. You can pick out the best boards with the straightest, clearest grain and reserve them for railings, trim, and other special parts of the deck.

Wood strips ¾ inch thick (in the form of 1 × 2s or 1 × 3s) make good stickers or spacers when stickering a load of lumber. The weight of the wood helps to keep lower boards or planks straight. Make sure to place stickers at intervals that prevent each layer of boards from sagging. This will help keep boards straight. Stones, bricks, or other weights placed on top of the pile help to stabilize uppermost pieces.

DRAWING 2–1: STORING LUMBER

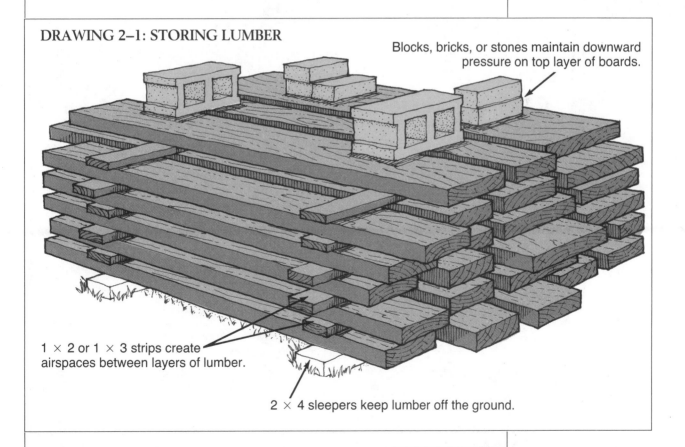

Blocks, bricks, or stones maintain downward pressure on top layer of boards.

1 × 2 or 1 × 3 strips create airspaces between layers of lumber.

2 × 4 sleepers keep lumber off the ground.

applied when the wood is suitably dry. Borate treatment has only limited effectiveness against mold and fungus, so it's not recommended for posts or other deck members that will be in contact with the ground. Tim-borized wood is currently available on a limited basis at selected lumberyards (see Sources on page 238).

ESTIMATING AND ORDERING WOOD

The sizes, lengths, and quantities of wood that go into a deck all depend on the deck's design. Like the design of your deck, your lumber order can be broken down into several categories. Framing lumber will be used for the posts, beams, joists, and other structural parts of the deck (see chapter 5). Decking material can be ordered separately if you have limited space for storage at the building site (see chapter 6 for specific information on different types of decking). Finally, many decks need railings and stairways; some designs even call for privacy screens and trellises. It makes sense to divide your estimate into these categories.

Once the estimate is complete, you can start to compare prices at dif-

DRAWING 2–2: LUMBER ORDER WORKSHEET

	HOW MANY	DIMENSION & LENGTH	USE
FRAMING	3	4 × 4 × 8'	POSTS
	1	2 × 10 × 16'	LEDGER
	2	2 × 10 × 16'	BUILT-UP BEAM
	9	2 × 8 × 10'	JOISTS
STAIRS	2	2 × 12 × 6'	STAIR STRINGERS
	2	2 × 10 × 8'	STAIR TREADS
RAILINGS	2	4 × 4 × 12'	RAILING POSTS
	4	2 × 4 × 8'	RAILS
	4	2 × 4 × 10'	RAILS
	72	2 × 2 × 3'	BALUSTERS
DECKING	50	2 × 6 × 8'	DECKING BOARDS

By breaking your lumber order into categories, you can purchase it in stages to save storage space on site.

ferent lumberyards or home centers. Remember that wood varies greatly in quality. Before dismissing a higher price, it's smart to compare the grades of lumber being sold. You might want to hand-pick some of your material, choosing straight, clear stock for railings, trim boards, and other highly visible parts of the deck. Some lumber dealers will allow a customer to pick through the stock; others won't.

For large orders, or if you don't have access to a truck, you'll have to arrange for delivery to the site. Find out if there will be a delivery charge for your order. It's also important to establish the dealer's policy regarding the return of unusable material. You can expect a few inferior boards in an order, but important members, such as a 6 × 6 post, should be replaced free of charge if they're too warped, twisted, or cracked to be used.

CHAPTER 3

FASTENERS AND HARDWARE FOR DECK CONSTRUCTION

Decks and other outdoor structures place difficult demands on the fasteners and hardware that hold them together. Rust protection is a primary concern. Without it, steel can oxidize rapidly, staining nearby wood, losing its strength, and actually promoting decay around the fastener. Outdoor fasteners also have to cope with wood that is constantly expanding and contracting as it absorbs and releases moisture. This kind of movement can cause conventional nails to work loose and show their heads in less than a season of exposure. Fortunately, there's a good selection of

fasteners and hardware for outdoor construction. The details in this chapter will enable you to choose what's right for your project.

NAILS

There are many types of nails manufactured for outdoor building; some are designed specifically for decks. A special treatment, called hot-dipped galvanizing, coats common steel nails with rust-resistant zinc. You can recognize hot-dipped nails by their bumpy, silver-grey coating. The rough surface of a hot-dipped nail makes it

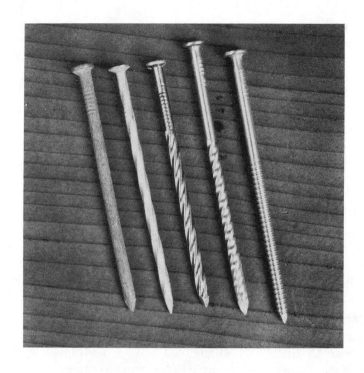

Photo 3–1: Nails used in deck construction must resist both corrosion and withdrawal. From left: *galvanized common nail, galvanized spiral-shank nail, galvanized spiral-shank nail with resin coating (used in pneumatic nail guns), stainless steel spiral-shank nail, and stainless steel ring-shank nail.*

difficult to drive into wood; but it's also difficult to withdraw.

For added withdrawal resistance, special decking nails have spiral shanks as well as hot-dipped galvanizing. These nails are also available in cartridge form for use in pneumatic nail guns. A thin resin coating on the cartridge nails makes them work more easily in the gun. When a nail is driven, friction heats the resin, which then bonds to the wood, creating an even stronger connection.

While hot-dipped nails are highly corrosion resistant, stainless steel nails are corrosion-proof. For deck construction, you can buy both spiral-shank and ring-shank stainless steel nails in several different sizes. Because these nails are made from solid stainless steel, they can be twice as expensive as hot-dipped nails. But in situations where extra corrosion protection is needed (on a deck near the ocean, for example), stainless steel is a wise choice.

Nailing Guidelines

For a strong connection, it's best to nail a thinner member to a thicker member. The nail should be long enough to penetrate the base or receiving piece to a depth at least twice the thickness of the thinner piece. Nail sizes are given by a *d* designation, which translates verbally as *penny*. This sizing system is based on a 2d nail with a 1-inch-long shank. Shank length increases by ¼ inch with each d size. Thus, a 10d nail has a 3-inch-long shank. And 20d nails, the longest normally used in deck construction, are 4 inches long.

Splitting the wood can be a problem when nailing near the edge or end of a board. To reduce the chances of splitting, you can blunt the point of the nail with several blows from the hammer before driving it. A pointed nail pushes the wood fibers apart, while a blunted nail tears a hole as it's driven. Blunting usually is necessary only at the ends of board. Don't do it to every nail; it reduces the nail's holding power. A more foolproof and more time-consuming way to prevent splitting is to predrill the nail hole in the piece that's being fastened down. In softwoods, the drill bit diameter should be close to half the diameter of the nail shank.

BUGLEHEAD SCREWS

Originally developed for installing gypsum wallboard, these versatile fasteners are now used for all kinds of woodworking and carpentry projects. They're still called drywall screws by some manufacturers; other companies call them multipurpose screws or buglehead screws. This last term refers to the bugle-shaped taper beneath the flat head of the screw. The bugle shape makes it easier to drive the screw flush with the surface of wood, even if you don't predrill the hole and countersink the screw head. Unlike conventional flathead wood screws, buglehead

screws don't have a tapered shank.

Buglehead screws are available with either a Phillips head or a square recess for driving (and removing) the screw. Buglehead screws with a black-oxide finish usually have fine threads, and they're good for interior use. Exterior screws have a coarse thread and a hot-dipped galvanized coating. Many lengths are available, but the most common lengths used for deck construction are 2 inches, 2½ inches, and 3 inches. As with nailed connections, it's always best to fasten a thinner member to a thicker member. The screw should penetrate into the thicker stock a distance that equals or exceeds the thickness of the thinner stock.

Buglehead screws are especially well-suited to deck construction. Their holding power is superior to that of nails, and they look good. Also, it's easier to unscrew a damaged board than to pry up a board that's been nailed down. To drive screws quickly

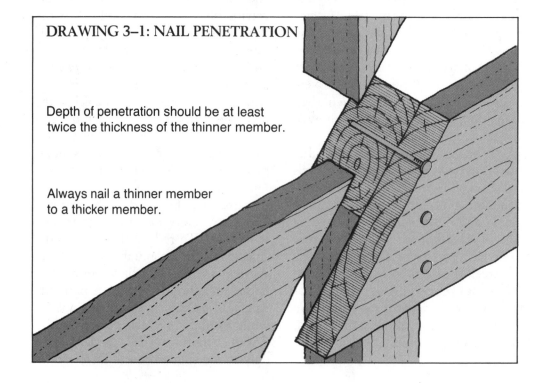

DRAWING 3–1: NAIL PENETRATION

Depth of penetration should be at least twice the thickness of the thinner member.

Always nail a thinner member to a thicker member.

Photo 3–2: Buglehead screws are galvanized to resist corrosion. They provide excellent holding power in deck construction. Screws are driven using a #2 Phillips-head bit, chucked in a variable speed drill or a screw gun.

and easily, you'll need a screw gun or a good variable-speed drill and a supply of #2 Phillips-head bits. If you use screws with a square-recess head, you'll need to get matching bits. Both types of bits are inexpensive, and they wear out, so it's smart to have at least several replacements on hand.

For screwed connections near the end of a board, or at delicate joints, predrill the screw hole before driving the screw. Drill bit diameter should be one-third to one-half the diameter of the screw shank. Photo 3-3 on page 26 shows a special attachment designed to fit over a Phillips-head bit (or square-drive bit) in the drill chuck. With this accessory, you can predrill screw holes and then drive screws im-mediately without switching bits in the drill.

LAG SCREWS

When it comes to fastening in deck construction, lag screws take over where buglehead screws leave off. Lag screws have thicker shanks (from $3/16$-inch diameter to $1/2$ inch and larger) and coarser threads than buglehead screws. For strength and appearance, a single lag screw can take the place of three or four buglehead screws. The lag screw's hex head enables you to fasten it down very tightly using a wrench. For this reason, lag screws are often used for major structural connections, such as fastening a ledger beam to the house or joining a joist to a post.

Lag screws are available in many lengths. Most hardware and building supply stores stock lags in lengths that range from 1 to 8 inches. As with other types of screws, the lag screw should be long enough so that at least half its length is in the base or bottom-most piece of wood. Holes for lag screws should always be predrilled, using a bit approximately half the diameter of the screw shank. To avoid splitting the wood if the lag screw is located close to the end of a board, it's a good idea to use a larger bit to predrill the hole in the top board. The bit diameter

should match the diameter of the lag screw just beneath its head. Always use a washer between the hex head and the wood. The washer distributes the pressure exerted by the screw, making the connection stronger while also reducing the chances of splitting the wood.

MACHINE BOLTS

Machine bolts, also known as lag bolts, are threaded to receive nuts, so they have to be used in *through-bolted* connections where the bolt extends all the way through the members being fastened together. Like lag screws,

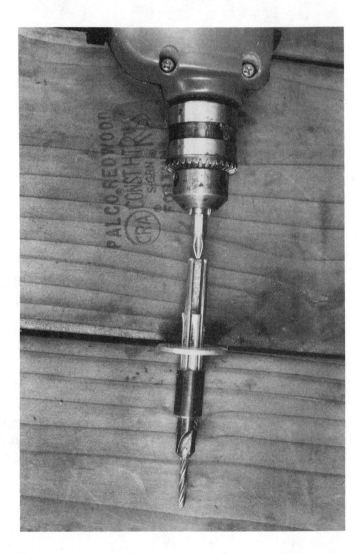

Photo 3–3: Predrilling screw holes is sometimes necessary to avoid splitting the wood. The steel fingers on this special bit fit around the Phillips-head bit and into the drill chuck. Without removing the Phillips-head bit, you can predrill, countersink, and even counterbore the hole. This speeds the process of drilling and driving.

Photo 3–4: Lag screws have hex heads and threaded shanks. They provide extra strength at major structural connections. Always use a washer between the head and the wood to spread the clamping force of the fastener. Holes for lag screws should be predrilled, and the screw can be driven using a wrench.

machine bolts have hex heads and come in different lengths and shank diameters.

Bolted connections are useful on major structural joints where two or more members need to be fastened together. Because a bolted connection uses a nut, through-bolted connections are generally stronger than screwed connections, since the threaded connection is in steel instead of wood. The bolt hole must be predrilled, using a bit whose diameter matches the shank diameter or exceeds it by no more than 1/8 inch. Washers beneath the hex head and the nut are important.

CARRIAGE BOLTS

Carriage bolts work just like machine bolts but have a round head in-stead of a hex head. Just beneath the head, the shank is square. When tapped into a snug-fitting hole with a hammer, the square shank seats in the wood, locking the bolt in place so that the nut can be tightened. A carriage bolt doesn't need a washer beneath the head, but a washer should still be used beneath the nut.

Carriage bolts provide the strength of a through-bolted connection, but the round head of the bolt is less obtrusive than the hex head of a lag screw. Carriage bolts are good to use on railing posts and in other places where a hex head might snag clothing or bruise fingers. The one limitation to using carriage bolts is that the nut should remain accessible after the deck is complete. If it doesn't, you won't be able to tighten or loosen the connection later.

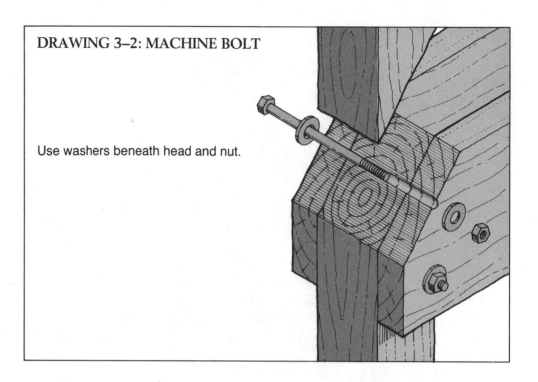

DRAWING 3–2: MACHINE BOLT

Use washers beneath head and nut.

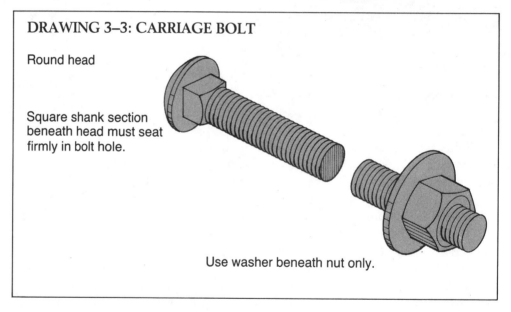

DRAWING 3–3: CARRIAGE BOLT

Round head

Square shank section beneath head must seat firmly in bolt hole.

Use washer beneath nut only.

FRAMING HARDWARE

In framing a deck, there are many situations where fasteners alone aren't adequate for joining structural members together. Joist hangers and other framing connectors are designed to provide strength at key connection points. These connectors can also com-pensate for structural members that aren't precisely cut. As a result, the added cost of using connectors can usually be offset by the time saved in assembling the frame.

Knowing a little about framing connectors can be helpful as you design the framework of a deck. In addition to the basic selection of connectors described below, there are all kinds of special connectors for different applications (see Sources on page 238).

Post and column bases are used to anchor vertical structural members (posts and columns) to a supporting pier or pad of poured concrete. As Drawing 3-4 below shows, some bases are designed to be cast into the concrete; others are meant to rest on the top of the pier. Adjustable bases can be raised or lowered slightly.

Post and column caps are designed to connect vertical structural members with beams, plates, and other horizontal members. Some caps are sized to fit only 4 × 4 or only 6 × 6 posts;

others can be adjusted for different size posts.

Joist hangers come in a variety of sizes and styles. All have a steel stirrup designed to hold the 1½-inch-thick dimension lumber used for floor and ceiling joists. Some joist hangers are designed with L-shaped flanges to fit over beams. Other hangers have special tabs for nailing and alignment. Special nails with short, thick shanks and hot-dipped galvanizing are available for use with joist hangers and other framing connectors. Often, the nails come with the connectors.

Beam hangers are designed to hold doubled or tripled joists, or a solid beam whose thickness exceeds 1½ inches. These connectors also come in different sizes and styles.

DRAWING 3–4: POST AND COLUMN BASES

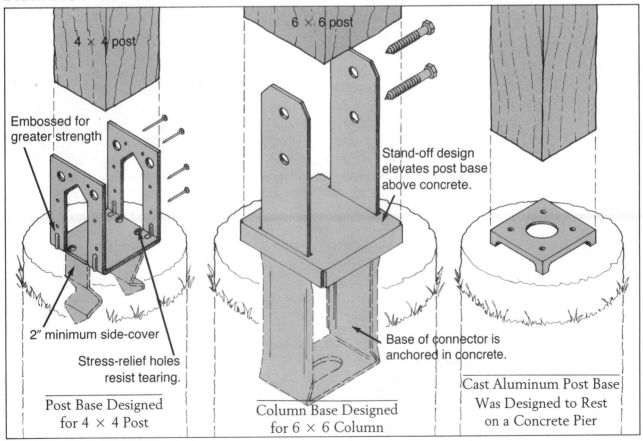

Embossed for greater strength

4 × 4 post

6 × 6 post

Stand-off design elevates post base above concrete.

2" minimum side-cover

Stress-relief holes resist tearing.

Base of connector is anchored in concrete.

Post Base Designed for 4 × 4 Post

Column Base Designed for 6 × 6 Column

Cast Aluminum Post Base Was Designed to Rest on a Concrete Pier

DRAWING 3–5: POST AND COLUMN CAPS

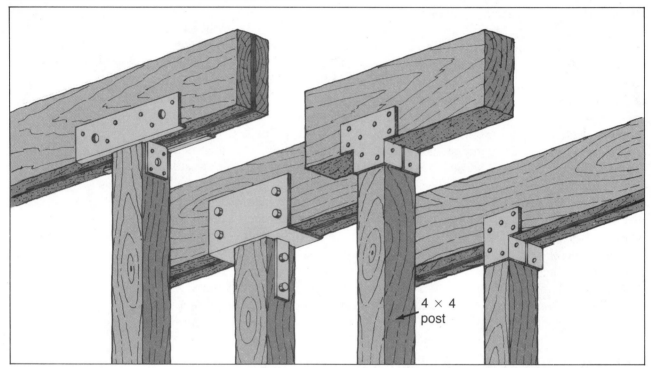

4 × 4
post

Hold-downs are required in earthquake-prone areas where extra resistance to racking, shifting, and uplift is required. Hold-downs can be used to anchor posts and plates to a concrete foundation or they can connect posts that are separated by floor framing.

Angled connectors are used where members must join at an angle other than 90 degrees. There are angled connectors for rafters as well as for joists. Some are prebent at the factory to fixed angles; others are adjustable.

Strap ties and *tie plates* can be used in many situations where two pieces need to be joined together.

MASONRY ANCHORS

In many deck projects, wood members have to be fastened to masonry walls, floors, or foundations. There are many different types of ma-

sonry anchors, but relatively few are well-suited to deck construction.

Expansion shields are installed in holes drilled in the masonry. They're designed to expand when a screw or bolt is tightened. *Sleeve anchors* and *wedge anchors* also work by expanding inside the hole until they lock firmly in place. These anchors are easier to install than expansion shields, since the diameter of the sleeve or wedge matches the diameter of the bolt that fits it. This enables you to drill through the wood member (that needs to be fastened to the masonry) and into the masonry at the same time, using a single masonry bit.

Concrete screws are made from extrahard steel so that they can thread their way firmly into a predrilled hole just slightly smaller than the screw's diameter. Several lengths and gauges are available. You can also choose between hex-head and Phillips-head screws.

DRAWING 3–6: JOIST HANGERS

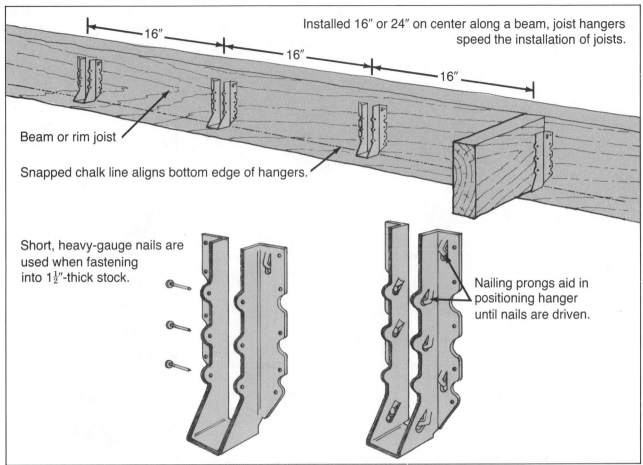

Installed 16″ or 24″ on center along a beam, joist hangers speed the installation of joists.

16″   16″   16″

Beam or rim joist

Snapped chalk line aligns bottom edge of hangers.

Short, heavy-gauge nails are used when fastening into $1\frac{1}{2}$″-thick stock.

Nailing prongs aid in positioning hanger until nails are driven.

DRAWING 3–7: BEAM HANGERS

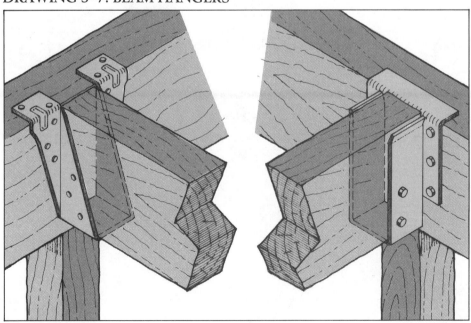

Toggle bolts are designed to be used in concrete block walls with hollow cores. *Masonry nails* are often used for attaching furring strips and other lightweight wood members to concrete, but they don't have sufficient withdrawal resistance to support the ledger beam for a deck.

DRAWING 3–8: HOLD-DOWNS

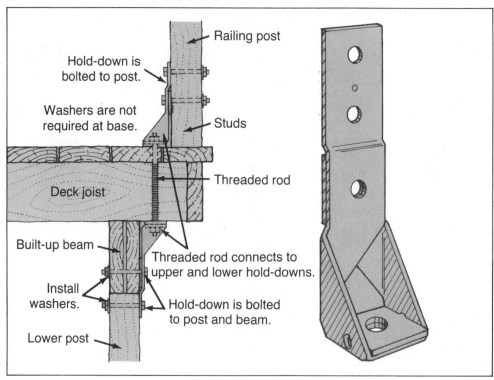

Railing post

Hold-down is bolted to post.

Washers are not required at base.

Studs

Threaded rod

Deck joist

Built-up beam

Threaded rod connects to upper and lower hold-downs.

Install washers.

Hold-down is bolted to post and beam.

Lower post

DRAWING 3–9: ANGLED CONNECTORS

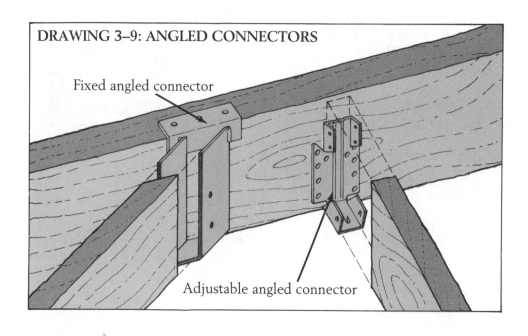

Fixed angled connector

Adjustable angled connector

Epoxy-based masonry fasteners rely on a chemical rather than a mechanical bond between the fastener and the masonry. With most of these fastening systems a special compound is injected into a predrilled hole. Then a length of threaded rod is forced into the hole so that the compound spreads around it. When the compound hardens, the rod is locked in place. Epoxy fastening systems are expensive but they're exceptionally strong and they aren't affected by moisture or vibration. They can be used to fasten a ledger board to the side of a pool. Epoxy is also a good solution near the edge or corner of a masonry wall where an expansion shield might cause a crack in the masonry.

DRAWING 3–10: STRAP TIES AND TIE PLATES

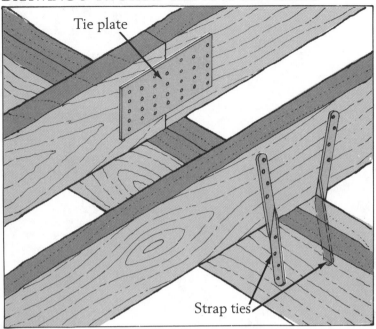

Tie plate

Strap ties

Photo 3–5: Masonry anchors. Clockwise from center: a toggle bolt, wedge anchor, sleeve anchor, concrete screws, and an expansion shield with lag screw and washer.

Photo 3–6: Lengths of threaded rod can be anchored to masonry by injecting an epoxy mixture into a predrilled hole prior to tapping the threaded rod into the hole. The two-part epoxy is mixed just before injection. When the epoxy cures, the threaded rod is chemically bonded to the masonry, and nuts can be tightened to pull the ledger firmly against the wall.

CHAPTER 4

TOOLS AND TECHNIQUES

Y̶ou don't have to spend a fortune on tools to build a great deck. With creativity, careful planning, and skillful execution you can turn out excellent work with a very basic selection of tools. But there's also more sophisticated equipment to consider, depending on your budget and the scale of your projects. In this chapter you'll find a comprehensive selection of tools to choose from, along with some basic techniques. The tools for building decks fall into three major categories: tools for layout, excavation tools, and cutting and joining tools.

TOOLS FOR LAYOUT

A *tape measure* is essential for just about any building project. For deck construction, a 25-foot or 30-foot tape length will handle both large and small projects. On a good tape measure, the first 12 inches of the tape will be divided into 32nds of an inch, enabling you to do fine layout work in addition to large-scale measuring. Tapes with ¾-inch-wide blades are lighter and more compact than 1-inch-wide tapes; but the wider blades are more rigid, so they can extend farther without folding. This can be a real advantage if

Photo 4–1: Tools for layout include, from left: *a bevel gauge, plumb bob, chalk line, and a 25-foot tape measure.*

you're measuring by yourself.

A builder's *chalk line* consists of a roll of string held inside a container full of powdered chalk. When stretched tight and snapped against a flat surface, the string leaves a straight, chalked layout line.

A *plumb bob* is a layout tool that relies on gravity, enabling you to drop a perfectly vertical line from any elevation. Suspended from a string, the heavy, inverted-cone body of the bob is designed to pinpoint the position of elevated members relative to a horizontal (or near-horizontal) plane. The plumb bob is useful for aligning posts or columns, especially where long distances are involved that might limit the accuracy of a level. Some chalk lines can also be used as plumb bobs.

Also called a bevel square or sliding bevel, the *bevel gauge* can be adjusted to any angle. Turning a thumbscrew locks the metal arm in place, allowing you to transfer angles precisely from one piece of wood to another.

Squares

Made in different sizes and styles, the *try square* is a small, fixed square intended for extremely precise, small-scale work. You can get by without one for deck building but if you have one, it will come in handy for testing other squares and adjusting power tools for exact 90-degree cutting angles.

The *combination square* is adjustable. The body of the square contains both 90-degree and 45-degree angles and it can slide up and down a 12-inch blade, locking in place with the turn of a thumbscrew. The movable body makes this tool ideal for transferring depth measurements or testing the depth of a mortise or lap joint.

Made from a single piece of steel or aluminum, the *framing square's* large size makes it useful for laying out stair stringers and rafters and for general squaring up on large boards or panels.

Angle squares, most commonly known by the brand name Speed-square, are the sturdy workhorses for

Photo 4–2: Several types of squares are useful in building a deck. Clockwise from top left: *a large angle square, a framing square, a try square, a combination square, and a small angle square.*

general framing and construction. Thick, strong, triangular castings of aluminum or plastic, angle squares are the only squares that can be knocked around and even dropped without breaking or becoming less accurate. The angle square's triangular shape enables you to lay out a 45-degree angle as quickly as a 90-degree angle. Using markings on the body of the square, you can also lay out angles other than 90 degrees.

Sometimes it helps to fabricate your own *site-made squares and gauges* as aids in doing particular layout work. With two straight-edged lengths of plywood, you can make an oversized square that's useful for large-scale layout work. Spread glue on the joint where one length of plywood overlays the other. Then use a framing square (or the 3-4-5 triangle method described below) to square the outside edges, and clamp the joint at a 90-degree angle. Finally, screw the joint together.

Using a similar technique, you can make an angle gauge to suit specific layout details. An octagonal deck, for example, requires a framework with eight corners that measure 135 degrees. A 135-degree gauge block will help you in laying out the framing for this deck shape.

The *3-4-5 triangle method* is a method that lets you check a right angle using your tape measure instead of a square. A triangle with one side measuring 3 units long, one side measuring 4 units long, and a 5-unit-long hypotenuse will contain a single 90-degree corner opposite the hypotenuse. This formula works with any multiple of the 3-4-5 ratio and at any

Photo 4–3: Cut from ¾-inch-thick plywood, this site-made gauge helps to lay out 135-degree angles used in building an octagonal deck.

scale. But the side measurements have to be exact. The 3-4-5 triangle method is most useful when you're doing large-scale layout that's beyond the accuracy of your framing square.

Levels and Transits

Also called a builder's level, *the dumpy level* is basically a telescope designed to swivel a full 360 degrees, defining a horizontal plane from which different layout heights can be measured. The level is usually mounted on a tripod. Once the tool itself is leveled by adjusting its feet against the tripod's platform, level layout work can begin.

Points above or below level are accurately established by siting through the viewfinder against a tape measure or a surveyor's measuring rod. When used with a plumb bob, the level can be positioned over post locations to give exact angular measurements between posts or framing members.

A *transit* works just like a level but can also pivot vertically to define vertical angles and elevations. When using either tool to lay out a deck, it is important to position the tripod on stable

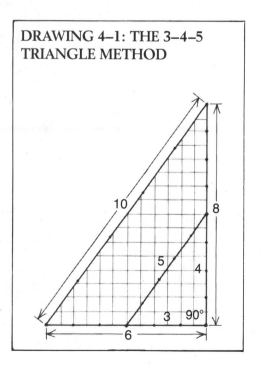

DRAWING 4–1: THE 3–4–5 TRIANGLE METHOD

Photo 4–4: A dumpy level, also called a builder's level, is used in conjunction with a tape measure or measuring rod to establish level lines on site. The level should always be set up in a secure place so that it won't shift or settle while readings are being taken. Here, two workers use the level to establish the height of concrete piers.

Photo 4–5: Basic, but very accurate, the water level is a low-cost alternative to an optical level. This level, available in kit form, consists of clear tubing that is connected to a small reservoir. Common food coloring, added to the reservoir, makes the water line more visible. Level marks can be made simply by moving the tubing to different locations. While this is being done, the reservoir position must remain unchanged, and water can't be lost or added.

ground (not in mud or sand) in a location where the view to different layout points will remain unobstructed. Layout with a transit or builder's level can be fast and extremely accurate once you master the technique of setting up the level and siting against a tape or rod.

With a length of clear tubing and a water supply, you can make a *water level* that can be just as accurate as a dumpy level or transit. When filled with water, both ends of the tubing will show the exact same water level when held up above the central portion of the tubing.

A conventional garden hose can be made into a water level by attaching a section of clear tubing to each end so that water levels will be visible. Manufactured water levels are also available.

To use a water level, one end of the tubing needs to be fixed against a post or other vertical member. The free end of the tubing can then be maneuvered to transfer the water level shown against the post to other points.

Hand Levels

You'll also need a couple of hand levels for a deck project. Small and light, a *line level* is designed to fit on a string that's stretched tightly between two points. The straightness of the string determines the accuracy of the reading, so, for best results, hang your line level from mason's twine or from an equivalent string that's strong and resistant to stretching. Always position the line level near the center of the string's span.

A 2-foot or 4-foot level is useful for positioning ledger boards, joists, and other horizontal members. The pocket-size *torpedo level* is a good tool for plumbing up concrete forms and keeping posts plumb as they're in-

Photo 4–6: Levels come in many sizes. The lightweight line level (front) *is designed to be hung from a taut string to lay out level marks. Larger, but still pocket-size, the torpedo level is good to use when installing posts and braces. Behind are 2-foot and 4-foot levels, which are useful for leveling beams and joists.*

stalled. If your torpedo level has a be-vel set at 45 degrees, you'll be able to use it for positioning diagonal braces.

DIGGING TOOLS

Nearly every deck project re-quires some sort of digging work. To sink posts or pour concrete piers or pads, you'll need a *posthole digger*. This double-handled tool is designed to cut and scoop the soil to create a circular hole.

For large projects where many holes have to be dug, a *power auger* will speed the job. The portable power au-ger shown in Photo 4-7 below is pow-ered by a gasoline engine and works like a giant drill. You still need a post-hole digger to clear dirt from the au-ger's holes.

If you run into rocks or roots while using the posthole digger, you'll need a large steel bar to get past these ob-structions. Sometimes called a *wreck-ing bar* or *breaking bar*, this tool is heavy enough to break stones apart in a hole so that they can be removed using the posthole digger. To deal with roots, you may need a small pruning saw or hand ax.

CUTTING AND JOINING TOOLS

Of all the cutting and joining tools used in deck construction, the portable circular saw or *Skilsaw* (a trade name of Skil Corporation), is easily the most important. You'll use the circular saw for everything from roughly sizing boards to making pocket cuts and pre-cise miters. In the following pages,

Photo 4–7: When many holes are required for a deck, the power auger can save time and energy. You'll still need a posthole digger to remove loosened soil and stones from the hole.

you'll find helpful information on choosing a saw, selecting the right blades, and making accurate cuts and basic joints.

Choosing a Circular Saw

With at least 11 manufacturers and dozens of models to choose from, buying a circular saw can be a confusing experience. Most popular with tradesmen and do-it-yourselfers alike are saws that take a 7¼-inch-diameter blade. With this blade size, maximum depth of cut (with the blade at 90 degrees) will be between 2¼ inches and 2⁷⁄₁₆ inches, depending on the model. Larger saws are available, with blade diameters of 8¼ inches, 9¼ inches, 10¼ inches and even 16 inches. These oversize saws are useful for cutting thick material such as posts and landscape timbers, but they're too unwieldy for general deck construction.

Among 7¼-inch saws, there are many small features that distinguish one model from another. A double-insulated saw is important for any kind of outdoor work. On some saws, you'll find a safety switch that has to be depressed before the trigger will work. Some people feel more secure with a safety switch, others find it an inconvenience. Saws without the extra switch have extra travel built into the trigger so that the saw won't turn on until the trigger is fully depressed. Changing blades will be a lot easier on saws equipped with an arbor lock. The lock prevents the blade from turning while you remove the nut from the arbor.

Worm-drive saws are popular among framing contractors for their power and durability and because the blade is more visible during use than on most other models. But worm-drives are the most expensive circular saws, and you probably don't need all that durability if you won't be subjecting the tool to long-term daily use.

Photo 4–8: The most popular circular saws for deck building take 7¼-inch blades. A broad, thick base, cast rather than stamped, gives this saw extra stability for deck work.

Also the extra weight of a worm-drive saw can be a disadvantage in some situations. For example, you'll appreciate a light saw if you have to trim off the top of a post that's already in place. Consider the size of the base, or *foot*, of the saw as well. A saw with a large base won't be as maneuverable in cramped quarters.

While you may not opt for a worm-drive saw, it's smart to spend the extra money on a professional quality saw for deck construction and all-around use. A contractor's saw will not only outlast a handyman saw, it will work more accurately and be easier to use. When shopping for a saw, don't judge the saw's power by its horsepower rating, since this is commonly measured under *no-load* conditions. A better indicator of power is the amount of amperage the motor draws. Low-cost saws usually have 9-amp or 10-amp motors with drive shafts and arbors running on roller or sleeve bearings. You'll be better off choosing a saw rated at 12 amps or 13 amps and made with ball bearings. The extra power is especially important if you plan to cut a lot of pressure-treated lumber, which is harder. Ball bearings make a saw more expensive, but increase durability significantly.

Plastic housings are no longer a sign of low quality on power tools. Today, the construction of metal parts in a saw will give a better indication of its quality. The first thing to examine is the foot or base of the saw. A thin, stamped-steel base won't be as stable or stay as flat as a thicker base that's extruded or cast.

Adjustments for angled cuts and for depth of cut are especially important. On cheaper saws, you'll find stamped wing nuts that are supposed to lock these adjustments. (Better saws have cast and threaded wing nuts or even levers.) Inexpensive rivets will be used at pivot points, sometimes showing detectable play between the base and the housing. These aren't good features. On a quality saw, look for large adjustment levers or cast and threaded wing nuts with firm locking action. These features will really affect the ease and precision of the tool.

Choosing a Blade

When it comes to achieving a smooth, precise cut, the blade you choose is even more important than the saw. Carbide-tipped blades are universally preferred over hardened or *high-speed* steel blades, especially for cutting pressure-treated lumber. Carbide holds its edge longer than steel, especially when difficult or prolonged cutting causes heat buildup in the blade. You can expect to pay two to four times more for carbide-tipped blades (over the price of a steel blade), but in return you'll get at least five times more cutting time before the blade needs sharpening.

It's smart to have a couple of different blades on hand to handle different cutting assignments in deck construction. Several companies make carbide-tipped blades designed especially for cutting pressure-treated wood. These *deck* blades typically have up to 24 teeth and they're excellent general *combination* blades. The combination label means that a blade can be used equally well to cut with the grain (ripping) or across it (cross-cutting). For a supersmooth edge, you'll do better with a 40-tooth (carbide-tipped) combination blade. Generally, the more teeth a blade has, the finer it will cut. But your saw has to work harder to move more teeth through the wood, so a blade with fewer teeth will cut faster. If you can, reserve your fine-cutting blade for situations where a supersmooth edge is called for.

Cutting Straight and Square

Keeping the saw straight and steady is also important for smooth, accurate cuts. Even in experienced hands, knots in the wood and motor vibration can easily cause a carefully made freehand cut to wander slightly off its line. Fortunately, there are a number of ways to guide your saw when extremely precise cuts are needed.

The first step in making a square cut is to square the blade to the base of the saw. Don't rely on the angle markings that are stamped into the saw base near its pivot points. These marks are just for ballpark purposes and their accuracy will vary from one saw to the next. To make sure the blade and base are square with each other, unplug the saw and loosen the angle adjustment. Then turn the saw over and set a Speedsquare or a try square against blade and base. Make sure that the body of the square extends between the blade's teeth, as shown in Photo 4-9 below. Tighten the angle adjustment when blade and base bear evenly against the square. Once you've squared up your saw like this, check the accuracy of the stamped markings. If necessary, you can make your own set of marks using a scribe or a small triangular file.

To use the Speedsquare as a cutoff guide, first mark the cutoff line on the stock using the square. Then slide the body of the square back on the stock, holding your circular saw with one edge of its base bearing against the

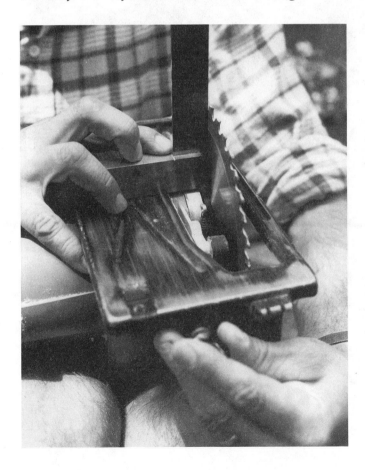

Photo 4–9: Square the base of the saw to the blade using a try square. Make sure the blade of the square extends between two teeth on the sawblade.

square edge of the Speedsquare. Adjust the square's position until the saw blade lines up on the correct side of the layout line. Now brace the square against the stock and make the cut, using the square's edge to guide the edge of the saw base.

There are several saw guides designed to work on the same principle as the Speedsquare, using a braced edge to guide the base of the saw. Most of these guides also can be adjusted to make cuts at angles other than 90 degrees.

For ripping or cutting close to the edge of a board, you can attach a rip fence to most saws and use this as a (continued on page 48)

Photo 4–10: Thick and durable, the angle square makes a fine cutoff guide when 90-degree or 45-degree angles need to be cut. Guide the base of the saw against the edge of the square when making the cut.

Photo 4–11: A saw protractor can be adjusted to guide the saw for different angled cuts.

CIRCULAR SAW JOINERY

You can do quite a variety of joinery work with the circular saw. Miters, lap joints, dadoes, and notches are fairly straightforward to make. You'll need a hammer and a sharp chisel in addition to the circular saw and whatever jig you choose to use.

Miter joints are cut in a single pass. Lap joints, dadoes, and notches require three distinct steps: kerfing, roughing out, and paring. Once you've marked the shoulders of a lap joint, dado, or notch, adjust the saw's depth of cut. On most lap joints, depth of cut should equal half the thickness of the pieces being joined, as shown in Drawing 4–2 below. It's good practice to make a test cut or two on scrap stock to make sure your setting is right.

(continued)

DRAWING 4–2: COMMON JOINTS FOR DECK CONSTRUCTION

End lap

Shoulder

45°

Lap miter

Miter

Mid lap

Dado

CIRCULAR SAW JOINERY—*Continued*

Once this is done, make a series of closely spaced kerfs in the waste area of the joint. The only kerf that needs to be square and straight is the one that makes the shoulder, so this is where you might want to use a Speedsquare to guide the saw.

When kerfing is complete, rough out the joint by chiseling off the thin waste pieces. If necessary, you can use the hammer with the chisel to break the pieces free, but keep the bevel side of the chisel pointing down. This gives you greater control over how deep the chisel cuts.

Chisel to the bottom of the joint only in its center portion; leave short ridges of waste near the edges. This material gets removed as you pare the joint down to its final dimensions. Do this with the chisel's bevel facing up. Use one hand to push the cutting edge into the waste and the other hand to keep the back of the chisel flat against the bottom of the joint.

With a little practice, it's possible to complete a lap joint, as shown in Photos 4–12 through 4–14 below and opposite in about five minutes. The same three-step technique is used to cut dadoes and notches with the circular saw. The only difference is, for a dado, you have to make two straight and square kerfs; one at each side of the dado. You'll need a narrower chisel to clean out a dado joint.

Photo 4–12: Step 1: Kerfing out. Working inside the layout lines for the notch, make a series of closely spaced kerfs. Cutting depth should match the planned depth of the notch.

Photo 4–13: Step 2: Chiseling out waste. With the bevel of the chisel facing down, rough out the shape of the notch.

Photo 4–14: Step 3: Paring to the line. Working with the chisel's bevel facing up, pare away shavings of waste to reach the layout lines of the joint.

guide. A steel arm on the fence slides into an opening in the saw base and is locked in position with a thumbscrew. If a rip fence doesn't come with your saw, most hardware stores have fences in stock. While convenient and easy to adjust, the rip fence depends on a straight, smooth edge to bear against. Another way to guide the saw for straight cuts is to simply clamp a straight board parallel to the cut line and use one edge of the board to guide the edge of the saw base.

One of the most useful jigs for making straight, exact cuts with the circular saw incorporates an edge guide that's glued to its own base. To make this jig you can use a thin, flat piece of wood (¼-inch-thick lattice molding works well) with one straight edge. To make the base, use an equally long piece of ⅛-inch-thick tempered hardboard about 12 inches wide. Glue the lattice molding along the full length of the hardboard base. Position the molding so that its straight edge will guide the saw base, allowing the blade to trim the hardboard perfectly straight along one side. Once you've made this trim cut with the saw, the jig is complete. To use it, simply line up the straight trimmed edge of the base with the cut line on stock. Adjust the saw's depth of cut to match the

Photo 4–15: To make precise straight cuts, you can use a shop-made straight-cutting jig. The jig consists of a straightedged wood guide strip glued on top of a ⅛-inch-thick length of hardboard. Trim the edge of the hardboard by running the saw along the guide strip. This allows you to position the saw blade along the cutting line.

thickness of the material, and use a couple of spring clamps to secure the jig while you make the cut.

Motorized Miter Boxes

These power tools are close relatives of the circular saw, since they consist of a circular saw body mounted on a pivoting assembly that's attached to a stationary base. Also called *chop saws* or *cutoff saws*, these tools are designed to make precise cross-grain cuts in boards, planks, and trim pieces. Chop saws are more expensive than portable circular saws, but they're popular among contractors because they make it possible to cut angles precisely and quickly.

Some chop saws rely on a large blade (10-inch diameter or larger) to cut wide boards at angles from 90 to 45 degrees. Other saws, such as Delta's Sawbuck model, take an 8-inch blade but are designed so that the motor housing slides on a pair of parallel bars. Unlike most chop saws, the Sawbuck can pivot in two planes to cut compound angles. Hitachi's Slide Compound Saw (model C8FB) and the Black & Decker DeWalt Crosscutter (model 1707) can also cut compound angles, and they're even more portable than the Sawbuck. All three of these

Photo 4–16: Motorized miter boxes or chopsaws facilitate quick, precise cutting. The DeWalt Crosscutter has a motor housing that can telescope on a pair of arms, making wide cuts possible. This saw can also make compound-angle cuts.

saws are especially useful for deck construction.

Other Saws

Another power tool that's useful in deck construction is the portable jigsaw or saber saw. The jigsaw can cut curves, make cutouts in deck boards, and complete angled cuts started with a circular saw. A handsaw is also good to have around, especially in situations where you need to complete a cut close to a wall or other obstruction that blocks your circular saw. A crosscut saw with 10 to 12 teeth per inch will work well.

Photo 4–17: A block plane does a good job of easing edges as a deck is built. With a sharp plane, sharp edges can be chamfered to improve the look and feel of a deck.

Chisels and Planes for Deck Builders

Smooth edges and close-fitting joints are fine details that give an elegant finish to a deck no matter how small or simple its design. With a few chisels and a block plane, you can trim visible joints for a tighter fit before fastening key pieces together. You can also soften hard edges that could catch clothing or detract from the deck's appearance.

A set of three chisels should handle most deck-related work. Blade widths of ¾ inch, 1 inch, and 1½ inches or 2 inches are good. Keep chisel and plane blades sharp. Pressure-treated wood will dull steel edges more quickly than untreated wood. Retract the blade of the plane when it's not in use, and protect chisel edges from getting dinged against other metal tools.

Other Tools for Deck Construction

For most deck projects, you'll need an *electric drill* with a ¼-inch or ⅜-inch chuck capacity. You'll also need a basic selection of bits. Variable speed control and a reversing switch are good features because they allow you to use the drill for driving and withdrawing screws. An adjustable clutch will protect the motor from being overloaded while also providing good control in driving screws. Battery-powered drills provide more freedom of movement than their corded counterparts. But to make a cordless drill truly convenient, you need a spare battery so that work won't have to stop while a spent battery is recharging.

There are some special power tools that deck builders use to achieve fine details and finishing touches in custom-built decks. With a *portable power plane* you can straighten the edge of a board, milling it smooth and square. You can also trim minute

Photo 4–18: The tool belt is as important to a carpenter as a briefcase is to a business executive. Heavy stitching and bartacked stress points distinguish well-made pouches. This three-pouch model holds nails, hammer, utility knife, angle square, pencil, tape measure, and torpedo level.

amounts from an edge or plane a beveled edge. A *belt sander* is also useful for smoothing surfaces that are rough or uneven, but it won't do as precise a job as a power plane.

Finally, a couple of hammers are called for, as well as a good tool belt. A 20-ounce framing hammer has the heft you'll need for driving 12d, 16d and 20d nails into beams and joists. Spiral-shank and ring-shank nails are more difficult to drive than smooth-shank nails, so a heavier hammer will make this work easier. If you're fastening railings, trim, and other lighter members, you might feel more comfortable using a 16-ounce hammer.

A good tool belt should hold your hammer, tape measure, pencils, utility knife, and Speedsquare and still have at least one pouch open for nails, screws, plumb bob, chalk line, and other transient items.

CHAPTER 5

FOUNDATION AND FRAMING

A deck's structural elements include joists, beams, ledger boards, posts, and concrete piers or pads. Ideally, all these parts should work together to keep the deck standing strong, year after year. A decking board is only as secure as the joists that support it. The joists, in turn, depend on beams for support. Beams bear on posts or directly on concrete piers or pads that distribute the weight of the deck at properly spaced intervals. All in all, it's a fairly complex system primarily because of the interdependence of the different structural parts. This chapter covers basic details for foundations and framing from design through construction. For unusual decks and special cases that demand more complex details, see the projects in chapter 8.

DESIGNING THE STRUCTURE

To comply with most building codes, a deck must be able to support a *live load* of 40 pounds per square foot (psf) and a *dead load* of 10 psf. The dead load is the weight of the structure itself, which might include railings, a trellis, built-in benches, and other per-

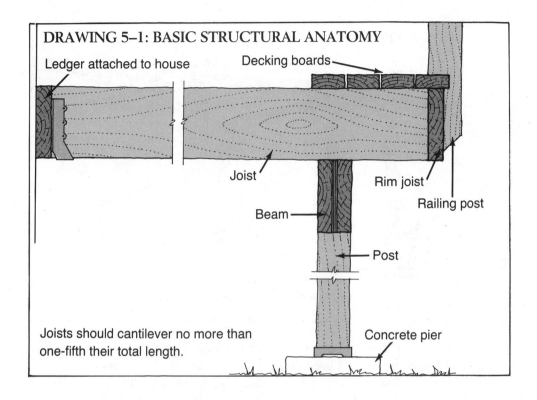

DRAWING 5–1: BASIC STRUCTURAL ANATOMY

Ledger attached to house

Decking boards

Joist

Rim joist

Railing post

Beam

Post

Concrete pier

Joists should cantilever no more than one-fifth their total length.

manent features. Live load applies to people, movable furniture, barbecue grills, and other impermanent items. Deck beams and joists must support these standard loads without deflecting more than $\frac{1}{360}$ of their span.

Four factors affect the load-bearing capabilities of a structural member:

- Size or dimension of the member
- Spacing between members
- Distance that the member spans between support points
- Species of wood used

All these factors must be considered when designing a deck. In some situations, you might want smaller structural members with short spans and close spacing between individual members. In other cases, longer spans are called for, with correspondingly larger structural members.

In designing most decks, it makes

sense to start at the top—with the decking boards—and work downward. The type of decking material you choose determines the spacing of the joists that the decking will be fastened to (for details on different decking material, see chapter 6). There are two common *on-center* spacings for deck joists: 16 inches and 24 inches. Joist spacing refers to the distance between the center of each joist, since this is the way layout marks are made on a beam or ledger where joists will be installed. Joists spaced 16 inches on center will actually be 14½ inches apart.

As shown in the joist spacing table on page 54, 16-inch centers are recommended to support redwood and cedar 2 × 4 decking. Also use 16-inch centers to support *one-by* deck boards (which actually measure ¾-inch thick) or *five-quarter* (1-inch thick) and *six-quarter* (1⅛-inch thick) stock. If you plan to use 2 × 6 deck boards, this decking can be installed over joists

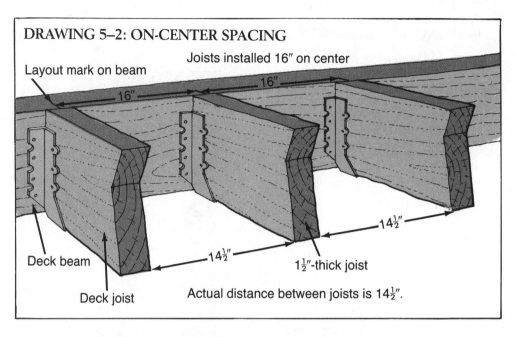

DRAWING 5–2: ON-CENTER SPACING

Joists installed 16″ on center

Layout mark on beam

16″   16″

Deck beam

14½″

14½″

Deck joist

1½″-thick joist

Actual distance between joists is 14½″.

spaced 24 inches on center. Southern pine and Douglas fir 2 × 4s are stiff enough to be installed over joists spaced 24 inches on center.

A note of explanation regarding the tables on pages 55, 56, and 57: While Douglas fir and larch are different species, they are graded together because they have the same structural properties. The same is true of hemlock and fir which are graded as *hem-fir*. The designation *Douglas fir South* refers to lumber that is milled from Douglas fir grown in Arizona, Colorado, Utah, Nevada, and New Mexico.

In the spans for deck joists table on page 55, you'll notice that Douglas fir-larch and southern pine, the prin-

JOIST SPACING

16 in. on Center	24 in. on Center
Redwood 2 × 4s	Redwood 2 × 6s (and larger)
Cedar 2 × 4s	Cedar 2 × 6s (and larger)
⁵⁄₄ and ⁶⁄₄ stock	Southern pine 2 × 4s (and larger)
Douglas fir 1× stock	Douglas fir 2 × 4s (and larger)
Southern pine 1× stock	

MAXIMUM ALLOWABLE SPANS FOR DECK JOISTS

Species	Joist Size (in.)	On-Center Spacing for Joists (in.)		
		16	24	32
Douglas fir-larch, southern pine	2 × 6	9'9"	7'11"	6'2"
	2 × 8	12'10"	10'6"	8'1"
	2 × 10	16'5"	13'4"	10'4"
Hem-fir, Douglas fir south	2 × 6	8'7"	7'0"	5'8"
	2 × 8	11'4"	9'3"	7'6"
	2 × 10	14'6"	11'10"	9'6"
Western pines and cedars, redwood, spruces	2 × 6	7'9"	6'2"	5'0"
	2 × 8	10'2"	8'1"	6'8"
	2 × 10	13'0"	10'4"	8'6"

cipal woods used to manufacture pressure-treated lumber, are among the strongest species. Western cedar and redwood are considerably weaker in terms of load-bearing capabilities.

This span table shows that longer spans (between support points on beams) are possible with larger joists. But closer on-center spacing can also allow for longer spans. These rules hold true for beams as well.

If you plan to cantilever the joists over a beam, use this rule: The cantilever should be no more than one-fifth the total span of the joist. For example, to calculate the maximum cantilever for a 10-foot joist: Multiply 10 feet by .2 to get 2 feet. This means the joist can extend 2 feet past the beam.

The spans for beams table on page 56 correlates beam sizes, spans, and spacings. There are several different types of beams used in deck construction. Solid beams usually have even nominal dimensions: 4 × 6, 4 × 10,

6 × 12, and so on. Built-up beams are made by fastening two or more *two-by* members together. Built-up beams will be at least as strong as solid beams of the same species and dimensions. In some areas, it's more economical to make your own beams on site instead of ordering solid stock.

When a built-up beam must fit over a 4 × 4 or 4 × 6 post, ½-inch-thick plywood spacers can be nailed between a pair of two-by members to give the beam a thickness of 3½ inches. This will match the actual thickness of nominal four-by stock. When plywood spacers are used, they should be cut from pressure-treated plywood and installed at an angle to shed water that falls between the two-by members.

Once specifications are set on decking, joists, and beams, you have to determine proper post sizes if beam loads are to be carried down to the foundation by posts. Post size has to

(continued on page 58)

MAXIMUM ALLOWABLE SPANS FOR BEAMS

On-Center Spacing for Beams (ft.)

Species: Douglas fir-larch, southern pine

Beam Size (in.)	4	5	6	7	8	9	10	11	12
4 × 6	Up to 6'								
3 × 8	Up to 8'	Up to 7'	Up to 6'						
4 × 8	Up to 10'	Up to 9'	Up to 8'	Up to 7'	Up to 6'				
3 × 10	Up to 11'	Up to 10'	Up to 9'	Up to 8'	Up to 7'	Up to 6'			
4 × 10	Up to 12'	Up to 11'	Up to 10'	Up to 9'	Up to 8'	Up to 7'	Up to 6'		
3 × 12		Up to 12'	Up to 11'	Up to 10'	Up to 9'	Up to 8'	Up to 7'	Up to 6'	
4 × 12			Up to 12'	Up to 11'	Up to 10'	Up to 9'	Up to 8'	Up to 7'	Up to 6'
6 × 10					Up to 12'	Up to 11'	Up to 10'	Up to 9'	Up to 8'
6 × 12							Up to 12'	Up to 11'	Up to 10'

Species: Hem-fir, Douglas fir south

Beam Size (in.)	4	5	6	7	8	9	10	11	12
4 × 6	Up to 6'								
3 × 8	Up to 7'	Up to 6'							
4 × 8	Up to 9'	Up to 8'	Up to 7'	Up to 6'					
3 × 10	Up to 10'	Up to 9'	Up to 8'	Up to 7'	Up to 6'				
4 × 10	Up to 11'	Up to 10'	Up to 9'	Up to 8'	Up to 7'	Up to 6'			
3 × 12	Up to 12'	Up to 11'	Up to 10'	Up to 9'	Up to 8'	Up to 7'	Up to 6'		
4 × 12		Up to 12'	Up to 11'	Up to 10'	Up to 9'	Up to 8'	Up to 7'	Up to 6'	
6 × 10				Up to 12'	Up to 11'	Up to 10'	Up to 9'	Up to 8'	Up to 7'
6 × 12						Up to 12'	Up to 11'	Up to 10'	Up to 9'

Species: Western pines and cedars, redwood, spruces

Beam Size (in.)	4	5	6	7	8	9	10	11	12
4 × 6	Up to 6'								
3 × 8	Up to 7'	Up to 6'							
4 × 8	Up to 8'	Up to 7'	Up to 6'						
3 × 10	Up to 9'	Up to 8'	Up to 7'	Up to 6'					
4 × 10	Up to 10'	Up to 9'	Up to 8'	Up to 7'	Up to 6'				
3 × 12	Up to 11'	Up to 10'	Up to 9'	Up to 8'	Up to 7'	Up to 6'			
4 × 12	Up to 12'	Up to 11'	Up to 10'	Up to 9'	Up to 8'	Up to 7'	Up to 6'		
6 × 10			Up to 12'	Up to 11'	Up to 10'	Up to 9'	Up to 8'	Up to 7'	Up to 6'
6 × 12					Up to 12'	Up to 11'	Up to 10'	Up to 9'	Up to 8'

DRAWING 5–3: BEAMS USED IN DECK CONSTRUCTION

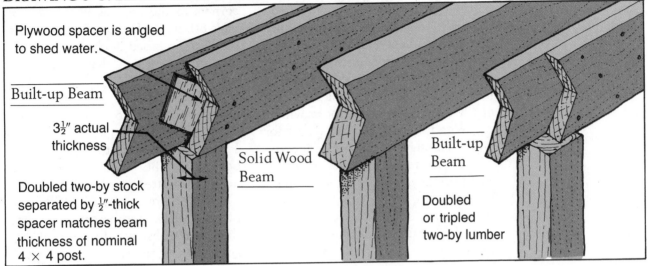

Plywood spacer is angled to shed water.

Built-up Beam

$3\frac{1}{2}''$ actual thickness

Doubled two-by stock separated by $\frac{1}{2}''$-thick spacer matches beam thickness of nominal 4×4 post.

Solid Wood Beam

Built-up Beam

Doubled or tripled two-by lumber

MINIMUM POST SIZES

Species	Post Size (in.)	Land Area in Sq. Ft. (beam spacing × post spacing)									
		36	48	60	72	84	96	108	120	132	144
Douglas fir-larch, southern pine	4 × 4	Up to 12'				Up to 10'			Up to 8'		
	4 × 6					Up to 12'				Up to 10'	
	6 × 6									Up to 12'	

Species	Post Size (in.)	36	48	60	72	84	96	108	120	132	144
Hem-fir, Douglas fir south	4 × 4	Up to 12'		Up to 10'			Up to 8'				
	4 × 6			Up to 12'			Up to 10'				
	6 × 6						Up to 12'				

Species	Post Size (in.)	36	48	60	72	84	96	108	120	132	144
Western pines and cedars, redwood, spruces	4 × 4	Up to 12'	Up to 10'		Up to 8'			Up to 6'			
	4 × 6		Up to 12'		Up to 10'			Up to 8'			
	6 × 6				Up to 12'						

increase as the load area increases or as post height increases (see the table on page 57). To calculate load area, multiply the on-center spacing between beams (10 feet, for example) by the on-center spacing between posts (12 feet in our example). For a load area of 120 square feet, 4 × 4 posts will be adequate for heights up to 8 feet for posts of Douglas fir or southern pine.

These tables should serve as guidelines as you make decisions about the size, span, and spacing of structural members. A single deck can be supported in a number of different ways. As you design a deck, make sure to err on the safe side. In other words, if a span falls between two joist or beam sizes, always use the larger, stronger member. It's also important, when designing a deck's structural system, to seek qualified assistance when it is needed. Spas or hot tubs that are incorporated into a deck will require their own separate foundations or supports. Follow the manufacturer's recommendations for these installations. Steep sites, difficult soil conditions, or the use of alternative wood species might require an engineer's expertise.

LAYING OUT THE FOUNDATION

Once post and beam locations are established, foundation layout can happen. Most decks rest on piers or pads of poured concrete. Precast or poured-in-place pads are used in warm climates where frostheaving isn't likely. In areas where the ground freezes during some part of the year, concrete piers have to be used to support a deck. The piers should extend to the frost line or below it so that freezing ground won't lift or shift the concrete.

A good way to pinpoint pier, pad, or posthole locations is to set up string lines. Strings can be held by stakes

driven into the ground at the planned corners of the deck as Photo 5-1 on page 60 shows. Use the 3-4-5 triangle method described in chapter 4 to adjust string lines so that corners are square.

It's also possible to run string lines off batter boards. To do this, you need three stakes and two short lengths of 1 × 2 or 1 × 4 stock to set up a batter board near the planned corner of a deck. The batter boards should be positioned 1 foot or so outside the planned deck perimeter. This way, they won't obstruct the work of digging holes for piers.

Using a tape measure and a plumb bob or level, you can pinpoint the locations of concrete piers. Mark each pier location with a spike. Later, when the hole has been dug and filled with poured concrete, you can measure off the string to position a metal post base before the concrete sets.

Use a posthole digger to make holes for your piers. With this double-handled, double-bladed tool, you can excavate a round hole with very straight sides. If you have more than a dozen or so holes to dig, you might consider renting a power auger or hiring an auger operator to dig your holes. In areas where cold winters are the norm, all holes should extend to the frost line or below it to prevent freezing soil from shifting the deck's foundation. Digging to a depth of 3 feet will put the base of a pier below the frost line in most parts of the United States. If you're unsure of the frost line depth in your area, your local building inspector will be able to tell you how deep to go.

INSTALLING PIERS AND POSTS

There are quite a few pier and post configurations used in deck construction. If pressure-treated posts are

DRAWING 5–4: PIER AND POST DETAILS

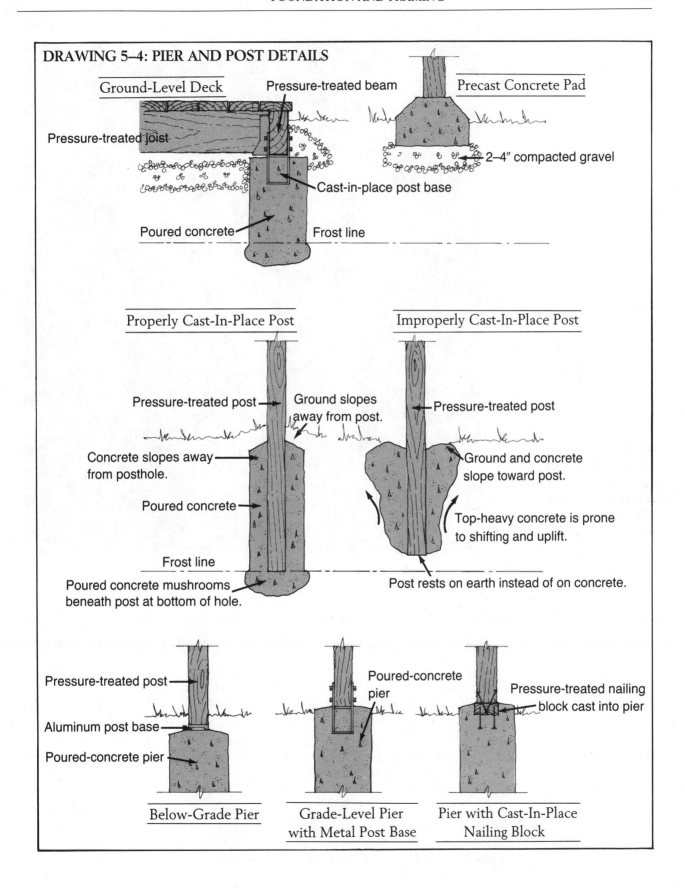

Ground-Level Deck

Pressure-treated beam

Precast Concrete Pad

Pressure-treated joist

2–4″ compacted gravel

Cast-in-place post base

Poured concrete

Frost line

Properly Cast-In-Place Post

Improperly Cast-In-Place Post

Pressure-treated post

Ground slopes away from post.

Pressure-treated post

Concrete slopes away from posthole.

Ground and concrete slope toward post.

Poured concrete

Top-heavy concrete is prone to shifting and uplift.

Frost line

Poured concrete mushrooms beneath post at bottom of hole.

Post rests on earth instead of on concrete.

Pressure-treated post

Poured-concrete pier

Pressure-treated nailing block cast into pier

Aluminum post base

Poured-concrete pier

Below-Grade Pier

Grade-Level Pier with Metal Post Base

Pier with Cast-In-Place Nailing Block

Photo 5–1: Wooden stakes can be used to set up string layout lines. Here, a level helps to establish the planned edge of a deck so that piers can be positioned.

used to support the deck framing, they can extend into the ground with at least the base of the post encased in poured concrete, as Drawing 5-4 on page 59 shows. This foundation detail is good for elevated decks where posts reach up 6 feet or more to support deck framing. The concrete *jacket* surrounding the post adds significantly to its rigidity. It's important to use the concrete correctly, however. Concrete works best at the base of the post. Avoid creating a concentrated *mushroom* of concrete around the post near grade level. This makes a top-heavy

profile that's prone to shifting and uplifting. The concrete, as well as the surrounding ground, should slope away from a cast-in-place post to encourage drainage.

When building an elevated deck with cast-in-place posts, it's usually easiest to install the posts so that they run longer than their finished length. Once all posts are in place, you can establish a level line and cut each post to its planned height. To install a post, first cover the bottom of the hole with 2 to 6 inches of poured concrete. Let this mix be fairly dry, so that it will set

Photo 5–2: Batter boards set up just outside planned deck corners make very accurate string layout possible. String position can be adjusted along the batter boards until the corner angle, defined by the intersection of string lines, is precise. A plumb bob, dropped from the intersection point, marks the exact corner of the deck.

up quickly. Tamp the concrete lightly so that it forms a relatively flat pad for the post to rest on.

The next step is to position the post on the concrete pad and brace it while the concrete is poured around it. Holding a level against two adjacent sides of the post, one worker can brace a post while another pours the concrete. This technique will work fine for posts that don't extend more than about 4 feet above the ground. For high posts, temporary braces should be used. First, wedge one or more stones against the post near the bottom of the hole to keep the post base from shifting. Then set up a pair of diagonal braces at right angles to each other so that you can plumb the post in two directions. The bottom of each brace is nailed to a short cleat, driven into the ground. The top of each brace is nailed to the post as your level indicates plumb position.

Once the second brace is nailed off, the post is fully braced and you can pour a fairly loose mix of concrete around it. Use a broom handle or a length of 1 × 1 stock to fill voids and work the mix around the post. Remember, it's not necessary to fill the hole all the way to grade level but the depth of the concrete should equal at least half the depth of the hole. Braces can be removed in three or four hours, but wait until the next day before fastening framing members to the post.

As an alternative to cast-in-place posts, you can use post anchors to fasten posts to concrete piers at or near grade level. These foundation details are good for low-level decks where extra post rigidity isn't needed. You might want to hide the concrete pier just slightly below grade level. On the other hand, if you're not using pressure-treated posts, piers should extend above grade level to protect posts from ground moisture.

In most situations, concrete piers can be poured using the hole as a form for the poured concrete (see "Working with Concrete" on page 70). The base of the hole should be dry and flat. If

Photo 5–3: Short posts can be held plumb by one worker while another secures the post with a jacket of poured concrete. To make sure the post is plumb, the torpedo level needs to be used against two adjacent sides of the post.

Photo 5–4: A high post should be held plumb with temporary diagonal braces until concrete hardens around the post base or until framing members are attached to keep it plumb. Install braces at right angles to each other, as shown here. The top end of each brace is fastened to the post. The bottom ends of the braces are fastened to wooden stakes that are driven securely into the ground.

the soil is loose near the top of the hole, you can use a square form made from 2 × 4s to contain the poured concrete at the top of the pier. Use a level when placing this square form around the top of the hole (see Photo 5-6 on page 63). Soil tamped in place around the form should keep it in place until the concrete sets.

In sandy or unstable soils, local building codes may require tubular fiber forms to be used for poured-concrete piers. These hollow, cylindrical forms (Sonotube is one brand) are available in diameters from 4 to 12 inches and in lengths from 4 to 10 feet. (Even larger sizes are used on commercial construction projects.) An 8-inch-diameter form is commonly used as a base for a 4 × 4 post; 10-inch-diameter forms are usually adequate to support 6 × 6 posts. To use tubular forms for poured-concrete piers, first make a hole for each form. Be sure to

Photo 5–5: A post that doesn't extend below grade can bear on a concrete pier at or near grade level. A steel framing connector cast into the top of the pier has holes in both exposed sides so that the connector can be fastened to the post.

Photo 5–6: Made from dimension lumber, a square form can be used at the top of a hole dug for a poured-concrete pier. It's good practice to level the top edges of the form.

dig down to the frost line or below it. Before positioning the form, spread 2 to 4 inches of gravel at the bottom of the hole. Then place the form in the hole and mark a cutoff line where you want the top of the pier to be. It's possible to have a form extend a foot or more above grade, but this usually calls for steel reinforcement bars, commonly known as *rebar*, to be installed inside the form prior to pouring the concrete. Check with your building inspector or a structural engineer concerning reinforcing requirements for exposed above-grade concrete piers.

Cut your forms to length by hand, using a crosscut saw. Then position each form in its hole, bracing it plumb and level by backfilling around the form. Finally, fill each form with freshly mixed concrete. When the forms are filled, install metal post or column bases as required. Once the concrete sets, any part of the form that appears above grade can be peeled away with the help of a utility knife.

There are some situations that call for the tops of concrete piers to be level

THE WELL-CRAFTED CORNER

Strength and appearance are both important at the perimeter of the deck. Doubling up the rim joists is good practice. There are a number of rim joist details that work well and also look good. Three different details are shown below.

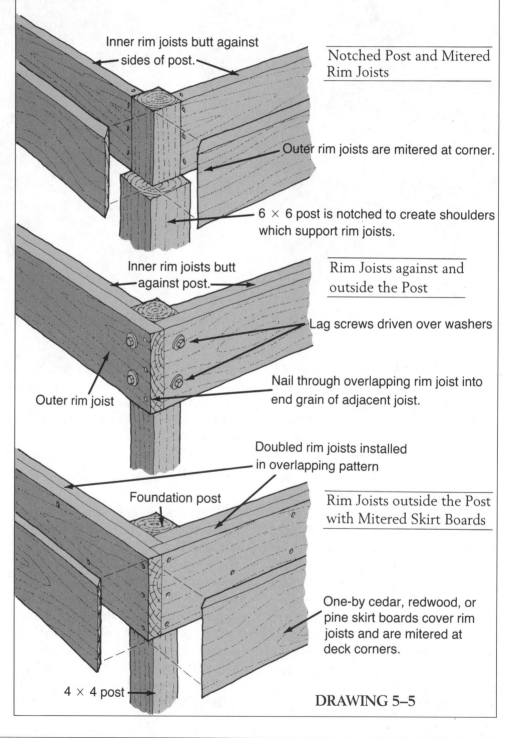

Inner rim joists butt against sides of post.

Notched Post and Mitered Rim Joists

Outer rim joists are mitered at corner.

6 × 6 post is notched to create shoulders which support rim joists.

Inner rim joists butt against post.

Rim Joists against and outside the Post

Lag screws driven over washers

Nail through overlapping rim joist into end grain of adjacent joist.

Outer rim joist

Doubled rim joists installed in overlapping pattern

Foundation post

Rim Joists outside the Post with Mitered Skirt Boards

One-by cedar, redwood, or pine skirt boards cover rim joists and are mitered at deck corners.

4 × 4 post

DRAWING 5–5

Photo 5–7: Tubular fiber forms are often used to make poured-concrete piers. Here, a steel post base is cast into the top of a pier contained in a fiber form. String lines are used to align the position of the post base in the freshly poured concrete.

with each other. For example, you may be planning a ground-level deck on a fairly level site. Instead of supporting posts (which can be cut to different heights as required), the piers will need to support a single beam. To make the tops of the piers level with each other, first secure the tubular forms in their holes, allowing the top of each form to extend several inches higher than the piers will be. Now use a water level, transit, or builder's level to mark the desired pier level on the outside of each form. Taking care not to shift the form, insert one or more nails in predrilled holes through each form on the level mark. These *grade nails*, which extend inside the forms, will serve as level indicators when forms are filled with concrete. Once the concrete has set, peel back the form sections that extend above the pier.

ATTACHING A LEDGER BOARD TO THE HOUSE

A deck's connection to the house is critical. In most cases, deck joists will be connected to a ledger board that is fastened to the wood framing or masonry of the house. It's important for the top edge of the ledger to be straight and level, so it's smart to reserve a straight, clear board for this key structural member. Two people can easily hold the ledger level for marking a level line and masonry anchor holes, and also while fastening the ledger. If you're installing the ledger yourself, you might find it easier to use a water level to make a couple of marks on the house (at opposite ends of the ledger location) where the top edge of the ledger will be; then snap a line to connect these marks. If you don't have a water level, you can use a 4-foot or 6-foot level to mark where the top edge of the ledger will be. It's also possible to fasten one end of the ledger to the house and then place a long level on the ledger's top edge as you adjust the free end of the ledger up and down until the top edge is level.

There are several ways to fasten a ledger to the house. Choosing the right one depends largely on the construction of the wall where the ledger will be installed. As a general rule, the ledger board should be at least as wide as the joists that will be fastened to it. Use fasteners in pairs when fastening

the ledger against any material. Each pair should be more or less vertically aligned, with pairs spaced 2 to 3 feet apart.

Using masonry anchors, a pressure-treated ledger can be fastened directly against most masonry walls, as Drawing 5-6 below shows. If trapped moisture between the ledger and the masonry could cause a problem (as in an old brick or stone wall, for example), then several aluminum or galvanized steel washers can be used as spacers between the ledger and the wall, as Drawing 5-7 on the opposite page shows. Vary the number of washers to compensate for an uneven wall surface. To promote drainage between ledger and wall, install the first decking board flush with the back edge of the ledger, as shown in Drawing 5-7.

Installation details for wood-framed walls are a bit more complex.

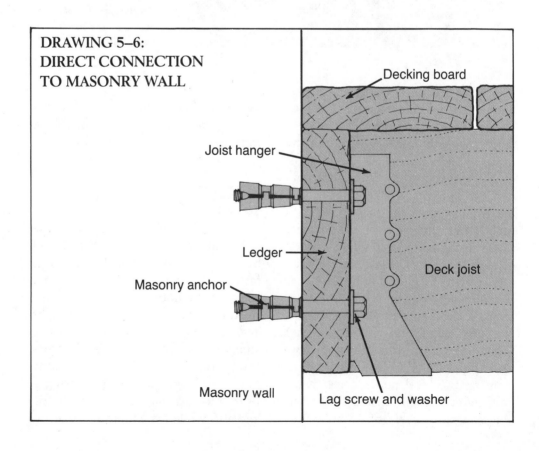

DRAWING 5–6:
DIRECT CONNECTION
TO MASONRY WALL

Decking board

Joist hanger

Ledger

Masonry anchor

Deck joist

Masonry wall

Lag screw and washer

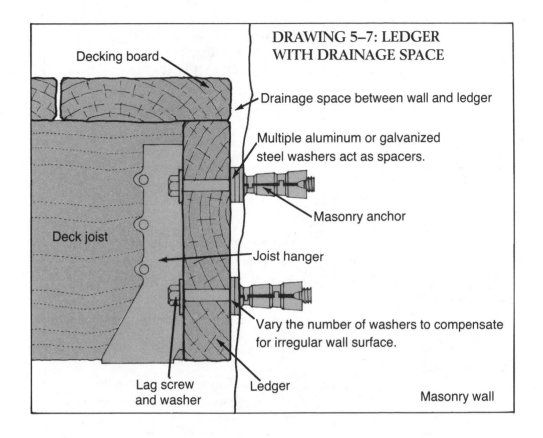

DRAWING 5–7: LEDGER WITH DRAINAGE SPACE

Decking board

Drainage space between wall and ledger

Multiple aluminum or galvanized steel washers act as spacers.

Masonry anchor

Deck joist

Joist hanger

Vary the number of washers to compensate for irregular wall surface.

Lag screw and washer

Ledger

Masonry wall

In most cases, it's best to remove the exterior siding so that the ledger can be fastened directly against the exterior sheathing. Remove enough siding above the ledger to allow the first deck board to fit under the siding, as Drawing 5-8 on page 68 shows. Once the siding is removed, nails in the exposed sheathing will reveal the location of studs, joists, and rim joists. It's important for the ledger to be screwed to these structural members rather than just to the sheathing. As Drawing 5-8 shows, lag screws should penetrate through the sheathing and at least 1½ inches into a stud, joist, or plate.

After the ledger is screwed to the wooden wall of the house, flashing needs to be installed. To flash a ledger board you'll need a roll of aluminum sheet flashing at least 5 or 6 inches wide. Ledger flashing should be continuous and calls for the aluminum to be bent in a Z profile. The top edge of the flashing is tucked at least 2 inches under the exterior siding. There's a right-angled bend where the flashing meets the top edge of the ledger. The remaining inch or so of flashing is bent down over the ledger board. This flashing detail protects the house from moisture damage. Treat the flashing carefully because it forms a critical barrier. Instead of nailing it in place, let the pressure of the siding and the weight of the first deck board hold the aluminum in position. Avoid nailing or screwing through the flashing when installing deck boards.

BUILDING THE FRAME

When the ledger has been installed and piers and posts are in place, the deck's frame can be completed by installing beams and joists. Joist hang-

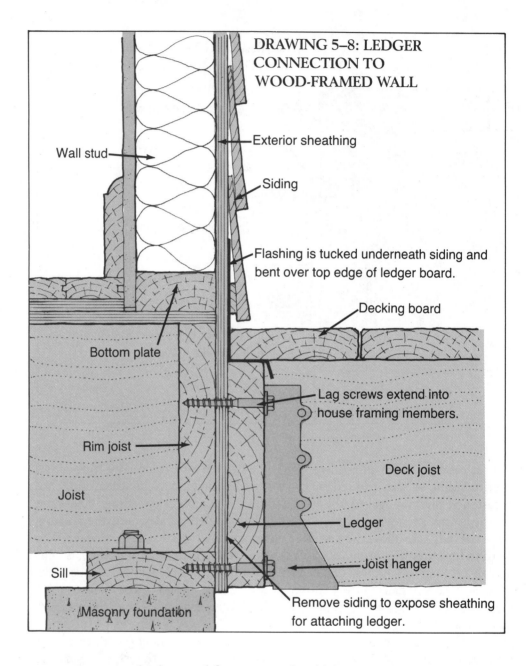

DRAWING 5–8: LEDGER
CONNECTION TO
WOOD-FRAMED WALL

Wall stud

Exterior sheathing

Siding

Flashing is tucked underneath siding and
bent over top edge of ledger board.

Decking board

Bottom plate

Lag screws extend into
house framing members.

Rim joist

Deck joist

Joist

Ledger

Sill

Joist hanger

Masonry foundation

Remove siding to expose sheathing
for attaching ledger.

ers, post caps, and other steel framing connectors can be used to make most of these structural connections (see chapter 3). But it's also possible to join structural members using just nails, lag screws, and bolts. Drawing 5-9 on the opposite page shows notching the joists to fit around a secondary ledger, a good substitute for joist hangers. A secondary ledger should be no larger than a 2 × 2 or 2 × 3 board, and joists should be toenailed to both the primary and secondary ledgers. For tips on toenailing, see "Toenailing Tips" on page 72.

In many elevated decks the joists can cantilever beyond a beam that runs at a right angle to the joists, as shown in Drawing 5-1 on page 53. If this is the case, the top edge of the beam should be a joist's width below the top edge of the ledger.

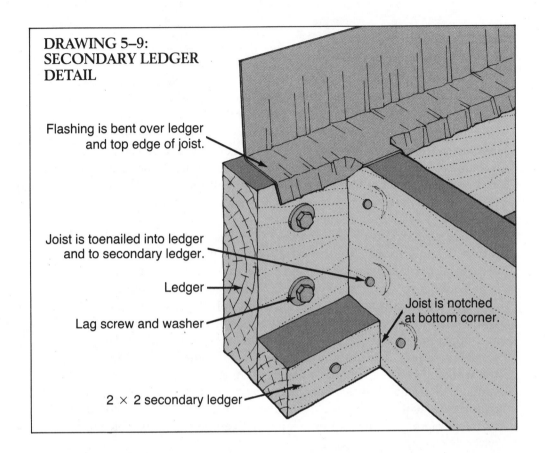

**DRAWING 5–9:
SECONDARY LEDGER
DETAIL**

Flashing is bent over ledger
and top edge of joist.

Joist is toenailed into ledger
and to secondary ledger.

Ledger

Lag screw and washer

Joist is notched
at bottom corner.

2 × 2 secondary ledger

In other deck designs, the beam and its support posts will be at the perimeter of the deck. Perimeter posts can extend above the deck to form part of the railing structure. With this framing detail the joists are usually fastened against the innermost face of the beam so the top edge of the beam needs to be level with the top edge of the ledger. It pays to take extra care when installing ledgers and beams. If these members are level and properly aligned, joist installation will be quick and accurate.

Before you install a joist, hold the end up to your eye and look down each edge. Often you'll notice a slight curve. The joist is fine to use, just make sure you install it with the curve or *crown* facing up. This puts the crown in compression under load. When the deck is finished and begins to support its live load, this weight will tend to straighten out crowned joists. If you install joists with the crown down, you'll be creating a head start toward a sagging deck.

WORKING WITH CONCRETE

Concrete is a crucial part of most deck projects. Without it, we'd have a much more difficult time creating a solid foundation for the deck structure. Sand, portland cement, and gravel are the dry ingredients in concrete. Portland cement is the binder. Sand and gravel provide strength and also take up space, giving the concrete 60 to 75 percent of its hardened volume. Technically known as *fine aggregate*, the sand in concrete needs to be clean and well-graded, containing a mix of particles up to ¼-inch in diameter. Likewise, the *coarse aggregate* in concrete should contain stones that range in size from ¼ inch to about 1½ inch.

The proportions of sand, cement, and aggregate can be varied to suit different applications. A good ratio for deck piers is (by volume) 1 part cement, 2 parts fine aggregate, and 3 parts coarse aggregate.

Water is the catalyst in concrete. When added to cement, it begins a process called *hydration*, the chemical reaction that hardens the mix. The water used to make concrete should be clean enough to drink. Salt, silt, and other impurities (in the aggregate as well as the water) significantly weaken concrete. The amount of water added to the dry ingredients affects the workability and strength of concrete. A soupy mixture with too much water will result in weak concrete. For pads and footings, a fairly dry consistency will set up quickly and cure to a strong base. For poured-concrete piers, you need a looser mix that can be placed in holes or forms without leaving voids or empty pockets.

ESTIMATING

To calculate how much concrete you'll need to fill a hole or tubular form, use the following formula: $0.7854 \times$ hole or form diameter (squared) $\times$ depth of form or hole (in inches). This calculation will give you volume in cubic inches. For volume in cubic feet, divide by 1728. A cubic yard equals 27 cubic feet.

For most small- and medium-size decks, you'll have to mix your own concrete. You can combine the ingredients yourself or, at greater expense, use bags of premixed concrete, which contain all the dry ingredients. An 80-pound bag of premixed concrete will yield a little less than ⅔ cubic feet of concrete.

MAKING THE MUD

Mix your concrete in a wheelbarrow or a mason's tub. For large jobs, where more than a dozen holes must be filled, you might want to use a cement mixer. Most tool-rental agencies have mixers available.

A hoe and a long-handled shovel make excellent companions when doing concrete work. The hoe is good for mixing concrete, while the shovel is good for moving it around once it reaches workable consistency. Rubber boots and gloves are also helpful. Wet or dry, concrete is very rough on the skin.

Whether you're mixing by hand or machine, always start with the dry ingredients first. Even bagged concrete mix should be turned over a few times before adding water to make sure that sand, cement, and gravel are homogeneous. Add water gradually until the consistency is right; then pour your piers. If you're using post or column bases, embed them at the top of the pier while the concrete is still wet. Make sure that bases align with the layout of posts.

While it's still wet, rinse concrete from mixer, wheelbarrow, and shovel surfaces. Be sure to protect unused dry ingredients from moisture. It's a good idea to seal partially full bags of concrete or cement in plastic bags and keep these in a dry place.

Once poured, concrete piers should remain undisturbed for at least 24 hours before weight is put on them. In extremely dry weather, keep piers wet by misting them with water or by covering exposed concrete with damp burlap. Concrete loses its strength if it is allowed to dry out too quickly.

Photo 5-8: A hoe is the best tool for mixing concrete.

TOENAILING TIPS

Toenailing is a standard method for fastening the edge of one framing member against the face of another. It's a quick, relatively strong connection that is often made when face nailing or end nailing isn't possible (see Drawing 5–10 below). Joists and blocking are often toenailed to other joists or to beams. For deck construction, where framing members will regularly shrink and expand due to changing moisture conditions, it's good practice to reinforce toenailed connections with cleats, secondary ledgers, or steel framing connectors.

To toenail a board properly, nails must be driven at an angle, penetrating through the joining edge of one piece and into the face of a supporting member. Ideally, half the length of the nail will be in each member. It takes some time to gain proficiency in toenailing one board to another. First, lay out the locations of joists or other members to be toenailed. Start

DRAWING 5–10: NAILING GUIDELINES

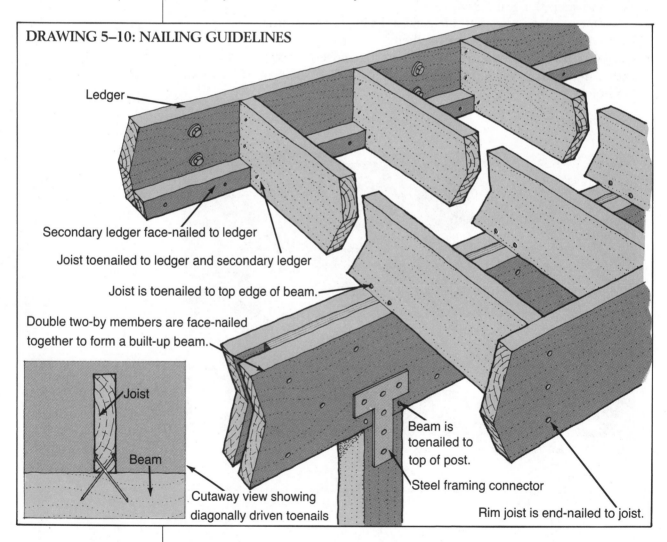

Ledger

Secondary ledger face-nailed to ledger

Joist toenailed to ledger and secondary ledger

Joist is toenailed to top edge of beam.

Double two-by members are face-nailed together to form a built-up beam.

Joist

Beam

Cutaway view showing diagonally driven toenails

Beam is toenailed to top of post.

Steel framing connector

Rim joist is end-nailed to joist.

with two 8d nails on each side of a joist, driving them into the wood at about a 45-degree angle. Place opposing nails so that they won't hit each other when driven. The points of the nails should enter the wood about 1½ inch back from the end of the board.

Driving nails at an angle will cause the board to shift, so you should start nailing one side with the board deliberately offset from its layout lines by about ¾ inch. As you nail, the board will move a little bit at a time. When it crosses its layout lines in the opposite direction, it's time to begin nailing from the opposite side. With experience, you can anticipate the movement that occurs and eventually end up with both sides toenailed and the board aligned with its layout.

A helpful trick to control board movement while toenailing is to hold your Speedsquare against one edge of the board while nailing the other. This braces the board and also keeps it square with the piece you're nailing into.

Screws can also be *toed*, or driven at an angle, to fasten the end of one board against the face of another. This is a common way to install rails between posts when building a railing. Shifting is less of a problem when toeing screws, but you may want to predrill the screw hole to avoid splitting the end of the board.

Photo 5–9: Toenailing takes practice. Nails are driven from both sides of the board at an angle to extend through the end of the board and into a joining member. Here, a joist is toenailed to a beam and to a 2 × 2 ledger that is nailed to the beam. An angle square held against joist and beam can help to control joist movement while nails are driven.

CHAPTER 6

PUTTING DOWN THE DECK

When the foundation and framework of a deck are complete, the decking itself can go down. The decking boards make up the most visible part of a deck. Because they're underfoot and directly exposed to the elements, decking boards take a great deal of punishment. (For information on maintaining decks, see chapter 9.) Doing a good job of selecting and installing decking boards will make a big difference in the overall appearance of the finished deck. This chapter is broken down into three parts: selecting what type and species of decking to use, deciding on an installation pattern, and installation details.

TYPES OF DECKING

Wood used for decking comes in two basic thicknesses. Nominal *two-by* boards used for decking actually measure 1½ inches thick. Nominal *five-quarter* (often written as ⁵⁄₄) stock used for decking is 1 inch thick. Porch flooring, which is installed without gaps between boards, is usually ¾-inch-thick *one-by* stock, milled with tongue-and-groove edges. As the name indicates, porch flooring is intended

Photo 6–1: Decking options. From top to bottom: *⁵⁄₄ × 4 treated southern pine with radiused edges, 2 × 4 treated southern pine, ⁵⁄₄ × 6 redwood with radiused edges, 2 × 6 redwood, and 2 × 6 treated southern pine.*

for outdoor floors that are protected by a roof. Porch flooring is not for open decks that must have gaps to let rain fall through.

Douglas fir and southern pine are the two principal pressure-treated woods available in both two-by and ⁵⁄₄ form. Lacking the strength of fir or southern pine, redwood and cedar decking are used mostly in two-by form.

It's best to stick with narrow widths in decking boards. Wider boards expand and contract farther than narrow boards, exerting more pressure against the nails or screws that hold them down. This makes wide boards more prone to splitting and warping. Widths of 3½ inches (as in a nominal 2 × 4) and 5½ inches (the actual width of a 2 × 6) are most popular for decking material. Decking

boards are available with square edges, or with *eased* edges that have been rounded over slightly in the milling process. Eased edges are usually desirable because they look good and are less prone to raise splinters and split with age.

The thickness and width of your decking should be matched to the spacing between deck joists. More details on joist spacing for different types of decking are given in chapter 5. The joist spacing table on page 54 shows that 16-inches on-center spacing is recommended for redwood or cedar 2 × 4s. Douglas fir or southern pine 2 × 4s are strong enough to be installed over 24-inch centers.

Beyond the structural requirements, choosing the type of wood to use for decking depends on budget and personal preference. Pressure-treated southern pine is often used as a decking surface. This material is strong and economical. Most pressure-treated wood is also guaranteed against rot and insect infestation. Dimensional instability is southern pine's chief drawback. Even boards that are kiln-dried after pressure treatment (KDAT) are prone to cracking, warping, and cupping with prolonged exposure to sun, rain, and freezing weather. Fortunately, you can counteract these tendencies to some degree with good fastening techniques and regular applications of water-repellent preservative.

Redwood, cedar, and (in some regions) cypress are alternatives to pressure-treated pine decking. It might be a good idea to install redwood, cedar, or cypress decking if you don't want infants or toddlers to have direct contact with a pressure-treated surface. All three species are naturally decay resistant. In addition, redwood and cedar have very good dimensional stability. (When kiln-dried, cypress is also dimensionally stable.) These woods resist cupping, cracking, and warping better than most other species. This performance comes at a price, how-

ever. Redwood and cedar can cost two or three times as much as pressure-treated pine or fir. This price difference varies in different locations and also depends on the grades of lumber available.

No matter which species of wood is used, a decking board should always be installed *bark side down*. This means that the growth rings visible in the end grain of a board should show a downward or concave arc, as Drawing 6-1 below shows. When installed bark side down, boards are more resistant to cupping as a result of uneven moisture absorption. If cupping does occur, the cup will face upward instead of downward, eliminating projecting corners and allowing water to run off the boards instead of collecting.

End-to-end joints between decking boards can cause difficulties. When two boards butt together over a single joist, nails have to be driven very close to the ends of the boards, angling into the joist. This frequently causes board ends to split. Water damage is a more severe problem. Runoff from the top of the deck can be trapped between boards on top of the joist or beam. Dust and debris will also collect in this

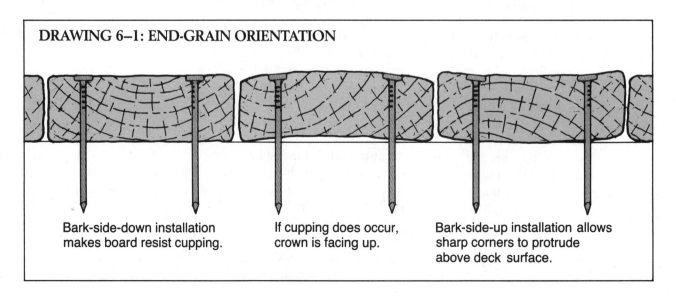

DRAWING 6–1: END-GRAIN ORIENTATION

Bark-side-down installation makes board resist cupping.

If cupping does occur, crown is facing up.

Bark-side-up installation allows sharp corners to protrude above deck surface.

area, retaining moisture for long periods of time. The eventual result is mildew and decay. Even pressure-treated wood can fail prematurely under these conditions.

Fortunately, there are ways to avoid butting deck boards together over a single joist or beam. One approach is to use long decking boards, so that butt joints aren't required. This is an advantage of redwood. Redwood boards as long as 20 feet are readily available. But if avoiding butt joints isn't possible, it's smart to plan for them to fall over a doubled joist or built-up beam. Separate the paired two-by members with a pressure-treated spacer— either plywood or solid wood. Angle the spacer, as shown in Drawing 6-3 on page 78 so that water can drain away.

This butt-joint detail requires more time and material, but it will make a deck last longer and look better. Water can't become trapped between decking boards. Also, board ends can bear on a broader surface and nails can be driven straight, with less risk of splitting the wood.

In most situations, the perimeter of a deck looks best when decking boards are allowed to overhang framing members, as shown in Drawing 6-4 on page 78. An even overhang of between ¾ inch and 1½ inches creates a pleasing shadow line around the edge of a deck, giving the entire structure a lighter feel. Sharp corners on the overhang can be softened with a belt sander, a block plane, or a router with a roundover bit.

DECKING PATTERNS

The pattern you create with decking can be simple or complex. Besides aesthetics, pattern choices depend on the decking material you're using and on the framing members that will support it. As discussed in chapter 5, the layout and spacing of joists will limit the pattern choices you have, so decking patterns really need to be determined as you're designing the framework that will support decking boards.

In a rectangular deck, decking can be installed parallel with the length or width of the deck, depending on how

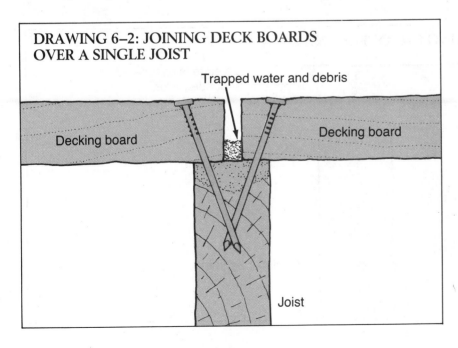

DRAWING 6–2: JOINING DECK BOARDS OVER A SINGLE JOIST

Trapped water and debris

Decking board

Decking board

Joist

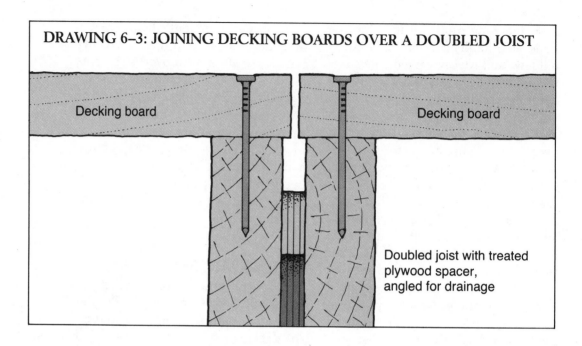

DRAWING 6–3: JOINING DECKING BOARDS OVER A DOUBLED JOIST

Decking board

Decking board

Doubled joist with treated
plywood spacer,
angled for drainage

the joists run. You can create an interesting pattern by alternating 2 × 4 boards with 2 × 6 boards.

A popular alternative to this conventional treatment is a pattern angled at 45 degrees, with angled board ends meeting over doubled joists. A series of angled runs creates a herringbone pattern.

Decking can be installed in a parquet pattern, providing that joists are located to support each parquet section. A parquet pattern is a good way to cover a large area using relatively short decking boards. More cutting will be required, so it will take a little longer to complete a parquet pattern deck.

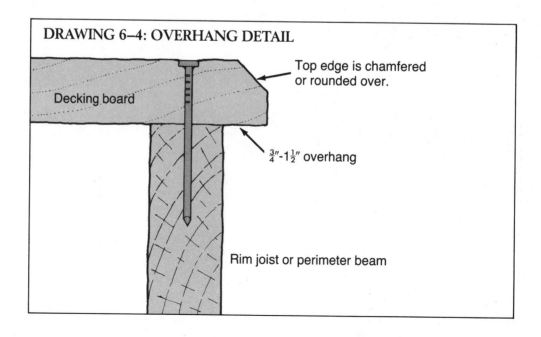

DRAWING 6–4: OVERHANG DETAIL

Top edge is chamfered
or rounded over.

Decking board

$\frac{3}{4}$"-$1\frac{1}{2}$" overhang

Rim joist or perimeter beam

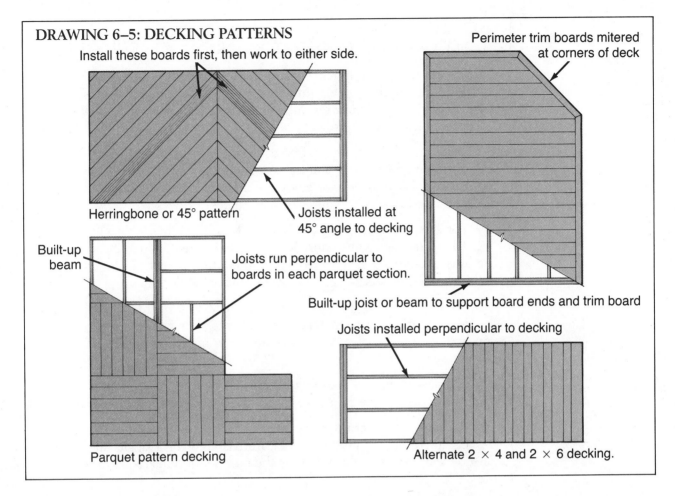

DRAWING 6–5: DECKING PATTERNS

Install these boards first, then work to either side.

Herringbone or 45° pattern

Joists installed at 45° angle to decking

Built-up beam

Joists run perpendicular to boards in each parquet section.

Parquet pattern decking

Perimeter trim boards mitered at corners of deck

Built-up joist or beam to support board ends and trim board

Joists installed perpendicular to decking

Alternate 2 × 4 and 2 × 6 decking.

Perimeter trim boards can dress up a deck, especially if these boards are mitered where they meet at the corners of the deck. To frame decking with perimeter boards, a secondary rim joist must be installed to support the ends of the decking boards that butt against the perimeter boards. This detail is shown in Drawing 6-6 on page 81.

BOARD BY BOARD

Compared to the work of building a deck's foundation and framing, installing decking boards is fairly easy. If you're working on a large deck, it may make sense to use an air-powered nail gun to fasten down decking boards. If you don't own an air compressor and pneumatic nailer, these tools are available from many tool rental outlets.

Be sure to use only rust-resistant fasteners to install decking. Galvanized outdoor screws or special decking nails, as described in chapter 3, will do the best job of holding down the deck. Wherever a decking board crosses a joist or beam, anchor it with two nails or screws.

Avoid driving nails or screws below the surface of a decking board. This increases your chances of splitting the wood and also creates a depression where water can collect. Instead, drive fasteners flush with the wood surface. If you don't want to risk splitting a board when driving a nail or screw near its end, blunt the end of the nail before driving it or predrill the hole.

CALCULATING COVERAGE FOR DECKING BOARDS

To estimate how much decking lumber to order for a given deck, multiply the length by the width to determine the square footage. Then use one of the conversion formulas given below to determine how many linear feet of lumber to order.

- For 2 × 4 boards, or any boards that are $3\frac{1}{2}$ inches wide:
  10 square feet will require about 34 linear feet of boards, so divide the square footage to be covered by 10; then multiply by 34. For example, a 200-square-foot-deck requires 680 linear feet of decking.

- For 2 × 6 boards, or any boards that are $5\frac{1}{2}$ inches wide:
  10 square feet will require about 22 linear feet of boards, so divide the square footage to be covered by 10; then multiply by 22. For example, a 200-square-foot deck requires 440 linear feet of decking.

- For an alternating pattern of 2 × 6 and 2 × 4 boards:
  Multiply the square footage to be covered by 1.5. This figure will tell you how many linear feet of 2 × 6s and how many linear feet of 2 × 4s to order.

- For boards that are installed diagonally:
  Add 5 percent to the above formulas to account for extra waste.

- For parquet pattern decking:
  Calculate how many linear feet are required for a single unit of the pattern; then multiply this figure by the number of units required to cover the deck.

To promote drainage, it is important to have gaps between decking boards. Gap width should be between ⅛ inch and ¼ inch. If you are installing kiln-dried decking or decking that has air dried to a moisture content below 14 percent, use a couple of 16d nails as spacers between boards when laying down the deck. This should create an even gap that will shrink or widen slightly as boards absorb and release moisture.

Green or unseasoned decking and pressure-treated decking that hasn't been kiln-dried after pressure treatment should be installed with board edges butting together. As the wood dries out, edge-to-edge shrinkage will create gaps. Installing these boards with gaps would be a mistake because later shrinkage will cause the gaps to be too wide.

If your deck is connected to the house, the first decking board to install is usually the one nearest the house. In a diagonal or herringbone pattern deck, install the longest diagonal board first; then install a neighboring board on either side and work across the deck with shorter and shorter diagonal courses.

At the perimeter of the deck, let decking boards run long, at least several inches beyond rim joists or beams. Once the entire deck or deck section is installed, you can use a chalk line to snap a cutoff line along the entire side of the deck (see Photo 6-2 below). Then trim off the waste pieces using a circular saw (see Photo 6-3 below).

Marking and trimming the boards all at once saves time, and results in a smooth, even line at the edge of the deck.

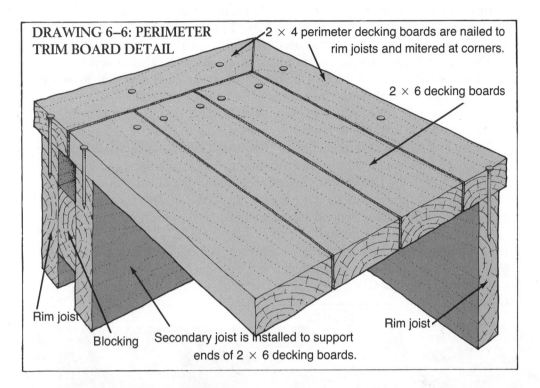

DRAWING 6–6: PERIMETER TRIM BOARD DETAIL

2 × 4 perimeter decking boards are nailed to rim joists and mitered at corners.

2 × 6 decking boards

Rim joist

Blocking

Secondary joist is installed to support ends of 2 × 6 decking boards.

Rim joist

Photo 6–2: When installing decking boards, let the boards run beyond the rim joist. Establish a cutoff line by snapping a chalk line.

Photo 6–3: With a circular saw and a fine cutting blade, trim decking boards in place following the chalk line.

NO NAILS

Deck Board Ties are designed to eliminate face-nailing in decking board installation. The surface of the deck can be free of nail or screw heads. Apart from the clean look of decking that seems to float on its framing, a nail-free surface means longer life for decking boards.

These fasteners must be used with 1½-inch-thick decking. To use Deck Board Ties, toenail both edges of a starter decking board to deck joists, as shown in Photo 6–4 below. If necessary, use a nailset to recess the nail heads flush with the edges of the board.

Next, nail the ties to the edge of the board that will fit next to the starter board. Install one tie for each joist that the board will cross, and locate ties within several inches of the joists (see Photo 6–5 below). The ties have a T-shaped profile, and the top of each T is designed to fit against the underside of the decking boards. To install the second board, fit the free ends of the ties under the edge of the starter board; then toenail the opposite edge of the second board to the joists (see Photo 6–6 below). Repeat this process to install the rest of the boards.

Deck Board Ties are made by Simpson Strong-Tie Co. Depending on quantities purchased, each fastener will cost between 15 and 20 cents. A similar product is called Dek-klips.

Photo 6–4: Step 1: Toenail starter board to joists. Nail through both edges of the starter board and into joists.

Photo 6–6: Step 3: Install remaining boards. After butting fasteners under and against installed board, toenail the exposed edge to joists.

Photo 6–5: Step 2: Install deck board hardware. Steel ties are nailed to board edge near each joist location. The free edges of the T-shaped fasteners will fit underneath the starter board.

GETTING IT STRAIGHT

Curves aren't uncommon among decking boards. As an imperfection, curves are less serious than twisting, bowing, and cracking. In most cases, it's possible to straighten a curved decking board as it is installed. Decking lumber that is green or unseasoned is often flexible enough so that curved boards can be straightened by hand pressure alone as the board is installed. Maximize your straightening leverage, as shown in Drawing 6–7 below, first fastening the straightest end of the board to at least two joists. The curve should bend out away from decking boards that have already been installed.

When hand pressure alone isn't sufficient to straighten a curved board, pipe clamps can sometimes be useful as long as there's a solid surface for the clamping feet to bear against. Avoid driving pry bars into joists and levering them back against a curved board as a straightening method. This usually damages the board and is only effective in straightening slight curves.

When hand pressure isn't effective and pipe clamps can't be used, you'll get good results with a simple straightening jig like the one shown in Drawing 6–7. The jig has two parts—a straight 2 × 4 brace about 8 feet long, and an angled wedge about 4 feet long. The wedge can be made from 2 × 6 or 2 × 8 stock. To use the jig, first fasten the straightest end of the curved decking board to at least two joists. Now, temporarily nail or screw the brace across two or more joists next to a board section that needs to be straightened. The brace should be positioned at an angle that approximates that of the wedge. When the brace is secured, drive the wedge between the brace and the curved decking board. Nail or screw down the decking board when it's straight, then loosen the wedge by tapping on its narrow end. To straighten long curves, you may have to repeat this process a couple of times along a single board.

DRAWING 6–7: STRAIGHTENING DECKING BOARDS
TWO METHODS ARE SHOWN. BOARD CURVES ARE EXAGGERATED FOR CLARITY.

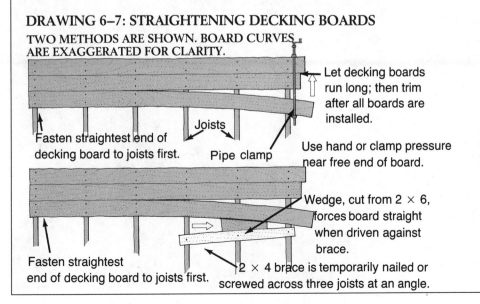

Let decking boards run long; then trim after all boards are installed.

Fasten straightest end of decking board to joists first.

Joists

Pipe clamp

Use hand or clamp pressure near free end of board.

Wedge, cut from 2 × 6, forces board straight when driven against brace.

Fasten straightest end of decking board to joists first.

2 × 4 brace is temporarily nailed or screwed across three joists at an angle.

CHAPTER 7

STAIRS, RAILINGS, AND BUILT-IN BENCHES

To make a great deck takes more than size and shape. Also important are built-in details that add convenience, safety, comfort, and style. Stairs, railings, and built-in benches all qualify on these counts. In fact, these elements offer excellent opportunities to distinguish a deck with good proportions and well-crafted joinery.

STAIRWAY DESIGN

Some elevated decks don't require stairways. A deck built off a second floor bedroom or study, for example, will be more private without an exterior stairway to ground level. Where stairways are required in a deck design, it is important to anticipate traffic patterns on the deck and plan stairways accordingly. (For more information on analyzing traffic flow, see chapter 1.) Depending on the activity areas served by the deck, two small stairways may provide more convenience than a single large one. On the other hand, a narrow stairway can look badly out of scale when built near the middle of a large deck.

There are a few important differences between interior stairways and the exterior stairways that are part of many deck designs. First of all, a deck stairway must be every bit as weather-resistant as the rest of the deck. Pressure-treated framing members should be used for an exterior stair. Stair treads, since they are replaceable and not in direct contact with the ground, can be of weather-resistant wood such as cedar or redwood, but pressure-treated treads are frequently used as well.

Size and scale also change when you move outside. There's more room outside, so stairways can be broadened and extended if necessary. By adding width to a stairway or incorporating a landing, space can be made for potted plants, benches, or built-in planters.

Interior stairways usually have both treads and risers. In an exterior stairway, risers are often eliminated because they inhibit drainage and make it more difficult to sweep debris away. A stairway without risers is a little easier to build.

There are several types of stairways to choose from. A straight stairway is easiest to build but requires a rectangular area, usually along the side or end of a deck. Landed stairs offer good flexibility in design, since the size of the landing and the configuration of the stairway can both be varied. Like a landed stairway, a winding stairway enables you to turn a corner when connecting two levels. If space is extremely cramped around an elevated deck, a prefabricated spiral stairway may be the only solution.

DRAWING 7–1: TYPES OF STAIRS

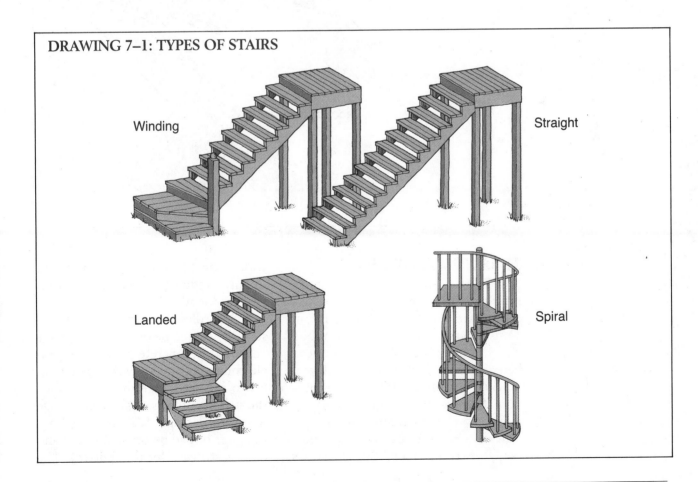

Winding   Straight

Landed   Spiral

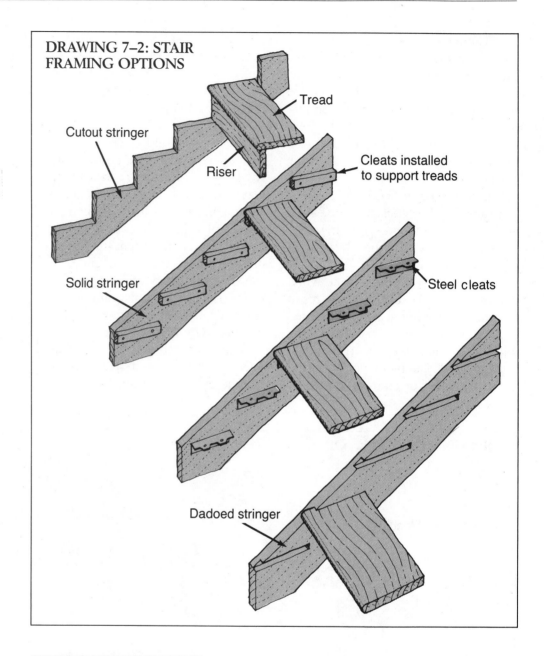

DRAWING 7–2: STAIR FRAMING OPTIONS

Cutout stringer

Tread

Riser

Cleats installed to support treads

Solid stringer

Steel cleats

Dadoed stringer

STAIR FRAMING OPTIONS

There are several ways to frame a stairway, all of which use stringers, also called carriages. Cutout stringers can be used with or without risers. Wood cleats, fastened to solid carriages, can be used to support stair treads. Metal brackets also are available for this purpose. Still another option is to cut dadoes in stair carriages to support the stair treads. Stair carriages are normally used in pairs. But stairways wider than 4 feet or higher than 5 feet usually require a central cutout stringer for added stiffness.

Regardless of type, an exterior stairway should be built with stringers anchored to concrete piers or to a single concrete pad. Allowing the stringers to rest on the ground will reduce the stability of the stairs and encourage moisture damage. It's smart to pour the piers or pad before measuring and cutting stringers for the stairway. The

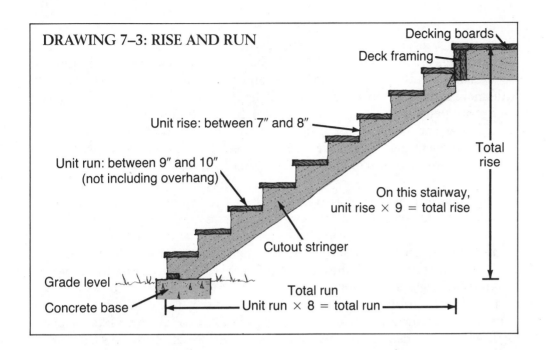

DRAWING 7–3: RISE AND RUN

Decking boards

Deck framing

Unit rise: between 7" and 8"

Unit run: between 9" and 10"
(not including overhang)

On this stairway,
unit rise × 9 = total rise

Cutout stringer

Total rise

Grade level

Concrete base

Total run
Unit run × 8 = total run

STAIR LAYOUT

There are a few building code guidelines that apply to both interior and exterior stairways. Headroom at any point on the stairway should be at least 80 inches. There should be a handrail on at least one side of the stair. If the stair is open on both sides, you'll need two handrails with balusters. Handrail height should be about 30 inches above the stair treads.

The first thing to do when laying out a stairway is to divide the *total rise* (vertical distance) and *total run* (horizontal distance) into comfortable tread widths and riser heights. There are a couple of helpful rules you can use to make these calculations. First, remember that the vertical distance between treads (called *unit rise*) should be between 7 inches and 8 inches.

Tread width *(unit run)*, not including any overhang or nosing, should be between 9 inches and 10 inches. Added together, unit rise and unit run should equal between 17 inches and 18 inches.

It usually takes some figuring before unit rise and unit run can be calculated for a particular stairway. Remember to account for the thickness of the decking material in determining total rise. As an example, assume total rise is 63 inches. Dividing 63 by a desired unit rise of 7½ inches yields an uneven tread number of 8.4. But if 63 is divided by a unit rise of 7⅞ inches (7.875 inches), the result is an even 8. A stairway with 8 risers will have 7 treads, so if unit run is set at 10 inches, the total run will equal 70 inches.

MAKING A CUTOUT STRINGER

Stair stringers usually start out as 2 × 10 or 2 × 12 dimension lumber. If cleats or brackets are used to support the treads, these can be fastened in place after stringers are cut or even after stringers are installed.

Making a cutout stringer takes a little more time. The tools you'll need are a sharp pencil, a framing square, a circular saw, and a hand crosscut saw. Lay out the cutting lines using the framing square, as shown in Photo 7-1 below.

Set the square with its corner facing into the body of the board. Using the measurements on the blade and *tongue* of the square, align unit rise and unit run with the edge of the board and mark the right-angled cutout. Repeat this layout for the full run of the stairway, always making a right-angled mark where unit rise meets unit run. At the base of the stringer, mark a level cutoff line parallel with the lowermost unit run mark.

Once both boards are marked, most of the cutting can be done with a circular saw. To avoid overcutting where the rise and run meet, use a hand crosscut saw to finish up the cuts and complete the stringer's sawtooth shape. Fasten the top of each stringer to the deck framing using cleats or steel framing connectors. Make sure stringers are parallel and level with each other.

Once stringers are in place, fasten the treads down, one by one. Treads with *eased*, or slightly rounded-over edges, are better looking and also a little safer to use. To round-over square-edged treads, use a router and either a ⅜-in. or ½-in. roundover bit. If you don't have a router, sharp corners can be eased with a block plane.

Instead of using a single wide tread for each step, it's better to install two boards across stringers or between cleats to make a single step. This creates a drainage space between boards, which is important. Also, a single wide

Photo 7–1: The corner of the framing square is used to lay out cuts for a stair stringer. For this stair, the 9-inch mark on the square is lined up with the edge of the 2 × 12 to mark unit run. The 8-inch mark on the square (unit rise) is also lined up over the edge.

Photo 7–2: With a circular saw, cut toward the corner of each step. The bottom of the stringer (front) has already been cut to fit around a 2 × 4 cleat that will be fastened to a concrete pad.

tread will cup or warp more severely than a pair of narrower boards. In the stairway shown in Photo 7-4 on page 90, each step actually is made up of three boards: a pair of 2 × 6s and a 2 × 4 that's nailed against the outer edge of the 2 × 6. The broad face of the 2 × 4 gives each step a bold *nosing*. The gap beneath the 2 × 4 is filled by a 1 × 3 board, creating a pleasing shadow line.

RAILINGS

Long before decks became popular, carpenters had developed innumerable ways to build railings for porches and stairways. This means there are many design possibilities for deck railings. All deck railings, however, are supported by posts, and all railings must meet specific building code requirements. In most designs, rails extend between posts, supporting vertical balusters. The top rail can stand on its own or be covered by a cap piece, which is sometimes beveled to help it shed water.

Most building codes require a railing if the finished deck surface sits 30 inches or more above grade. Standard railing height is 36 inches. Balusters should be spaced no farther apart than 6 inches. This 6-inch spacing rule also

Photo 7–3: Finish up each triangular cutout with a handsaw.

Photo 7–4: On this stairway, each tread contains three boards: a pair of 2 × 6s and a 2 × 4 that's nailed against the outer edge of the 2 × 6. The broad face of the 2 × 4 gives each step a bold nosing. The gap beneath the 2 × 4 is filled by a 1 × 3 board, creating a pleasing shadowline.

applies to railings that have intermediate horizontal rails instead of balusters.

Regardless of railing type, railing posts come first in design and construction. Without secure posts, the entire railing can never be strong. There are several structural options for railing posts. First, they can be foundation posts that extend from the ground, supporting beams and joists as well as railing members. Alternately, posts can be fastened to framing members, extending up through the decking boards to become principal railing supports.

Another option is for posts to be bolted to the rim joists or skirt boards that define the perimeter of the deck. Posts in this configuration usually are notched to make the connection stronger and more attractive. An angled notch, combined with a horizontal support and a front leg, can be used to frame a combination bench and railing that leans out beyond the deck perimeter. Both types of notched posts are available in precut form at many lumber yards that carry decking material.

Railing Option 1

The railing shown in Photo 7-6 on page 92 has 4 × 4 posts, 2 × 4 rails, 2 × 2 balusters, and a 2 × 6 cap for the top rail. The balusters are available at most lumber yards as nominal 2 × 2 stock. It's also easy to make your own by ripping 2 × 4 stock in half. Baluster ends are beveled at a 45-degree angle. This gives the railings a well-crafted look, and beveled ends shed water better than square-cut ends.

This railing is easy to build. Rails can meet posts squarely or at an angle. Top rails should be screwed flush with the tops of the posts, as Photo 7-7 on

Photo 7–5: A post with an angled notch, combined with a horizontal support and a front leg, can be used to frame a combination bench and railing that leans out beyond the deck perimeter.

Photo 7–6: This railing is built using 4 × 4 posts, 2 × 4 top and bottom rails, 2 × 2 balusters, and 2 × 6 cap pieces. Baluster ends are beveled at a 45-degree angle.

Photo 7–7: Using 2½-inch-long screws, fasten top rails to posts so that the top edge of each rail is flush with the post top. Screws will have to be toed, or driven at an angle, into posts.

Photo 7–8: On this railing, 2 × 4 top and bottom rails are installed with their sides positioned horizontally. Balusters made from 2 × 2s are centered between both rails.

the opposite page shows. Drive 2½-inch-long screws at an angle through the sides and ends of the rails and into the posts. Predrilling screw holes will prevent splitting as screws are driven.

Bottom rails should be screwed in place about 3½ inches from the deck surface, again by angling screws through rails and into posts. Make sure that top and bottom rails are vertically aligned with each other. Once rails are in place, balusters can be installed. One 2½-inch screw at each baluster end should be sufficient to hold it in place. Installing the cap completes the railing. At the corners of the deck, cap pieces should be mitered where they meet over posts.

Railing Option 2

The railing shown in Photo 7-8 on the opposite page also has 2 × 4 rails and 2 × 2 balusters, but they're configured a little differently. Rails are installed with the face sides of the 2 × 4s positioned horizontally. Bal-usters are centered along the faces of both rails. When building this type of railing, first cut rails to fit between posts and cut balusters to length. Then preassemble rails and balusters flat on the deck. Finally, position the railing section between posts and screw rails to posts. Posts can be topped off with a small cap.

Railing Option 3

In some railing designs, posts extend above railing cap pieces, showing off ornamental tops. In the railing shown in Photo 7-9 below, there's no need for a bottom rail because the balusters are fastened directly against the rim joist. Balusters are beveled on bottom ends only. The top rail and cap are cut from 2 × 4 stock; both members are screwed to the posts they connect to.

Exotic options in railing treatments include steel cable rails and clear acrylic panels. For a more traditional-style railing, specially milled compo-

Photo 7–9: No bottom rail is required for this railing. Balusters are fastened against the rim joist. Posts with ornamental tops extend above 2 × 4 top rails and caps.

UNCONVENTIONAL RAILINGS

Conventional rail and baluster configurations work well for many decks, though they definitely obstruct the view. This is fine if privacy or traditional details are important. But sometimes an elevated deck offers beautiful vistas, and you may want your railing to be as minimal as possible without compromising the safety of the deck. Here are two designs for railings that will make the best of a deck's vantage point. Before you build any unconventional railing, check with your building inspector to make sure it meets your local building code.

Steel cable can be used, in combination with standard wood posts and a wood cap rail, to make a railing that's safe and unobtrusive, creating a

Photo 7–10: High-strength cable can be used to make a nearly invisible railing. The cable is installed horizontally, held in holes that are drilled in 4 × 4 posts. Corners require a pair of posts, as shown.

nents are available in pressure-treated wood, as well as in cedar, redwood, and fir. These components include both short and long posts that are decoratively turned, post caps, contoured handrails for stairways, cap pieces, top and bottom rails, and turned balusters. For a decorative post treatment you can do yourself, see "Making a Decorative Post" on page 96.

Photo 7–11: Clear acrylic panels can take the place of railing balusters, providing an unobstructed view. The ¼-inch-thick acrylic is installed in grooves that are cut in posts and cap pieces.

distinctive high-tech appearance (see Photo 7–10 on the opposite page). Installed horizontally through holes drilled in railing posts, the thin-gauge, high-strength cable (diameters of ⅛ inch and ³⁄₁₆ inch are typical) is tightened and secured using special turnbuckles and other fittings that are part of the system.

Corners, building connections, and other details require special treatment using cable-railing components. To be safe and to look good, cable tension should be around 150 pounds. For source-of-supply information on cable railings, see Sources on page 238.

Another strategy for railings that don't block the view calls for clear acrylic panels to be installed between posts (see Photo 7–11 above). In the design shown here, grooves milled in posts and rails hold ¼-inch-thick acrylic panels in place at the edge of the deck. Acrylic expands and contracts with temperature changes, so it's important for grooves to allow for at least ¼-inch of panel movement. Each panel is fitted into side and bottom grooves before the top rail is installed.

Railing Option 4

As Photo 7-12 on page 96 shows, the turned balusters (some manufacturers call them spindles) are designed to be installed between specially milled top and bottom rails. Baluster ends can be cut at an angle to fit between rail members on a stairway. Turned railings and balusters help a deck design blend with traditional architecture.

Photo 7–12: Milled components for traditional-style railings include contoured top and bottom rails, turned balusters or spindles, and decorative posts.

MAKING A DECORATIVE POST

Posts that extend above a deck railing need some sort of decorative treatment. Posts with factory-milled tops are available at many lumber yards, but you can do your own decorative work using a circular saw and a square. The 4 × 4 post shown here has a pointed cap with a decorative groove just beneath it (see Photo 7–13 below).

Photo 7-13: A decorative post such as this one can be made with a circular saw.

To make this decorative cap, first use your square to establish cutting lines on all four faces of the stock. The pointed top requires a pair of 45-degree-angle cuts on each face (see Photo 7–14 below). Make these cuts with the circular saw set for maximum depth of cut, and be sure to use a sharp blade designed to produce smooth finish cuts. If necessary, use a handsaw to complete the cuts for the top.

The groove is made with depth of cut set at about ½ inch. Depending on groove width, make repeated passes with the blade until waste is removed between layout lines (see Photo 7–15 below). If necessary, use a chisel to smooth the bottom surface of each groove. Use this technique to make as many grooves as you like.

Photo 7–14: After laying out 45-degree angle cuts on the post, make two angled cuts on each face of the post. Adjust the circular saw for maximum depth of cut.

Photo 7–15: To groove the top of the post, adjust depth of cut to about ½ inch and make a series of closely spaced passes on each side of the post. Clean up the grooves with a chisel.

Photo 7–16: This built-in bench, located at the deck perimeter, takes the place of a railing.

BUILT-IN BENCHES

On many decks, built-in benches can be used instead of railings. Benches are often combined or integrated with railings to make a seating area at the edge of the deck. The bench shown in Photo 7-16, at left, is made from red-wood. Of course, the same design could be built using cedar or pressure-treated lumber.

In this design, 2 × 4 crossmembers form the seating and backrest surfaces. These 2 × 4s are fastened to bench support frames, which are spaced 4 feet on center. Each support frame can be assembled flat and then secured to the deck by attaching the rear support member to the rim joist of the deck.

A RAILING OF AWNING

Awning material, stretched tightly between a frame of steel tubing, is an unconventional railing that offers privacy instead of broad vistas. In the design shown here, steel tubing has been custom-bent to fit two adjacent sides of this elevated deck. The ends of each tubing section extend below the decking where they are securely fastened to framing members. Awning material, reinforced and grommeted at the edges, is stretched and tied inside the tubing frame.

Photo 7-17: Awning material and steel tubing create an unusual railing.

To build each support frame, first cut all parts to size. As Drawing 7-4, below, shows, the 2 × 8 back is sloped for comfort and also notched out to fit against the rear support member. Seat supports for the frame are paired 2 × 6s, sandwiched around the back and around a diagonal seat brace. The seat brace is very important in this design since it provides sufficient strength for the seat to cantilever over the deck surface.

When all frames have been assembled, fasten each one to the deck and to the rim joist. Lag screws will strengthen the rim joist connection. Then connect the frames by attaching 2 × 4 bench cross members.

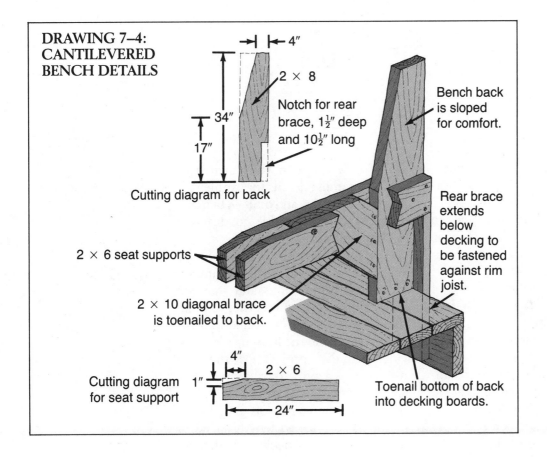

DRAWING 7–4: CANTILEVERED BENCH DETAILS

4″

2 × 8

34″

17″

Notch for rear brace, 1½″ deep and 10½″ long

Bench back is sloped for comfort.

Cutting diagram for back

Rear brace extends below decking to be fastened against rim joist.

2 × 6 seat supports

2 × 10 diagonal brace is toenailed to back.

4″

2 × 6

1″

Cutting diagram for seat support

24″

Toenail bottom of back into decking boards.

CHAPTER **8**

DECK-BUILDING PROJECTS

In this section of the book, you'll find a design portfolio of interesting decks and a selection of 12 deck-building projects. The design portfolio presents a diverse selection of deck ideas that should inspire your own design efforts. The selection of projects also offers a broad range of possibilities presented in step-by-step fashion. Some of the projects involve basic construction principles discussed elsewhere in the book. Other projects contain more complex construction details. Regardless of scale or complexity, in each project you'll find tips and techniques that you can apply when building your own deck.

Houses and backyard landscapes vary, so you'll probably need to adapt certain details shown here to suit conditions at your house and site. For example, if your site isn't as level as the one shown in a particular project, you'll need to modify post and foundation details, referring back to the information in chapter 5.

Another way to use this part of the book is to pick out particular details from one or more projects and incorporate them in your own deck design. Framing details for cantilevers, multi-level decks, and built-in benches are especially adaptable to different deck projects.

A lumber order is provided for each project. This is the list of lumber, in nominal dimensions and standard lengths, that you would order to build the featured deck. Finished dimensions are given in the framing plan provided with each project. Use these dimensions as a guide during the design and construction process; don't use them to precut beams, joists, and other members to finished length ahead of time. Even if your deck is identical in size to one shown here, slight variations in lumber thickness and width or in pier height or location make it necessary to cut members to size as they're installed.

A hardware order also appears with most projects. This lists items like joist hangers, post bases, machine bolts, and special brackets or fixtures, but stops short of nail and screw quantities.

Sometimes a great view is justification enough for a deck design. This second-story deck was part of a new home design. The railing posts are also foundation posts. The decking boards are redwood. Design by Tedd Benson Woodworking.

A cobblestone courtyard is the base-level anchor for different deck levels that cascade down this gentle slope. Built-in benches follow the angular forms of deck levels, creating a pleasing geometric pattern. Here, bark chips are an effective ground cover. Design by Jim Babcock. Photo courtesy of California Redwood Association.

Integrating different design elements can bring a great deck into being. Here, railing posts extend to support a trellis over this cedar deck. Solid cedar skirt boards hide the under-deck area. And the patio proves that brick and wood go well together. Design and construction by Allen Enterprises. Photos by Mitch Mandel.

This ground-level deck complements a Colonial-style house. Good landscaping and a brick patio integrate this deck with its surroundings.

A walkway leads to the two-level deck at the back of this house. Locating the walkway between deck levels is convenient as well as attractive.

A landed stairway adds elegance to this basic elevated deck. The deck uses 6 × 6 support posts instead of 4 × 4 posts to make the deck look stable and strong. Photo courtesy of Osmose Wood Preserving, Inc.

A bi-level deck is a wise choice in situations like this, when small changes in elevation must be resolved. This deck steps down gracefully from doorway level to grade. Photo courtesy of Archadeck.

There's always room for a deck, however small. Asymmetrical in plan and in railing design, this diminutive deck is reached by two sets of sliding glass doors that open into the kitchen.

When extended horizontally, a stairway can become a major design element, creating a terrace effect. Here, boards cover the ends of decking boards at upper and transition levels. Photo courtesy of Archadeck.

Sometimes a great tree calls for a jog in a deck's plan. Photo courtesy of Hickson Corporation.

A tree is the centerpiece of this elevated deck built from pressure-treated lumber.

A 45-degree corner adds drama to this deck plan. Lattice panels are used to screen off the under-deck area. Design and construction by Allen Enterprises.

Built around a pool, this deck offers excellent drainage, good footing, and fine looks. Photo courtesy of Osmose Wood Preserving, Inc.

Fences or screens are important when a deck design includes a spa or hot tub. Here, concentric steps on two levels integrate the hot tub. Photo courtesy of Hickson Corp.

A pair of posts, angled braces, and a beam are aesthetic as well as structural elements in this multi-level deck design. Here, a white stain is used to distinguish the second-story deck from lower levels. Design by Eli Sutton.

Gray stain, used on exterior trim and on the deck, integrates both the house and the deck.

Pressure-treated lumber is an especially wise choice when a deck is built at the edge of the water. Photo courtesy of Osmose Wood Preserving, Inc.

This redwood entry deck, with its built-in benches, is a project you can complete in a weekend. See page 118.

This two-level deck covers a nondescript concrete slab. Its pressure-treated framing is covered with redwood rim joists and decking boards. For instructions on how to build it, see page 122.

A simple built-in bench can enhance any deck. Construction details begin on page 132.

It can be difficult to deck around an aboveground pool. This design works well because it combines a small upper-level bathing area with a larger ground-level deck. See page 136.

Many decks could use a privacy screen like this one. It consists of a lower panel of vertical 2 × 6s, and an upper frame that surrounds a lattice panel. See page 152.

Spas go well with decks, but demand special structural details to accommodate the added weight of the water. Construction information begins on page 156.

Repetitive elements create harmony in this design, which includes built-in benches, a trellis, a fence, and an octagonal table. For instructions on building the trellis, fence, and table, see page 182. Photo courtesy of California Redwood Association.

This distinctive deck dramatically transforms a raised-ranch house. The shingled deck wall and open roof trusses unify the deck with the house. Stairways, decking, trim, and lattice panels are finished with white stain. Plans start on page 170. Design by Vincent Babak. Construction by Luxeder Clan.

On this severely sloped site, a two-level deck takes the place of a backyard. Walkways, supported by cantilevered beams, lead back to grade level. Stretched tightly between posts, stainless steel cable takes the place of conventional balusters. Deck projects this complex usually require design assistance from a structural engineer. For details, see page 194. Photo by Muffy Kibbey.

Converted to a residence, this stone barn gains a graceful entry deck that is built around a tree and between the walls of an old stone foundation. See page 204.

PROJECTS

PROJECT 1

ENTRY DECK

This small entry deck, with its decked walkway and simple benches, is a nice alternative to a brick or concrete surface. The deck is particularly appropriate in the setting shown here because it blends with the natural wood siding of the house. This deck is 6 feet deep and 7 feet across, but the size can easily be altered to fit different spaces.

1   **Attach ledger boards to the house.** To prevent trapped water from damaging house siding and framing, flash the two ledgers carefully. In this situation, the siding should be removed up to a level that will be just above the level of the finished deck. This way, the ledger can be fastened directly against the exterior sheathing, and the decking board closest to the house can extend under the siding. Bend the ledger flashing over the top edge of the ledger, and tuck it up under the siding. (See chapter 5 for flashing details for different wall surfaces.)

2   **Put in concrete foundation pier.** This deck has only one corner that is not supported by the house, and this corner gets its support from a foundation post bearing on a poured-concrete pier. Extend string lines from both ledger boards to lay out the location of the pier. Use the 3-4-5 triangle method described in chapter 4 (see page 36) to adjust string lines so that corners are square. Use the same string lines to position a post base in the top of the poured concrete before it sets.

3   **Install the foundation post.** Fasten the 4 × 4 foundation post to its post base when the concrete has set. The top of the 4 × 4 foundation post needs to be level with the top of the ledgers. To do this, start by cutting the post several inches too long. When the concrete has set, fasten it to the post base, making sure it is plumb. Then use a line level to mark the ledger height on the post and cut the post off in place.

4   **Install joists.** Install the two rim joists that define the deck's perimeter. Face-nail them to the pier post and into the ends of the ledgers. Double up each rim joist by adding an inner 2 × 8, as shown in Drawing 8–1. Install the joists 16 inches on center.

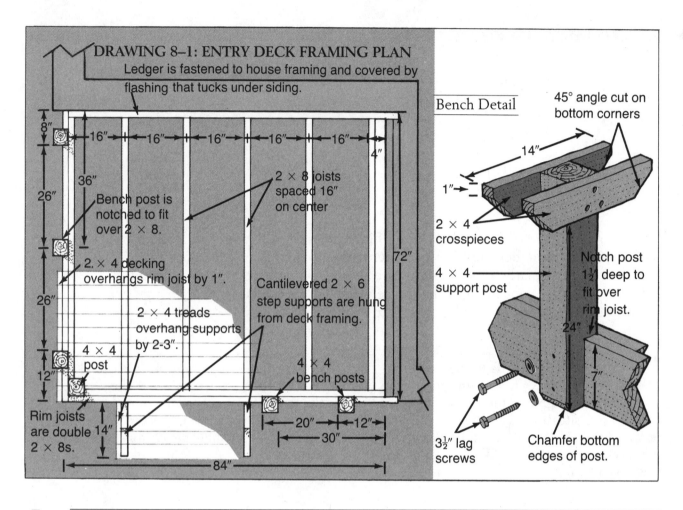

DRAWING 8–1: ENTRY DECK FRAMING PLAN

Ledger is fastened to house framing and covered by flashing that tucks under siding.

8"
16" 16" 16" 16" 16"
4"

36"
26"
Bench post is notched to fit over 2 × 8.

2 × 8 joists spaced 16" on center

2 × 4 decking overhangs rim joist by 1".

Cantilevered 2 × 6 step supports are hung from deck framing.

26"
2 × 4 treads overhang supports by 2–3".

4 × 4 post

12"
4 × 4 bench posts

Rim joists are double 2 × 8s.

14"

72"

20" 12"
30"
84"

Bench Detail

45° angle cut on bottom corners

14"
1"
2 × 4 crosspieces

4 × 4 support post

Notch post 1½" deep to fit over rim joist.

24"
7"

3½" lag screws

Chamfer bottom edges of post.

---

5   **Cut and install bench support posts.** Cut a notch 7 inches long and 1½ inches deep in these five posts. Then make a 45-degree-angle chamfer cut on the bottom end of each post. The chamfer softens the bottom corner of each post, adding to the deck's well-crafted appearance. You can make the chamfer cuts using a handsaw or you can use your circular saw with the base adjusted for a 45-degree-angle cut.

Post positions are shown in Drawing 8–1. Fasten each post to its rim joist with a pair of 3½-inch-long, ⅜-inch-diameter lag screws. Once posts are in place, it's best to finish the deck itself before completing the benches.

6   **Install step supports and step.** Using steel tie plates, hang two 5-foot-long 2 × 6 step supports from underneath two joists. Extend the step supports 14 inches beyond the rim joist. By cantilevering the supports, the step seems to float, and ground contact is avoided.

7   **Install decking.** The decking used on this project is 2 × 4 redwood. The boards run parallel to the step. Begin by installing the deck board closest to the house. Tuck it under the exterior siding to rest on the ledger flashing. Nail down the rest of the decking, leaving ⅛ inch between boards. If decking boards aren't dry, no airspace between boards is necessary. Allow decking boards to overhang rim joists by 1 inch and notch boards to fit around bench support posts.

Lumber Order

AMOUNT	MATERIAL	PART
2	4 × 4 × 8' treated	1 foundation post and 5 bench posts
1	2 × 8 × 7' treated	ledger
1	2 × 8 × 6' treated	ledger
2	2 × 8 × 7' treated	rim joists
2	2 × 8 × 6' treated	rim joists
5	2 × 8 × 6' treated	joists
2	2 × 6 × 6' treated	stair supports
30	2 × 4 × 8' redwood	deck boards, seat crosspieces, and seating boards

Hardware

1 foundation post base
4 steel tie plates
10 pcs. 3½ × ⅜-in.-dia. lag screws

8   **Assemble benches and step from 2 × 4 stock.** Like the bench posts, the bench crosspieces have 45-degree-angle cuts along their bottom corners (see Bench Detail, Drawing 8–1). Make these cuts after cutting the crosspieces to a finished length of 14 inches. Then fasten the crosspieces across the tops of the bench support posts, and complete benches by installing four 2 × 4 bench slats on each one.

The slats for the bench to the right of the stairs run from the edge of the steps to the right end of the deck, about 39½ inches. The slats for the bench on the left side of the deck run the full length of the left side, about 6 feet. Finally, fasten 2 × 4 treads to step supports. The treads should be about 38 inches long, overlapping the supports by 2 or 3 inches.

PROJECT 2

TWO-LEVEL DECK OVER CONCRETE PATIO

This two-level deck was designed to cover an existing concrete patio while extending the usefulness and visual interest of the backyard.

The 10 × 16 patio was poured when the house was first built about 15 years ago. The patio was still in good condition, but its hard, flat surface did little to enhance the comfort or appearance of the house. A deck transformation was called for. In many cases, if a brick or concrete patio is cracked or buckled, it's easier to build a deck over the patio than to demolish and dispose of the old masonry.

Covering an area of about 214 square feet, this deck actually extends beyond the end of the old patio, angling around a tree and stepping up to become a two-level design that's well-integrated with the backyard landscape. Built-in benches on both levels add comfort and convenience.

Below you will find two separate construction sequences—one for the lower deck, the other for the upper deck. One reason for this is that it makes sense to build this deck in two stages. The other reason is that you might want to build only the lower level.

Building the Lower-Level Deck

1   **Install the treated 2 × 6 ledger for the lower level.** This house has vinyl siding, so the first step is to remove enough siding so that the ledger can be fastened directly against the exterior sheathing. Use lag screws that extend into the rim joist of the house. Bend ledger flashing over the top edge of the ledger and under the trimmed-back siding. See chapter 5 for more information about ledgers and how to install them against various siding materials.

2   **Lay out, dig, and pour the concrete piers.** There are six piers, each supporting a post at the deck perimeter beyond the existing patio. Because 4 × 4 redwood posts are used for this deck, the top of each poured-concrete pier should be about 1 inch above grade level. Place steel post base supports in the tops of the piers before the concrete hardens.

DRAWING 8–2: LOWER-DECK FRAMING PLAN

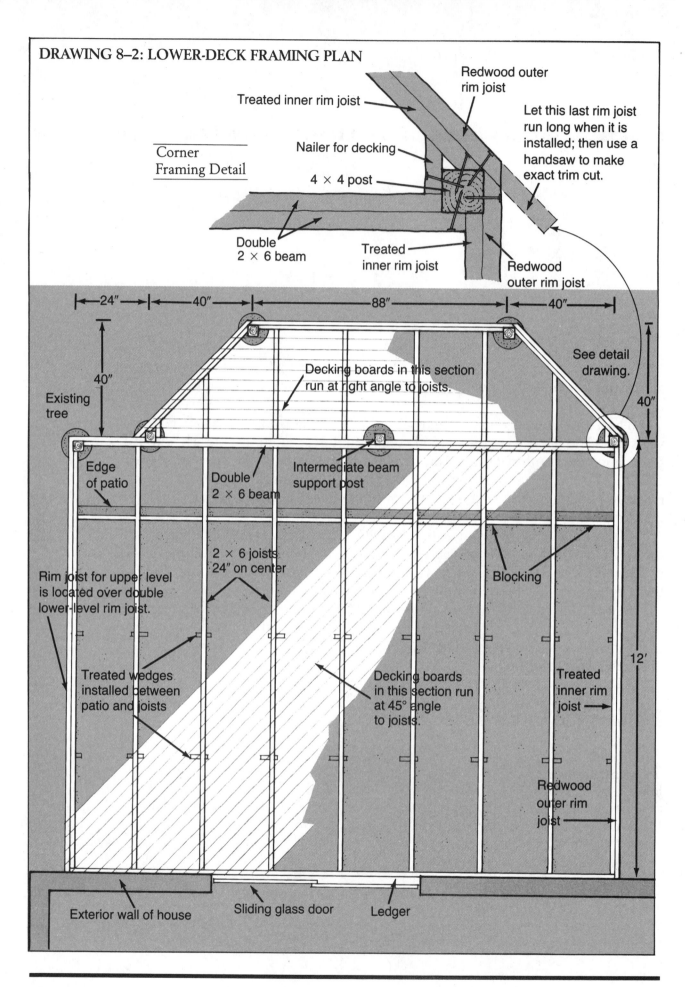

Corner
Framing Detail

Treated inner rim joist

Redwood outer
rim joist

Nailer for decking

Let this last rim joist
run long when it is
installed; then use a
handsaw to make
exact trim cut.

4 × 4 post

Double
2 × 6 beam

Treated
inner rim joist

Redwood
outer rim joist

24"   40"   88"   40"

Existing
tree

40"

40"

Decking boards in this section
run at right angle to joists.

See detail
drawing.

40"

Edge
of patio

Double
2 × 6 beam

Intermediate beam
support post

Rim joist for upper level
is located over double
lower-level rim joist.

2 × 6 joists
24" on center

Blocking

12'

Treated wedges
installed between
patio and joists

Decking boards
in this section run
at 45° angle
to joists.

Treated
inner rim
joist

Redwood
outer rim
joist

Exterior wall of house

Sliding glass door

Ledger

Lumber Order

AMOUNT	MATERIAL	PART
1	2 × 6 × 16' treated	ledger
1	4 × 4 × 8' treated	8 short posts for lower and upper decks
2	4 × 4 × 8' redwood	4 posts
10	2 × 6 × 12' treated	joists and rim joists
1	2 × 6 × 12' redwood	outer rim joist
2	2 × 6 × 16' treated	beam (double 2 × 6)
1	2 × 6 × 16' treated	inner rim joists for angled section
1	2 × 6 × 18' redwood	outer rim joists for angled section
1	2 × 6 × 16' treated	joists for angled section
2	2 × 6 × 10' treated	blocking and wedges
520 linear ft.	2 × 6 redwood	decking and built-in bench
4	2 × 6 × 8' redwood	built-in bench
2	2 × 4 × 20' redwood	top and bottom rails
36	2 × 2 × 3' redwood	balusters
1	2 × 6 × 20' redwood	railing cap

Hardware
6 steel post bases
20 joist hangers

3 Install the lower-level posts. Two of the posts are short pieces of treated wood that support the beam under the decking. Four others are redwood because they extend through the deck to become railing posts. After the concrete sets, fasten each post to its post base. Let the railing posts run long and hold them plumb with temporary braces.

4 Cut and install the rim joists that butt against the ledger on either side of the deck. Note that all rim joists for the lower level are double 2 × 6s; the inner 2 × 6 is pressure treated, while the outer 2 × 6 (which shows on the finished deck) is redwood. As shown in Drawing 8–2, the redwood rim joists should be face-nailed to the ends of the ledger, while the treated rim joists are toenailed against the face of the ledger and face-nailed to the redwood rim joists. The top of the rim joists should be level with the top of the ledger.

If the patio is sound, it can provide extra support for rim joists as well as joists. But since most patios are sloped slightly away from the house, you'll need to install shims between the patio and the bottom edges of framing members. Cut wedges from scrap pieces of treated lumber and use the wedges in pairs, driven under the bottom edge of each joist from each side of the joist. Adjust the shims until the top of the rim joists are level with the top of the ledger.

5   **Install the double 2 × 6 beam.** This beam runs parallel to the ledger, about 2 feet beyond the end of the patio. Cut a 16-foot 2 × 6 to fit between the two posts that are now supporting the installed rim joists. Level the 2 × 6 across the intermediate beam support post and nail it in place. Then build up the sections of 2 × 6 between the posts to form the double beam.

6   **Frame the angled section at the end of the deck.** Cut and install the treated inner rim joists for this section first. If pier and post installations are accurate, the angled end-cuts for the sides of this section should measure close to 45 degrees, as shown in the detail on Drawing 8–2. Level and toenail the inner rim joists against the posts. Then cut and install the six short joists in the angled section of the deck. Use joist hangers at the beam and face-nail through the rim joists. Mark, cut, and install the redwood outer rim joists. As shown in Drawing 8–2, these outer 2 × 6 members will run by the outside of the post, overlapping each other. Make the angle cut on the last 2 × 6 installed at the corner *after* the piece is nailed in place, using a handsaw. This is a fairly foolproof way to make an exact angle cut. Be sure to nail the outer rim joists to the posts and to inner rim joists.

7   **Cut and install the 2 × 6 joists for the lower level.** The joists are spaced 24 inches on center. Use joist hangers at ledger, beam, and rim joist connections. Top edges of joists should be level with top edges of the beam and rim joists. If necessary, install treated shims between the patio surface and the bottom edges of the joists, as shown in Drawing 8–2. Cut the posts off level with each other 34 inches above the rim joists.

8   **Install blocking between joists.** Locate the treated 2 × 6 blocking near the end of the patio. Blocking can be staggered to allow face-nailing instead of toenailing. In addition to stiffening the deck, blocking will keep small animals from getting between the deck and slab. For drainage, keep the blocking about ¼ inch above the slab.

9   **Install diagonal decking on lower level.** If outdoor lights or receptacles will be added around the deck, snake wires along and between joists before the decking goes down. The boards on the rectangular section of the deck run diagonally at a 45-degree angle to the joists. Install the longest board course first, as shown in Drawing 8–2, using the straightest decking board (or boards) in your supply. Install this decking course along a snapped chalk line to make sure it runs at a 45-degree angle to the joists, and as straight as possible. When the first course is down, install the rest of the diagonal boards, working on either side of the first course. Let these boards run long, beyond the double 2 × 6 beam and the rim joists. When the rectangular section of the deck is done, trim off the excess with a circular saw. Cut along a chalk line snapped to allow a 1-inch overhang at the deck perimeter. Where diagonal decking runs over the double 2 × 6 beam, trim the decking so the outer 2 × 10 remains exposed. For this last cut, set your depth of cut to ⅛ inch or so more than the thickness of your decking.

10   Install decking in the angled section of the deck. These decking boards should run at a right angle to the joists. Notch boards to fit around posts, and let the decking run long. Trim the perimeter of this section after all the decking is down, allowing a 1-inch overhang.

11   Build the bench frame. As shown in Drawing 8–3, framing members are screwed to the posts in the angled section. End cuts for framing members will be either 90 degrees or 45 degrees. At the inner corners of the bench, two additional posts are required. These short posts bear directly on the decking and can be toenailed in place.

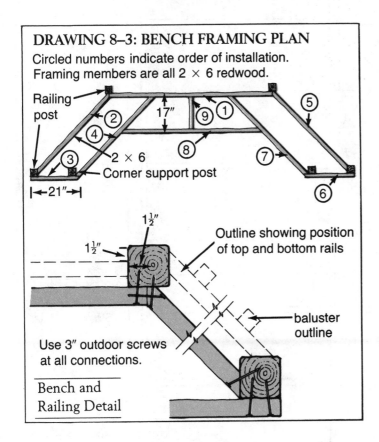

DRAWING 8–3: BENCH FRAMING PLAN
Circled numbers indicate order of installation. Framing members are all 2 × 6 redwood.

Railing post

Corner support post

2 × 6

17"

21"

1½"

1½"

Outline showing position of top and bottom rails

baluster outline

Use 3" outdoor screws at all connections.

Bench and Railing Detail

12   Install rails and balusters. Like the bench framing members, top and bottom rails require angled end cuts to fit between railing posts. Space 2 × 2 balusters 6 inches on center.

13   Cut and install railing cap pieces. The redwood 2 × 6 cap pieces are mitered where they meet over posts. For more information on railing designs, see page 89.

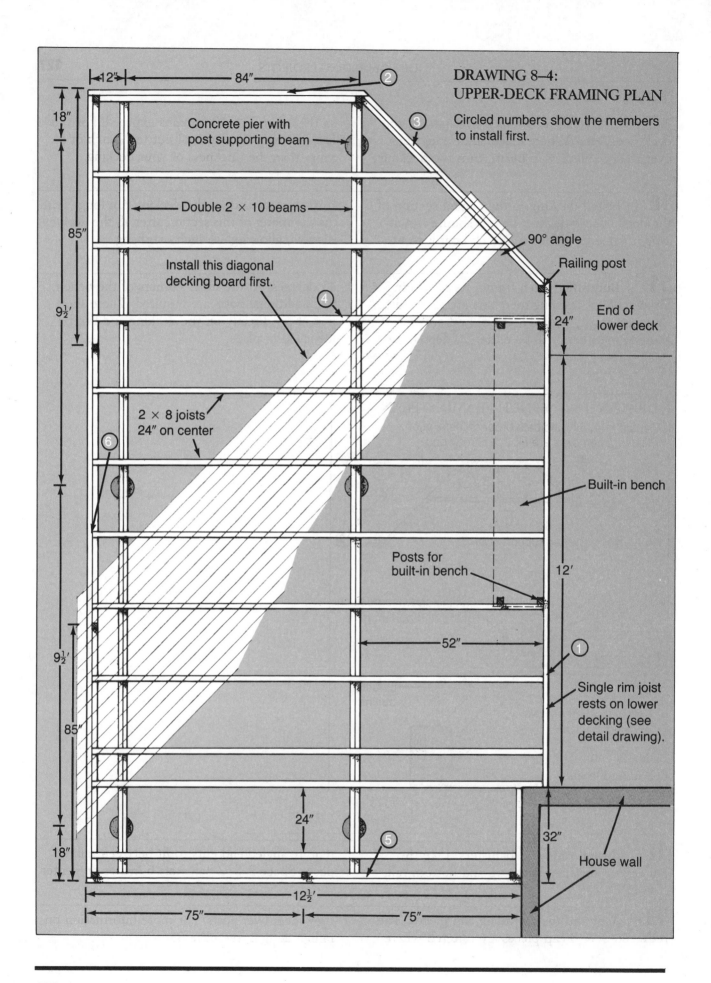

DRAWING 8–4:
UPPER-DECK FRAMING PLAN

Circled numbers show the members to install first.

Concrete pier with post supporting beam

Double 2 × 10 beams

Install this diagonal decking board first.

2 × 8 joists 24" on center

90° angle

Railing post

End of lower deck

Built-in bench

Posts for built-in bench

Single rim joist rests on lower decking (see detail drawing).

House wall

12"
84"
18"
85"
9½'
52"
24"
12'
9½'
85"
24"
18"
32"
12½'
75"
75"

Building the Upper-Level Deck

Lumber Order

AMOUNT	MATERIAL	PART
4	2 × 10 × 22' treated	beams for upper level*
1	2 × 8 × 12' treated	rim joist
2	2 × 8 × 12' redwood	rim joists
1	2 × 8 × 10' redwood	rim joists
2	2 × 8 × 14' redwood	rim joists
3	2 × 8 × 14' redwood	rim joists number 1,2,3,4
13	2 × 8 × 14' treated	joists, inner rim joists, blocking, and ledger
1	2 × 8 × 22' redwood	rim joist number 5
4	4 × 4 × 8' redwood	8 railing posts
1	4 × 4 × 8' redwood	2 bench posts
1	2 × 4 × 14' redwood	top and bottom rails
8	2 × 4 × 8' redwood	top and bottom rails
2	2 × 4 × 12' redwood	top and bottom rails
1	2 × 6 × 22' redwood	railing cap
1	2 × 6 × 8' redwood	railing cap
1	2 × 6 × 8' redwood	railing cap
1	2 × 6 × 14' redwood	railing cap
555 linear ft.	2 × 6 redwood	decking
124	2 × 2 × 36" redwood	balusters

*If 22-ft.-long 2 × 10s aren't available, see text and drawing for alternative built-up beam.

Hardware

6 steel post bases
1 joist hanger
16 pcs. 5½ × ¼-in.-dia. carriage bolts

1 **Pour the concrete piers for the upper deck.** As shown in Drawing 8–4, the six piers are laid out in pairs, 7 feet on center. Each pair is 9½ feet apart. This arrangement allows for an 18-inch overhang at both ends of the deck.

2 **Cut and install the posts and double 2 × 10 beams.** The short posts sit in aluminum post bases set on the piers. Adjust the height of each post so that the tops of the beams will be level with the decked surface of the lower deck. Each beam is 22 feet long, and made by doubling up 2 × 10s. Beams can be assembled from shorter 2 × 10s, but joints should be staggered on either side of the center support posts, as shown in Drawing 8-5. Toenail the beams to the posts.

3 **Cut and install the first three rim joists.** These redwood 2 × 8s will define three sides of the upper deck. The first rim joist to install rests on the decking along the edge of the lower deck. Toenail it to the decking boards, as shown in Drawing 8–5.

Now cut and install the 8-foot-long outer rim joist number 2 at the narrow end of the deck. One end of this joist will overhang the beam by 10½ inches, defining a 90-degree corner of the deck. Make the outside edge of the rim joist flush with the end of the opposite beam, and allow the rim joist to run long for now.

Cut and install rim joist number 3 for the angled section of the deck. This piece requires 45-degree-angled end-cuts that can be accurately marked by placing the 2 × 8 over the two joists that it will join.

After installing rim joist number 3, use its outside face as a guide to trim the 45-degree angle on the end of rim joist 2.

4   **Install the short upper-deck ledger and rim joist number 4.**   Trim back the siding and flashing and install the ledger, as discussed in step 1 for the lower deck. Cut the 12-foot, 6-inch rim joist number 4 to finished length; then nail it to the ledger and to both beams.

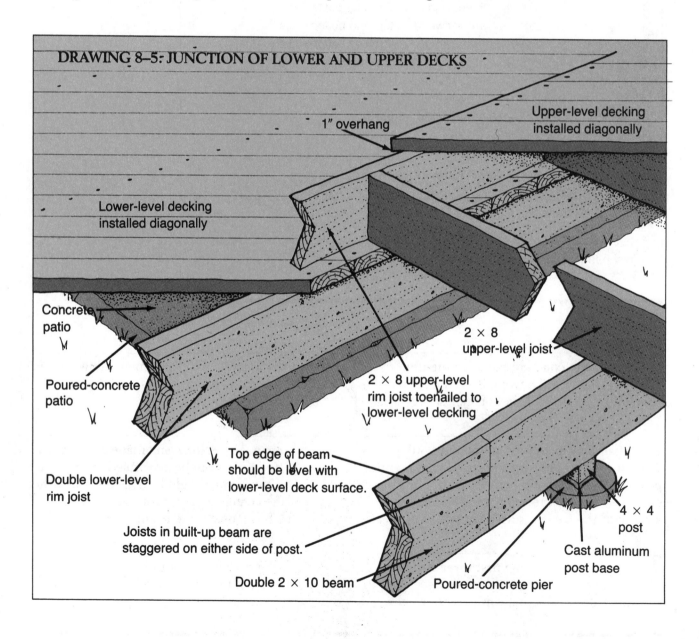

DRAWING 8–5: JUNCTION OF LOWER AND UPPER DECKS

1" overhang

Upper-level decking installed diagonally

Lower-level decking installed diagonally

Concrete patio

Poured-concrete patio

Double lower-level rim joist

2 × 8 upper-level joist

2 × 8 upper-level rim joist toenailed to lower-level decking

Top edge of beam should be level with lower-level deck surface.

Joists in built-up beam are staggered on either side of post.

Double 2 × 10 beam

Poured-concrete pier

4 × 4 post

Cast aluminum post base

5   **Cut and install the joists.** On the tops of both beams and rim joist 1, make marks every 24 inches for the joist spacing. Make 45-degree cuts on one end of the two beams that will meet rim joist number 3. Put the joists in position and check that they are square to the beams. Snap a chalk line across the tops of the joists 9 inches from the outside face of the beam that is farthest from the house. Cut each joist, put it back in position, and face-nail it to rim joist number 1. One joist is not attached to rim joist number 1. Instead, it is attached to the short ledger with a joist hanger. Check that the joists are square to the beams and toenail them to the beams.

6   **Install the longest rim joist.** Cut rim joist number 5 to fit between rim joists numbers 2 and 4. Nail through the face of rim joist number 5 into the joists.

7   **Install the railing posts.** Cut the posts to 43 inches long and install them so that 36 inches of post extends above joists. Use two 5½-inch-long, ¼-inch-diameter carriage bolts through the rim joist into each post.

8   **Cut and install inner rim joists and blocking.** Install the pressure-treated inner rim joists and blocking, as indicated in Drawing 8–4.

9   **Install four posts for the upper-level bench.** For more details on how to build this bench, see the built-in bench project on page 132.

10   **Install upper-level decking.** As on the lower level, this decking goes down diagonally over joists. Make the first course a long one that runs over the angled section, as shown in Drawing 8–4. Then install decking boards on either side of this course, notching boards to fit around posts.

11   **Install top and bottom rails between railing posts.** These 2 × 4 rails must be cut to fit between posts. Fasten them, toeing screws by driving them at an angle through the rail and into the side of the post. For more specific information on building the railing for this deck, see page 89.

PROJECT 3

BASIC BENCH

This basic bench could be a welcome feature on many decks. The lumber order is for an 8-foot-long bench, but without changing construction details you can adjust length and width to suit your needs. A wide, low version would serve equally well as a coffee table. By adding a pair of intermediate posts every 8 feet, you can make the bench any length.

This bench is built into the deck so its posts extend below the decking where they are fastened to framing members. To build a freestanding version of the bench, which can be moved around, make all posts 15 inches long.

The bench shown here is made from pressure-treated yellow pine. As an alternative, you might choose a good outdoor wood such as cedar, redwood, or cypress.

1 **Install posts.** Install the posts first, after the deck has been framed, but before decking boards have been nailed down. Using lag screws, fasten the bottom of each post to a joist or beam. The tops of the posts can run long.

2 **Install decking.** Install decking boards, cutting them to fit around the posts. Blocking between joists may be necessary to support deck boards that fit against posts.

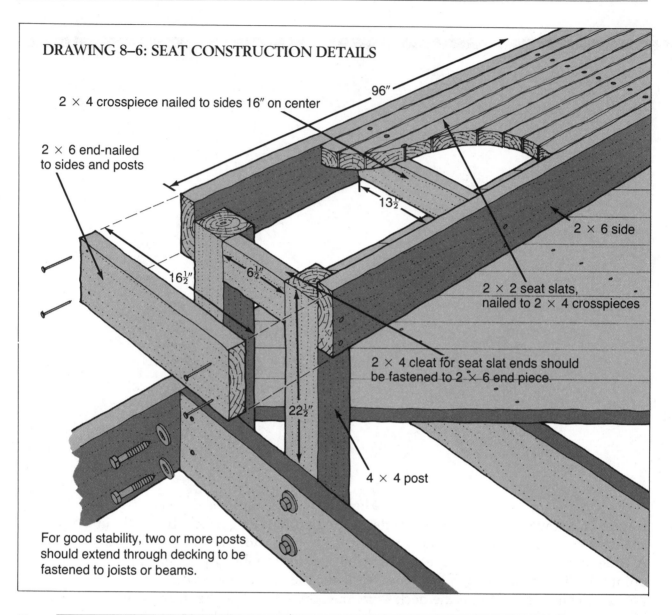

DRAWING 8–6: SEAT CONSTRUCTION DETAILS

2 × 4 crosspiece nailed to sides 16" on center

2 × 6 end-nailed to sides and posts

96"

13½

2 × 6 side

16½"

6½"

2 × 2 seat slats, nailed to 2 × 4 crosspieces

22½"

2 × 4 cleat for seat slat ends should be fastened to 2 × 6 end piece.

4 × 4 post

For good stability, two or more posts should extend through decking to be fastened to joists or beams.

3   **Cut posts.** Cut the posts off level with each other and 15 inches above the deck surface. Cut 2 × 4 cleats to fit between posts at each end of the bench; then toenail cleats to posts. Make the top edges of the cleats flush with the tops of the posts.

4   **Install side pieces.** Cut both 2 × 6 sides to length and nail them in place. Make sure that the top edges of the sides are level and 1½ inches above the tops of the posts, as shown in Drawing 8–6. Attach the 2 × 6 ends next. When nailing the ends in place, drive nails into sides, cleats, and posts.

5   **Install crosspieces.** Cut and install the 2 × 4 crosspieces, spacing them 16 inches on center. Note that the top edges of the crosspieces should be 1½ inches below the top edges of side and end pieces, and level with the tops of posts and cleats.

Lumber Order

AMOUNT	MATERIAL	PART
1	2 × 6 × 8′	one side
1	4 × 4 × 8′	4 posts
1	2 × 4 × 8′	5 crosspieces and 2 cleats
1	2 × 6 × 12′	other side and both ends
11	2 × 2 × 8′	seat slats

Hardware

8 pcs. ⅜-in.-dia. lag screws, length as needed

6 **Install seat slats.** Cut and install the 2 × 2 seat slats, beginning on one side and working across the width of the bench. Drive a single nail or screw through the slat at each support point. Leave ⅛ inch between slats for drainage.

7 **Round the edges.** To finish the bench, ease all corners and edges with a block plane. Or, you can round these edges with a ⅜-inch roundover bit in a router.

PROJECT 4

DECK WITH ABOVEGROUND POOL

Aboveground pools present special problems to deck builders. A deck that serves this kind of pool must be structurally independent of it while at the same time providing safe access. Ideally, the deck can cover and protect the pool's filtering and circulation equipment without making it difficult to service. The deck should also enhance the pool's appearance, integrating it with the rest of the yard.

The deck and pool combination, shown on the opposite page, works particularly well for several reasons. First of all, it provides a platform that's large enough for sunbathing between dips in the pool. A broad deck like this one, abutting a small segment of the aboveground pool, usually works better than a narrow deck built all the way around the water. This deck was designed to fit a round pool 4 feet deep and 18 feet in diameter. With a few changes, this design could work well on aboveground pools of different sizes.

The problem with aboveground pools is that they stand out in the backyard like a sore thumb. This design uses three levels of decking to gracefully make the transition from pool to ground. Much of the aboveground pool is hidden from view by a small elevated pool deck. From there, it's four steps down to the largest portion of the deck and then one step down to the third level, which extends 20 feet from the house. Railings and other details are consistent, unifying the design. A washed gravel ground cover beneath both decks discourages grass and weeds in these areas and adds to the well-crafted appearance. Part of the area beneath the pool's deck is enclosed to protect pump and filter. The remaining area is open—a good storage place for patio furniture and other items.

It's best to lay out and build the deck with the pool and its equipment already in place. Avoid working with water in the pool, however, since this can be a safety hazard, especially if power tools are on-site. If you know exactly where the pool will go and where the pump and other equipment will be installed, it's possible to build the deck before the pool is in place.

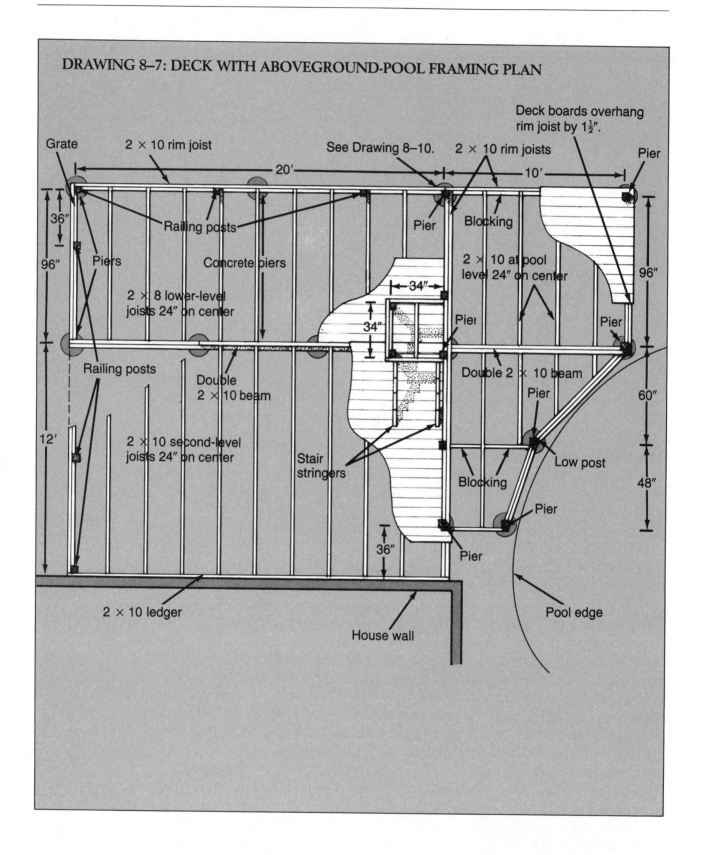

DECKS

Lumber Order

AMOUNT	MATERIAL	PART
5	2 × 10 × 20' treated	ledger, double beam, second-level rim joist, and lower-level rim joists
13	2 × 8 × 8' treated	lower-level rim joist, joists, and blocking
13	2 × 8 × 12' treated	upper-level joists and blocking
7	4 × 4 × 4' redwood	railing posts for lower- and second-level decks
11	4 × 4 × 8' redwood	foundation and railing posts for pool deck, including stairway landing
1180 linear ft.	2 × 6 redwood	decking and stair treads
1	2 × 10 × 18' treated	pool-level rim joist
3	2 × 10 × 10' treated	joists and blocking for angled section of pool deck
2	2 × 10 × 16' treated	angled rim joists adjacent to pool
2	2 × 10 × 10' treated	joists and blocking for stairway landing
1	2 × 12 × 8' treated	stair stringers
3	2 × 4 × 8' redwood	pool-level top and bottom rails
6	2 × 4 × 10' redwood	pool-level top and bottom rails
1	2 × 4 × 6' redwood	pool-level top and bottom rails
4	2 × 4 × 20' redwood	lower- and second-level top and bottom rails
4	2 × 6 × 20' redwood	railing caps
166	2 × 2 × 3' redwood	balusters
120 linear ft.	1 × 6 cedar tongue and groove siding skirt boards	

Hardware

72 pcs. 3 × ⅜-in.-dia. lag screws

26 joist hangers

2 steel framing connectors

1   **Install the ledger.** In this design, the top edge of the 2 × 10 ledger is 3 inches below the sill of the living room's sliding glass door. Remove exterior siding where the ledger and decking will be installed and fasten the ledger against the exterior sheathing, driving lag screws into house framing members. For specific details on installing and flashing ledger boards against different walls, see chapter 5.

2   **Put in the piers.** As shown in Drawing 8–7, there are a total of 12 piers in this design. Framing work will be easier if piers are level with each other and 7½ inches below the bottom edge of the ledger. This 7½ inches allows for the width of the lower level joists. See chapter 5 for more information about installing piers.

3   **Install the double 2 × 10 beam.** Build this beam by nailing together a pair of 20-foot-long 2 × 10s. The beam rests on four piers that are 12 feet from the house wall, as shown in Drawing 8–7. The top of the beam should be level with the bottom of the ledger. If necessary, use treated shims or wedges to elevate the beam to the proper level.

4   **Frame the lower level.** Start by installing the two 8-foot rim joists that are perpendicular to the beam. Then install the 20-foot rim joist that rests on three of the four outer piers. Use treated shims or wedges to make rim joists level with the double 2 × 10 beam.

Fasten joist hangers against the outside face of the double beam 24 inches on center. Then cut and install joists. One end of each joist will be held by a joist hanger. Secure the opposite end by nailing through the 20-foot-long rim joist.

5   **Frame the second level.** As shown in Drawing 8–7, this level also has three rim joists. As the drawing also shows, the 20-foot-long rim joist rests on the double beam, while the two 12-foot-long rim joists are fastened to the ledger and to the long rim joist.

Nail joist hangers to the ledger, spacing them 24 inches on center. Then cut and install joists. Nail through the outside face of the rim joist and into joist ends. Toenail the 20-foot-long rim joist to the beam.

6   **Install railing posts for lower- and second-level decks.** Precut seven posts to 44 inches. Secure each of these posts to the rim joists with at least four 3-inch-long, ⅜-inch-diameter lag screws through the outside of the rim joist into the post. Make sure the bottom of each post is flush with the bottom edges of the rim joist.

7   **Install posts for pool deck and stairway.** There are eleven 8-foot-long posts that bear directly on concrete piers. These include four posts that define the corners of the stair landing

DRAWING 8–8: STAIR FRAMING DETAILS

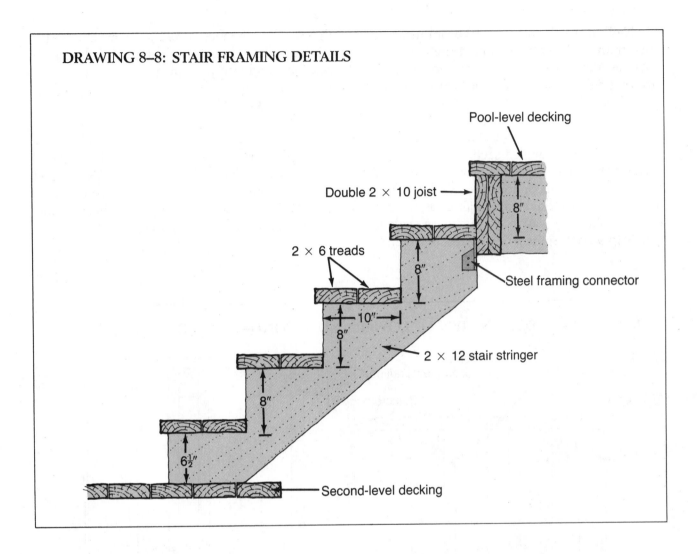

Pool-level decking

Double 2 × 10 joist

8"

2 × 6 treads

Steel framing connector

10"

8"

8"

2 × 12 stair stringer

8"

6½"

Second-level decking

and seven posts around the perimeter of the pool-level deck. The four corner posts will need to be braced plumb atop their piers, using temporary diagonal braces.

8   **Cut and install blocking on lower- and second-level decks.** Nail these short 2 × 8 pieces against joists, posts, and rim joists, as shown in Drawing 8–7.

9   **Install decking boards on lower and second levels.** These 2 × 6 redwood boards run perpendicular to the joists, and should extend 1¾ inch beyond rim joists. Notch decking to fit around posts.

10   **Frame the rectangular portion of the pool deck.** First install the 17-foot-long 2 × 10 that runs perpendicular to the house wall and is fastened to five posts. The top edge of this board should be level and about 2 inches above the height of the pool.

Nail up the double 2 × 10 beam next. Then frame the square section of the pool deck, installing rim joists and joists, as shown in Drawing 8–7. Rim joists extend past posts so that they can be face-nailed to them. Use joist hangers where joists joint the beam. Nail through rim joists and into joist ends.

11 **Frame the angled section of the pool deck on the pool side of the beam.** You'll need to make angled cuts on four pieces of 2 × 8 to create the two doubled rim joists that abut the pool. An easy way to lay out these angled cuts is to stretch some string tightly between posts. The string line will duplicate the angle cut that has to be made on the joist. Use a bevel gauge to transfer this angle to the edge of the 2 × 10. It will still be necessary to measure for the length of each framing member.

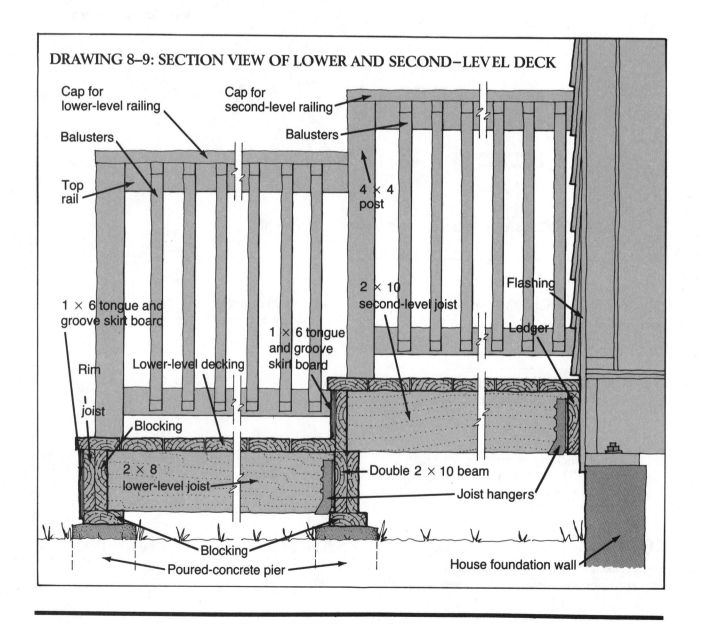

DRAWING 8–9: SECTION VIEW OF LOWER AND SECOND–LEVEL DECK

Cap for lower-level railing

Balusters

Top rail

Cap for second-level railing

Balusters

4 × 4 post

2 × 10 second-level joist

Flashing

Ledger

1 × 6 tongue and groove skirt board

1 × 6 tongue and groove skirt board

Lower-level decking

Rim joist

Blocking

2 × 8 lower-level joist

Double 2 × 10 beam

Joist hangers

Blocking

Poured-concrete pier

House foundation wall

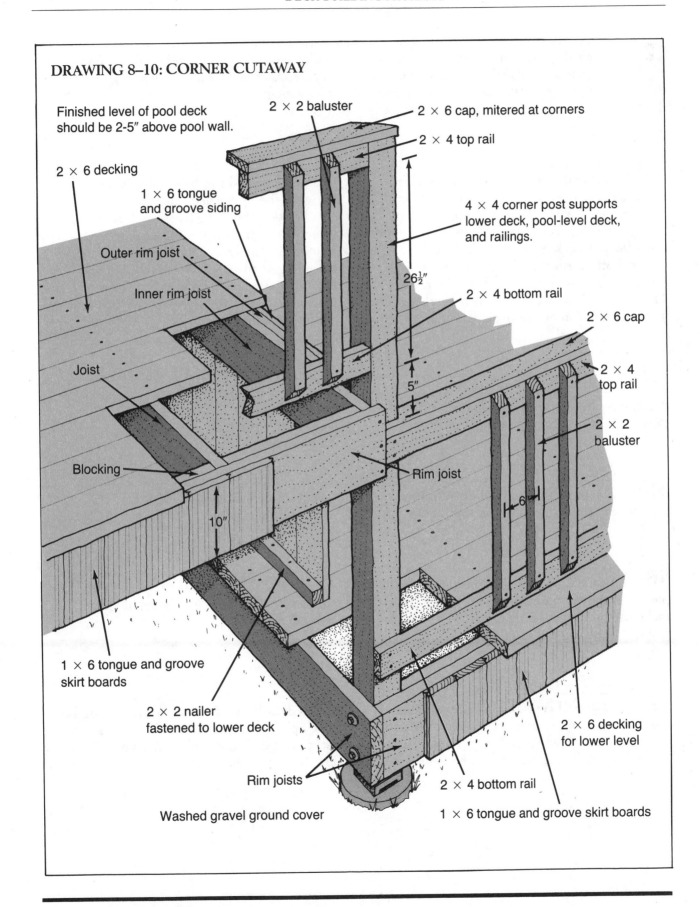

DRAWING 8–10: CORNER CUTAWAY

Finished level of pool deck
should be 2-5″ above pool wall.

2 × 6 decking

1 × 6 tongue
and groove siding

Outer rim joist

Inner rim joist

Joist

Blocking

2 × 2 baluster

2 × 6 cap, mitered at corners

2 × 4 top rail

4 × 4 corner post supports
lower deck, pool-level deck,
and railings.

26$\frac{1}{2}$″

2 × 4 bottom rail

5″

2 × 6 cap

2 × 4
top rail

2 × 2
baluster

Rim joist

10″

6″

1 × 6 tongue and groove
skirt boards

2 × 2 nailer
fastened to lower deck

Rim joists

Washed gravel ground cover

2 × 6 decking
for lower level

2 × 4 bottom rail

1 × 6 tongue and groove skirt boards

12   **Install the remaining joists.** Once the angled rim joists are installed, cut and install the remaining joists. Again, use joist hangers at the beam. Toenail joists against angled rim joists and face-nail remaining joists. Then frame the stairway landing and install blocking, as shown in Drawing 8–7.

13   **Cut and install stair stringers.** The short, fairly narrow stairway to the pool deck requires only 2 stringers, which are cut from 2 × 12 boards. As shown in Drawing 8–8, the stairs for this deck have open risers and 2 × 6 treads. Bottom riser height is 6½ inches; the remaining risers are 8 inches high. Treads are 11 inches wide including a 1-inch overhang. On your own version of this deck, you may have to adjust rise and run based on the distance between the upper deck and the pool deck.

Position the top edge of each stringer 8 inches down from the top edge of the landing framing, as shown in Drawing 8–8. Toenail the stringers to the second level deck and to the landing. For added strength, fasten a steel framing connector between the top of each stringer and the landing.

14   **Install pool-level decking.** The 2 × 6 decking boards go down perpendicular to the joists. Notch boards to fit around posts and allow for a 1¾-inch overhang at the deck perimeter. Install stair treads—a pair of 2 × 6s on each tread cutout.

15   **Cut posts for the pool deck to their final height.** For safety, cut the tops of the posts at least 35 inches above the deck.

16   **Attach 2 × 4 top and bottom rails to posts.** As shown in Drawings 8–9 and 8–10, make the bottom rail 5 inches above the deck and make the top rail flush with the tops of the posts. Butt the lower level rail into the second-level rim joists and posts, as shown in Drawing 8–9.

17   **Install rail caps and balusters.** Miter the 2 × 6 cap pieces where they join over posts, and fasten caps to posts and to top rails. Then cut and install 2 × 2 balusters. The balusters have 45-degree-angle cuts on both ends. Space balusters 6 inches on center, and fasten each end to its rail with a single 2½-inch galvanized buglehead screw.

18 **Cut and install skirt boards.** Nail these 1 × 6 tongue and groove boards vertically over all rim joists, as shown in Drawing 8–10. Skirt boards for the pool level are 10 inches long; those for rim joists on lower and upper levels are 7½ inches long.

Use 1 × 6 tongue and groove boards to build the solid wall between the pool deck and the lower and upper decks. Nail the boards to the pool-level rim joists and to a 2 × 2 nailer that's fastened to the lower decking, as shown in Drawing 8–10. Also, cut and install skirt boards to cover the outer stair stringer.

PROJECT 5

SECOND-STORY DECK

Elevated decks can offer the advantages of privacy, limited access, and dramatic views. The 240-square-foot deck shown here has an L-shaped plan with a privacy screen on the wide side. It's connected to the main level of the house by a pair of insulated glass doors. The broad section of the deck is 12 feet wide and cantilevers 3 feet beyond a 4 × 8 beam that runs parallel with the back of the house. The 6-foot-wide section of the deck is partially supported by a 4 × 6 diagonal brace that's fastened to the house and to the rim joist.

1 **Fasten ledger board to the house.** See chapter 5 for details on how ledgers are attached to different wall surfaces. Make sure the board is level and at a height that will allow the decking material to fit underneath the sill of the exterior door.

2 **Install piers.** Lay out, dig, and pour the four concrete piers that will support the foundation posts. The tops of the piers need not be level with each other but their centers should be 9 feet from the ledger. Before the concrete sets, anchor a steel post base in the concrete at the top of each pier.

3 **Install foundation posts.** Post height, when installed, should equal the height of the ledger's top edge less the height of the 4 × 8 beam and the height of the 2 × 10 joists that will be used to frame the deck, as shown in Drawing 8–12. That should total 16½ inches, but measure your lumber as dimensions can vary slightly. Keeping all posts plumb, install 2 × 4 diagonal braces between posts. Temporary braces should be used to prevent the posts from leaning toward or away from the house. These braces can be removed after several joists have been installed.

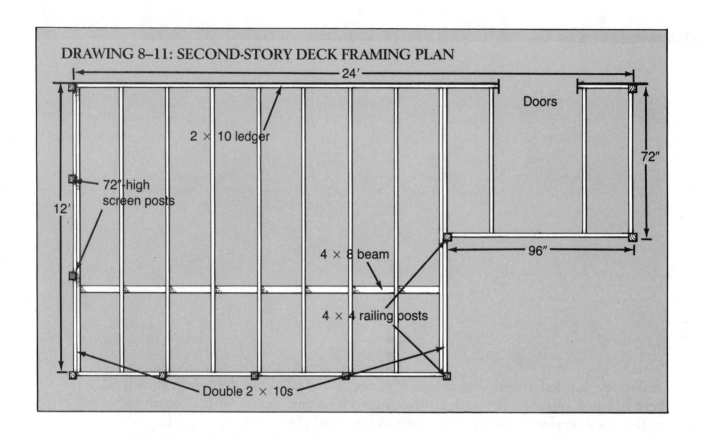

DRAWING 8–11: SECOND-STORY DECK FRAMING PLAN

24'

Doors

2 × 10 ledger

72''-high
screen posts

72''

12'

4 × 8 beam

96''

4 × 4 railing posts

Double 2 × 10s

4   **Install the beam and long joists.** Use steel post caps to fasten the 4 × 8 beam atop the posts. Then install the 2 × 10 joists 24 inches on center. Cut the joists to length on the ground and butt them into joist hangers where they meet the ledger board. Install double 2 × 10 rim joists at each end of the broad section of the deck. Use a double joist hanger for the double 2 × 10 nearest the door. To fasten the other double 2 × 10, face-nail the outer member to the end of the ledger and toenail the inner member against the face of the ledger. Be sure to nail double 2 × 10s to each other as well. Nail the 16-foot rim joist in place.

5   **Frame the 6-foot-wide section of the deck.** Install the rim joists first. The rim joist that runs parallel to the house should be nailed to a 2 × 6 cleat that is fastened against the double 2 × 10 beam, as shown in Drawing 8–13. Prop a temporary post under the free corner to keep the two rim joists level until the diagonal brace is installed. The 4 × 6 diagonal brace will require an angle cut at each end, which you can measure with a bevel gauge. It's a good idea to cut a sample brace from 2 × 4 stock, test-fitting it to make sure that the angle cuts are correct. Then transfer the same angles and length to the 4 × 6 brace.

Use two ⅜-inch-diameter lag screws to attach the bottom end of the diagonal brace to the wall. Use a 3-inch-long screw on top and a 2½-inch-long screw at bottom, as shown in Drawing 8–13. Use heavy-duty expansion shield masonry anchors if the wall is masonry. Counterbore the top screw 1 inch and the bottom screw ¾ inch. The counterbores reduce leverage on the screws and allow more threads to grip the wall. Fasten the top of the brace to the corner of the deck with lag screws and nails, as shown in Drawing 8–13. When the diagonal brace is installed, the joists can go in.

Lumber Order

AMOUNT	MATERIAL	PART
Note: All Lumber Is Pressure Treated.		
1	2 × 10 × 24'	ledger
4	4 × 4 × 8'	foundation posts
6	2 × 4 × 8'	diagonal braces for posts
1	4 × 8 × 16'	beam
11	2 × 10 × 12'	joists
1	2 × 10 × 16'	rim joist
5	2 × 10 × 6'	joists
1	2 × 10 × 8'	rim joist
7	4 × 4 × 4'	railing and privacy screen posts
1	4 × 6 × 8'	diagonal brace
4	4 × 4 × 8'	posts for lattice screen
540 linear ft.	2 × 6	decking
4	2 × 2 × 4'	top rails
1	2 × 2 × 8'	top rail
2	2 × 2 × 6'	top rails
4	2 × 4 × 4'	bottom rails
1	2 × 4 × 8'	bottom rail
2	2 × 4 × 6'	bottom rails
1	2 × 6 × 16'	railing cap
2	2 × 6 × 6'	railing caps
1	2 × 6 × 8'	railing cap
68	2 × 2 × 3'	balusters
3	4 × 8'	lattice screen panels, with channel molding

Hardware

4 steel post bases for support posts
4 steel post caps (1 for each post)
11 joist hangers
3 double joist hangers
14 pcs. 3½ × ⅜-in.-dia. lag screws and washers for railing and screen posts
2 pcs. 2½ × ⅜-in.-dia. lag screws and washers for diagonal brace
2 pcs. 3 × ⅜-in.-dia. lag screws and washers for diagonal brace
masonry anchors, if needed, for ledger and diagonal brace

6 **Cut and install railing and privacy screen posts.** Make 1½-inch-deep, 9¼-inch-long notches in the railing and privacy screen posts to fit against the perimeter of the deck, as shown in Drawing 8–12. Fasten posts to rim joists with 3½-inch-long, ⅜-inch-diameter lag screws.

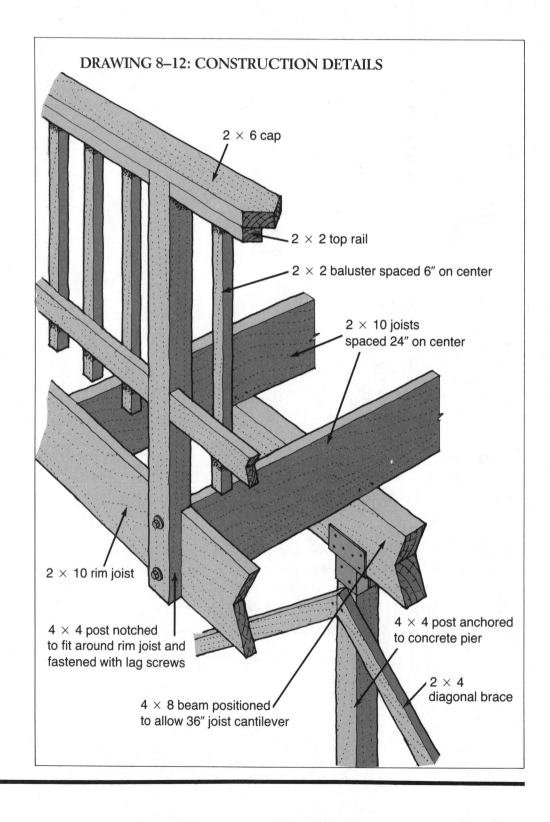

DRAWING 8–12: CONSTRUCTION DETAILS

2 × 6 cap

2 × 2 top rail

2 × 2 baluster spaced 6" on center

2 × 10 joists spaced 24" on center

2 × 10 rim joist

4 × 4 post notched to fit around rim joist and fastened with lag screws

4 × 8 beam positioned to allow 36" joist cantilever

4 × 4 post anchored to concrete pier

2 × 4 diagonal brace

7 **Install decking.** On this project, the decking boards run parallel to the house. The first board to install is the one at the deck perimeter. This board needs to be notched to fit around railing posts and to overhang the rim joist slightly. To mark the locations of the notches, place a 16-foot-long board across the joists with one edge butted against the posts. A notch depth of 2¾ inches will allow the decking board to overhang the rim joist by ¾ inch.

After the notched decking board is nailed (or screwed) down, work toward the house, installing the rest of the decking boards. If boards shorter than 16 feet are used, be sure to stagger joints in adjacent courses. If necessary, rip the last board (or boards) to fit against the house.

8 **Complete the railing.** Working on the deck, attach top and bottom rails to post edges. The 2 × 4 bottom rail should run level, about 12 inches above the deck surface. The outside face of the bottom rail, along with the outside edge of the top rail, should be flush with the outside face of the post. Toenail top and bottom rails between posts, then install the 2 × 6 railing caps next by screwing them to top rails and to the tops of the posts. Miter caps where they meet at the corners of the deck. Screw balusters to the inside of top and bottom rails, using a single screw at each connection point. Predrill the screw hole at the top of each baluster if splitting is a problem. Space balusters 6 inches on center, or as local building code dictates. Butt the top of each baluster under the cap. For details on building the lattice screen, see "Installing Lattice Screens" on page 166.

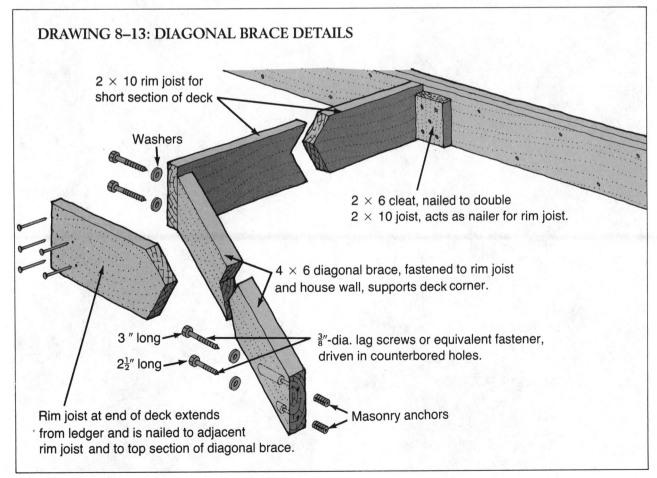

DRAWING 8–13: DIAGONAL BRACE DETAILS

2 × 10 rim joist for short section of deck

Washers

2 × 6 cleat, nailed to double 2 × 10 joist, acts as nailer for rim joist.

4 × 6 diagonal brace, fastened to rim joist and house wall, supports deck corner.

3 " long

2½" long

⅜"-dia. lag screws or equivalent fastener, driven in counterbored holes.

Masonry anchors

Rim joist at end of deck extends from ledger and is nailed to adjacent rim joist and to top section of diagonal brace.

PROJECT 6

PRIVACY SCREEN

Privacy screens are especially popular on suburban decks, where houses are close to each other and to the road. This screen offers an attractive way to set your deck apart from its surroundings. The screen shown here is 41½ inches high and 80 inches wide. The design is flexible, however, so height and width can be varied to suit your needs. The 2 × 6 vertical members give this screen strength where it counts—close to the deck surface where foot traffic, playful children, and furniture movement might damage lighter construction. Above the sturdy lower part of the screen, a frame of lattice provides a delicate balance. This screen is designed to be installed between 4 × 4 or 6 × 6 posts. The posts should extend through the decking boards and be bolted or screwed to framing members.

1   **Build the lower frame.** This section is easier to build if you nail it together on the flat, with the edges of the frame resting on the deck or on your workshop floor. As Drawing 8–14 shows, both rails are sized to fit between 4 × 4 posts. After cutting the top and bottom rail to length, cut both of the 2 × 4 stiles. Nail the frame together and keep it square with one or more temporary diagonal braces.

2   **Cut and install 2 × 6 vertical members between rails.** The 2 × 6s will be the same length as the stiles. As Drawing 8–14 shows, the 2 × 6s are positioned diagonally across the 3½-inch width of the rails. Line up opposite corners of each 2 × 6 with the edges of the 2 × 4 rails. and nail them in place through the rails. Overlapping the diagonal pattern slightly will create a more private screen.

3   **Install lower section.** When the lower section is complete, toenail it in place between support posts. Make sure that rails are level when installed. For ease in sweeping the deck clean, keep the bottom rail about 3½ inches above the deck.

DRAWING 8–14: PRIVACY SCREEN
CONSTRUCTION DETAILS

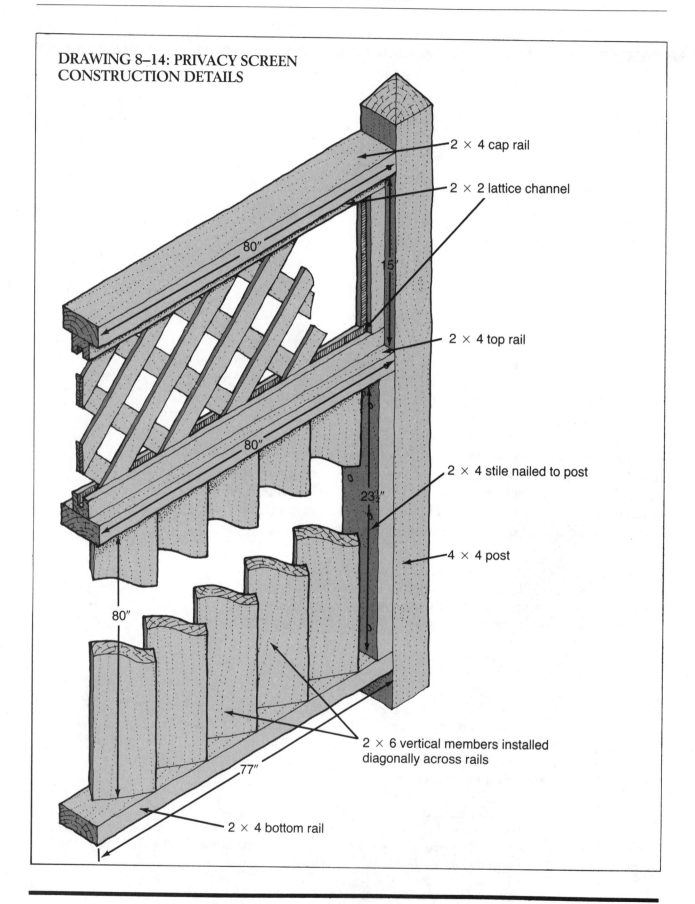

2 × 4 cap rail

2 × 2 lattice channel

80″

5′

2 × 4 top rail

80″

2 × 4 stile nailed to post

23½″

4 × 4 post

80″

2 × 6 vertical members installed
diagonally across rails

77″

2 × 4 bottom rail

Lumber Order

AMOUNT	MATERIAL	PART
1	2 × 4 × 8′	top rail
1	2 × 4 × 8′	bottom rail
1	2 × 4 × 4′	2 stiles
2	2 × 6 × 8′	vertical members
1	2 × 6 × 10′	vertical members
2	2 × 2 × 8′	lattice channel pieces
1	4 × 8′	lattice panel
1	2 × 4 × 8′	cap rail

4 **Install bottom molding channels.** In this screen, four lengths of channel molding form a frame for the lattice panel. As an alternative to the molding channel shown here, you can install the lattice as shown on page 169. Cut and install the bottom piece of molding first.

With a drill and ¼-inch bit, bore drainage holes through the bottom of the molding channel and through the top rail. Space holes about every 10 to 12 inches. This will prevent water from collecting in the bottom channel.

5 **Assemble lattice and frame.** Miter the side pieces of molding and nail them to the post. Then miter the top piece of molding to complete the frame. Cut the lattice panel to fit in the grooves of the frame. Then cut the cap rail to fit between posts and nail the top channel molding to the underside of the cap rail. Finally, slide the lattice into side and bottom channels and install cap rail and top channel molding as a single piece.

PROJECT 7

DECK AROUND A SPA OR HOT TUB

In many ways, decks and spas or hot tubs were made for each other. Offering excellent drainage and the forgiving feel of wood underfoot, a deck can connect the house with the hot tub while providing comfort and privacy during a soothing soak.

There are several basic options for combining a deck and spa or a deck and hot tub (see "Installing a Built-in Spa" on page 160). The deck shown here was designed to hold a freestanding spa in one corner. One advantage freestanding spas have over built-ins is that they can be removed without leaving a gaping hole in the deck. Without alteration, the deck can then be used for other purposes.

Regardless of the spa or hot tub used in a deck design, it is important to heed the manufacturer's recommendations regarding installation details. This freestanding spa rests directly on the deck surface, so it was necessary to reinforce the deck framing with closely spaced posts and extra beams in the area beneath the planned location of the unit.

The deck shown here is connected to the lower floor of the house by a walkway—a section of deck that starts out narrow at the doorway and flares out to meet the main deck area. Between the house and the main deck, bushes, shrubs, and flowers reach up to hide the foundation wall. At the opposite end of the deck, there's a stairway that leads down to the backyard. There's also an exterior stairway that leads up to a screened porch.

The backyard where this deck was built slopes away from the house. Foundation posts, cut to different lengths, keep the deck framing level. You'll have to adjust post height to fit the slope of your site.

1 Lay out forms and pour concrete piers. As shown in Drawing 8–15, this deck has 19 piers and a single pad for the bottom of the stairway. Tubular fiber forms could have been used in making the piers, but for this deck the builder decided to build square forms for the tops of the piers that extend above grade. Made from scrap pieces of two-by material, these site-fabricated forms eliminate the cost of fiber forms. Each square form is positioned on top of the hole dug for the pier. The top edges of the form should be level, as shown in Photo 5–7 on page 65. Make forms for the concrete pads as well.

The six piers that are closest to the house should all be level with each other, and 10¾ inches below the level of the finished deck. The remaining 13 piers can be formed up following

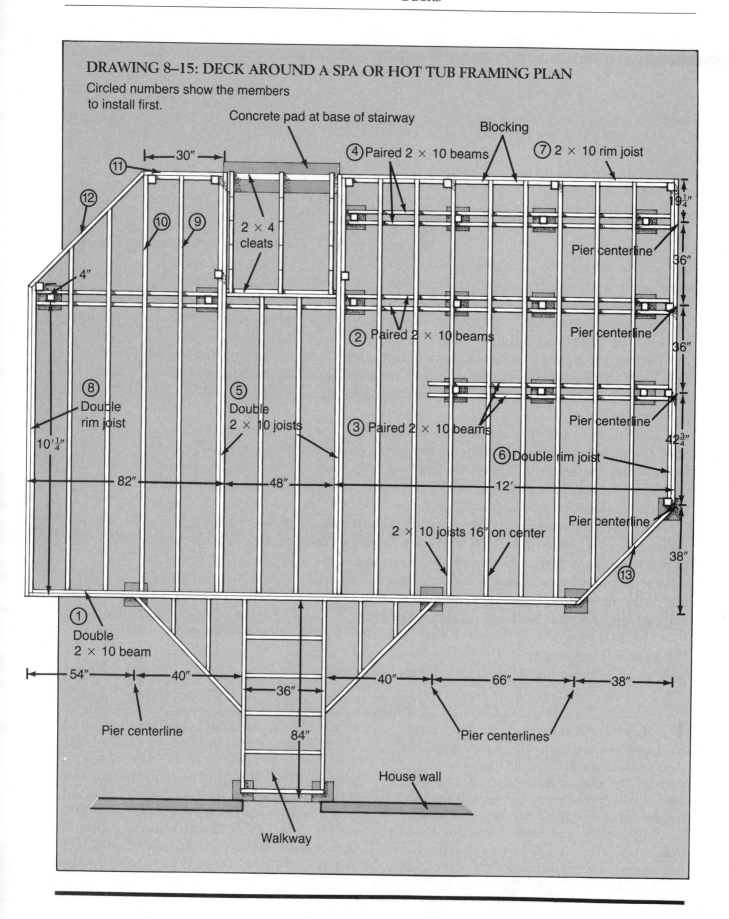

DRAWING 8–15: DECK AROUND A SPA OR HOT TUB FRAMING PLAN

Circled numbers show the members to install first.

Concrete pad at base of stairway

Blocking

④ Paired 2 × 10 beams

⑦ 2 × 10 rim joist

⑪

30″

⑫

⑩ ⑨

2 × 4 cleats

4″

$19\frac{1}{4}$″

Pier centerline

36″

② Paired 2 × 10 beams

Pier centerline

36″

⑧ Double rim joist

⑤ Double 2 × 10 joists

③ Paired 2 × 10 beams

Pier centerline

⑥ Double rim joist

$42\frac{3}{4}$″

$10'\frac{1}{4}$″

82″

48″

12′

2 × 10 joists 16″ on center

Pier centerline

38″

⑬

① Double 2 × 10 beam

54″ 40″ 40″ 66″ 38″

Pier centerline

36″

84″

Pier centerlines

House wall

Walkway

Lumber Order

AMOUNT	MATERIAL	PART
Note: All Lumber Is Pressure Treated.		
4	2 × 10 × 12'	double beam number 1
2	4 × 4 × 8'	foundation posts
2	4 × 4 × 12'	foundation posts
6	2 × 10 × 12'	paired beams numbers 2 and 4
2	2 × 10 × 10'	paired beams number 3
17	2 × 10 × 16'	joists and blocking
5	2 × 10 × 12'	rim joists numbers 6, 7, and 8
1	2 × 10 × 14'	rim joists numbers 11, 12 and 13
1	2 × 10 × 14'	walkway rim joists
2	2 × 10 × 16'	walkway joists and angled rim joists
1	2 × 10 × 10'	walkway joists
4	2 × 4 × 12'	diagonal foundation bracing
6	4 × 4 × 8'	railing posts
804 linear feet	2 × 6	decking
2	2 × 4 × 14'	rails
7	2 × 4 × 12'	rails
104	2 × 2 × 3'	balusters
1	2 × 12 × 18'	3 stair stringers
10	2 × 6 × 4'	stair treads

Hardware

3 steel post bases
96 pcs. 7½ × ⅜-in.-dia. machine bolts, with nuts and washers
2 double joist hangers
13 aluminum post bases for 4 × 4 posts
19 joist hangers
24 pcs. 4 × ⅜-in.-dia. lag screws with washers

the slope of the site, as shown in Drawing 8–16. After pouring the concrete for the three piers that will support the double 2 × 10 closest to the house, place steel post bases in the tops of these piers, aligning them to hold the beam.

Pour the remaining piers and the concrete pad for the stairway. These piers don't require cast-in-place framing connectors. Remove the wood forms after the concrete has set.

2 **Install the beam closest to the house.** This double 2 × 10 is identified as number 1 on Drawing 8–15. Make the double beam from four 12-foot 2 × 10s. First, draw a line

1½ inches from the end of one 2 × 10. Place the end of another 2 × 10 on this line and nail the two pieces together. Later, this will allow you to form an interlocking corner joint with

INSTALLING A BUILT-IN SPA

Built-in spas are designed so that the water level in the spa will be close to the level of the deck. Bathers can opt for total immersion or they can simply sit on the deck at the edge of the spa, dangling their feet in the water. Though a built-in spa appears to be supported by the decking boards, this isn't the case. A built-in spa or hot tub requires its own separate foundation, usually in the form of a concrete pad. The deck frame is built around the spa at an elevation that allows decking boards to fit right under the lip of the spa, as shown in Photo 8–1.

Wooden hot tubs often benefit from a multi-level design like the one shown in Photo 8–2. The top level is close to the waterline, while the

Photo 8–1: Well-designed installations make spas and hot tubs seem to be supported by the deck, but in reality, the weight of a water-filled spa or hot tub requires its own separate foundation.

rim joist number 8. On the other end, it lets you form a lap joint with the remaining two 2 × 10s that will form beam number 1. Let the other end of number 1 run long. Later you'll cut it to a 45-degree angle to join with rim joist number 13. After nailing the 2 × 10s together to make the beam, seat the beam in the post bases that are cast into the three concrete piers.

Then make sure that the top edge of the beam is perfectly level. If necessary, drive pressure-treated shims between the beam and the top of the post base to level the top edge of the beam. It's important for this first beam to be perfectly level, since all other beams will be leveled relative to the top edge of beam number 1.

3 **Install the 13 foundation posts.** The posts run in three rows that are parallel with the house wall. The outermost row contains four

posts; the middle row contains six; the inner row contains three. Attach aluminum post bases to the bottom of each post before placing it on

middle level acts as a step. Decking boards at all three levels extend up to the sides of the tub.

In any built-in design, pumps, plumbing, and electrical lines are kept out of sight beneath the deck. However, they must be accessible for maintenance and repairs. Always follow the manufacturer's instructions regarding wiring and plumbing for a spa or hot tub.

Photo 8–2: Two-level access works well for hot tubs like this one. The top level is flush with the top edge of the hot tub. The lower level, which surrounds half the tub, provides both a seat and a step. The hot tub itself requires its own foundation, usually in the form of a concrete pad. Framing for the deck and the surround is built around the hot tub. In this design, the walls of the surround are finished with the same horizontal channel siding used on the house.

its pier. The top of each post should be approximately level with the top of beam number 1, or slightly below it. Using temporary diagonal braces, secure two posts in each row so that they're plumb and equidistant from the house wall.

4 **Install paired 2 × 10 beams.** These beams, labeled 2, 3, and 4 on Drawing 8–15, run parallel with the house, and will support the deck joists. Beams number 4 are 12 feet long, ending at the long double joist at the side of the stairway. Beams number 3 are 10 feet long, ending one joist past a pier. These beams provide extra support for the hot tub. Paired beams number 2 are 23 feet long, running the full length of the deck. You'll need four 12-foot 2 × 10s to make beams number 2. Where the 2 × 10s for beams 2 butt together at the center post, support this joint with a 2 × 4 cleat bolted to the post beneath the beams. The top

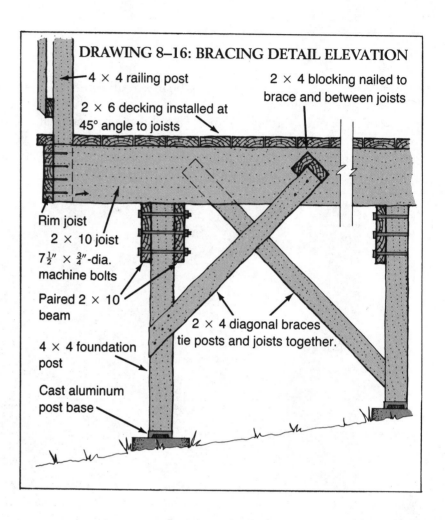

DRAWING 8–16: BRACING DETAIL ELEVATION

4 × 4 railing post

2 × 6 decking installed at 45° angle to joists

2 × 4 blocking nailed to brace and between joists

Rim joist

2 × 10 joist

$7\frac{1}{2}'' \times \frac{3}{4}''$-dia. machine bolts

Paired 2 × 10 beam

4 × 4 foundation post

Cast aluminum post base

2 × 4 diagonal braces tie posts and joists together.

---

edge of each 2 × 10 beam should be level with the bottom edge of beam number 1, as shown in Drawing 8–16.

Fasten each pair of beams to the two braced posts first; then the remaining posts will be easier to attach. Start by snapping a level chalk line defining the bottom of each beam. Tap a 16d nail into the line at each post. Drive the nail about halfway in. Put the posts up on the nails. Now you can tap on the tops of the beams and the bottom of the nails, bending the nails slightly until the beams are perfectly level. When they are, drill holes for 7½-inch-long, ⅜-inch-diameter machine bolts. Drill three holes per post connection; then install bolts with washers and nuts.

---

5 **Install double 2 × 10 joists.** These two sets of joists are labeled number 5 in Drawing 8–15. The outer joist in each pair is 14 feet 4 inches long; the inner joist is 1½ inches shorter. This difference creates a strong overlapping nailing pattern at the corner of the deck, as shown in Drawing 8–15.

Install the double joist members parallel with each other and 4 feet apart. Join one end of each double joist to beam number 1, using double joist hangers. Toenail these members to the top edges of the beams they cross.

6   **Install double rim joist.** This pair of 2 × 10s is labeled number 6 in Drawing 8–15. Make a 45-degree cut at the end of the double joist that will be closest to the house. As you

did in the previous step, make the inner member 1½ inches shorter than the outer one to create a strong corner joint.

7   **Install rim joist number 7.** Cut this 2 × 10 to fit between the outer members of the double 2 × 10s that extend to form two corners of the deck. Nail through number 7

into the ends of the inner members and nail through the outer members into the ends of number 7.

8   **Install rim joist number 8.** This double 2 × 10 should have a 45-degree-angle bevel cut on the end that's farthest from the house. Use

an overlapping joint at the corner where rim joist number 8 meets beam number 1.

9   **Install joists numbers 9 and 10.** Cut these joists to length. With joist hangers, attach one

end of each to beam number 1 and toenail the bottom of each joist to paired beams number 2.

10   **Install rim joists numbers 11 and 12.** First, cut rim joist number 11 to 34½ inches with a 45-degree cut on one end, as shown in Drawing 8-15. Nail it to joists numbers 9 and

10 and to the double 2 × 10 joist, as shown in Drawing 8–15. Install rim joist number 12, letting both ends run long. Trim the ends flush with the outside faces of rim joists numbers 8 and 11.

11   **Install rim joist number 13.** Lay rim joist number 13 against the 45-degree angle at the end of rim joist number 6 and across beam number 1. Mark the angle (approximately 45 degrees) at which it crosses number 1. Remove

number 13 and cut number 1 at that angle. Nail number 13 to the ends of numbers 6 and 1, letting numer 13 run long on both ends. Then trim the ends flush with the outside faces of numbers 1 and 6.

12   **Install joists and blocking in the main section of the deck.** Now that all beams and rim joists are in place, cut all the joists to fit and install these 2 × 10s 16 inches on center. Use joist hangers where joists join beam number

1. Toenail joists to beams. Nail through rim joists and into joist ends.

   When all joists are in place, cut and install blocking, as shown in Drawing 8–15.

13   **Frame the walkway section of the deck.** Frame the center ladder part first. As shown in Drawing 8–15, two piers near the doorway support one end of the ladder. Use joist hangers to fasten the opposite ends of these two rim

joists to the beam. Cut and install the two angled rim joists by toenailing them to the beam and to the ladder rim joists. Then face-nail and toenail the remaining four joists in this section into place.

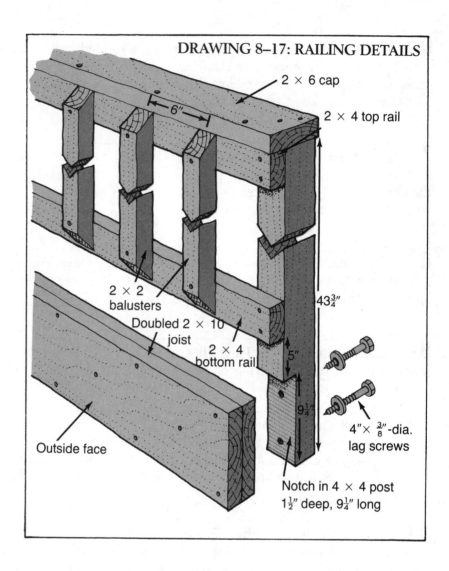

DRAWING 8–17: RAILING DETAILS

2 × 6 cap

2 × 4 top rail

6"

2 × 2 balusters

Doubled 2 × 10 joist

2 × 4 bottom rail

43¾"

5"

9¼"

4"× ⅜"-dia. lag screws

Outside face

Notch in 4 × 4 post 1½" deep, 9¼" long

14   **Install diagonal braces between posts and joists.** This extra bracing, shown in Drawing 8–16, is necessary because of the added weight of the spa. Nail one end of each 2 × 4 brace against a post. The other end can be nailed directly against a joist or to blocking that's nailed between joists, as shown in Drawing 8–16.

15   **Cut and install railing posts.** After cutting the 12 posts to a finished length of 43¾ inches, notch each post to fit around the inside of the rim joist, as shown in Drawing 8–17. Each notch should be 1½ inches deep and 9¼ inches long. Fasten posts to the inside of rim joists with 4-inch-long, ⅜-inch-diameter lag screws. Use two screws per post, except at deck corners, where an extra screw should be driven through the other rim joist and into the post.

16   **Lay down the deck.** The 2 × 6 decking boards are installed diagonally.

17 **Install rails and balusters.** Top and bottom rails are cut from 2 × 4 stock and fastened against the outside faces of the posts. Position the bottom rail 5 inches above deck framing. The top edge of the top rail should be flush with the tops of the posts.

Fasten 2 × 2 balusters to the rails, spacing them 6 inches on center. Drive a single nail or screw at each baluster/rail connection.

18 **Cut and install stair stringers.** Adjust the length and unit rise and run of the three stringers to fit the slope of the yard. Notch the ends of the stringers to fit over 2 × 4 cleats fastened to the deck and to the concrete pad at the base of the stair. Leave about 2 inches between double joists number 5 and the outer stringers.

19 **Install stair treads.** Each tread consists of two lengths of 2 × 6. Leave about ⅛-inch space between pairs of 2 × 6s for drainage.

PROJECT 8

INSTALLING LATTICE SCREENS

Lattice panels are very useful in deck construction projects. These lightweight 4 × 8-foot grids are made from lattice molding strips of wood or plastic about ¼-inch thick and 1½ inches wide. Panels can be made from pressure-treated wood, cedar, redwood, or plastic. Each panel contains two layers of strips oriented so that all the strips in one layer are parallel and spaced equally apart from each other. The two layers overlap at a 90-degree angle, forming a square grid that's stapled or nailed together. Vinyl lattice panels are fused together with a solvent during manufacture. A couple of different grid densities are available, as shown in Photo 8–3. It's also possible to buy stiffer, heavier lattice panels made from ⅜-inch-thick lattice strips.

With a screen made from one or more lattice panels, you can hide unsightly areas (under a raised deck, for example) or build a privacy screen around all or part of the deck. A lattice screen also makes an excellent backdrop for vines and other climbing plants.

Lattice panels usually have to be cut down for use in making screens, but they also can be used full-size. While lattice panels are versatile, they're also delicate, and their durability depends on careful handling and good installation procedures. If possible, store lattice panels flat until you're ready to use them. Standing panels on edge for long periods of time can cause them to bow or even to come apart. Avoid stepping on the lattice, since this may cause strips to break or separate from each other.

For appearance and durability, lattice panels should be installed in a frame of some sort. The frame hides and protects the edges of the panel. As shown in Drawing 8–18, there are several ways to build a frame when making a lattice screen. Wood cleats or lengths of quarter-round molding will do a good job of securing the panel. Channel molding will also work well as long as the width of the channel matches the thickness of the lattice panel. You can buy channel molding at many lumber outlets where lattice panels are sold. You can also make your own, using a router and a straight bit (bit diameter should equal the thickness of the panel) or a table saw and a dado cutter (adjust dado width to match the thickness of the panel).

Another installation method is to build a 2 × 3 subframe for the lattice panel, and install this frame between posts and rails. As shown in Drawing 8–18, the subframe is rabbeted to hold the panel and also to hold ¾-inch quarter-round molding, which is nailed in place along the edges of the panel.

Photo 8–3: Lattice panels have a number of uses in deck construction projects. More expensive, dense-pattern panels like the one at right can be used for maximum screening effect.

1 **Install backing cleats or channel molding.** To install a lattice screen between a post-and-rail framework, first fasten the backing cleats (or the subframe members) to posts and rails, using either galvanized finishing nails or bugle-head screws. If you use screws, predrill screw holes to avoid splitting the cleats.

If channel molding is used, install bottom and side pieces of molding with galvanized 4d finishing nails, but leave the top molding piece off until the lattice panel can be slid into side and bottom channels. Using a ¼-inch-diameter bit, drill drainage holes that extend through the bottom channel piece and also through the bottom rail. Space the holes about every 8 inches. Bottom rail drainage holes are also necessary if you're using cleats to install the lattice screen.

2 **Cut the lattice panel to fit inside its frame.** First, place the panel on a flat surface. Then mark cutting lines by snapping a chalk line or by running a pencil against a long straightedge. Place a board underneath the panel so that the cutting line is located over the board. Adjust your circular saw's depth of cut to match the thickness of the panel, then make the cut.

3 **Fit the panel in its frame or slide it into side and bottom channels if channel molding is used.** To hold the panel against backing cleats until the front cleats are installed, you can tack it to the backing cleats with several brads.

4 **Install front cleats or top channel molding.** Install the front cleats, holding each one firmly against the panel. If you're using channel molding, fasten the top piece of molding to the underside of the top rail, then install the top rail.

DRAWING 8–18: LATTICE PANEL INSTALLATION OPTIONS

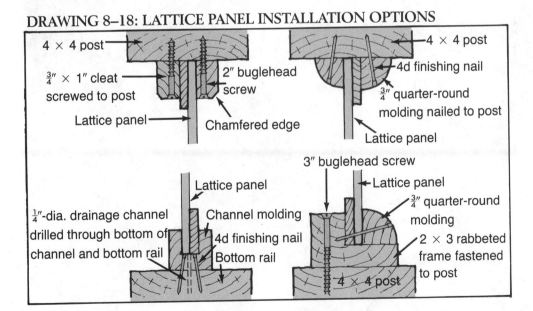

PROJECT 9

RAISED-RANCH DECK

Many raised-ranch houses (also called bilevel houses), like this one, were built with decks. But the original deck on this house didn't offer the size, style, or privacy the owners desired. They decided to replace it with one that would better suit their needs. The new design, which covers a little more than 500 square feet, includes some unusual features. Instead of a conventional railing, this deck has a solid wall that's built much like the wall of a house. The wall is covered on both sides with cedar shingles, the same siding treatment that covers the house. This waist-high wall yields far more privacy than an open railing with rails and balusters. Drainage openings, reminiscent of a traditional porch wall, are built into the deck wall at regular intervals.

A freestanding gable wall, with a broad opening onto stairs that lead to the backyard, is incorporated into the deck. Like the lower wall, the gable wall is covered on both sides with cedar shingle siding. Shingle courses on deck walls match those on the house, integrating both structures. To further unify deck and house, the slope of the deck's gable wall is the same as the slope of the house roof. A pair of exposed, site-made trusses that match the roof slope are installed between the deck gable and the gable end of the house. The trusses now support only a porch swing, but they could also support an awning if additional shade and shelter were desired.

To build a deck like this, you may have to adapt the height of the deck to suit the house you're working on. Likewise, the slope of your roof may differ from the 6-in-12 pitch on this house.

1 **Lay out the locations of the eight concrete piers.** As shown in Drawing 8–19, piers that support the cantilevered section of the deck are 9 feet from the edge of the house, spaced 8 feet on center. Dig holes for the piers and set tubular fiber forms in place. Allow the tops of the forms to extend several inches above grade. Set up wood forms for the concrete pads at the bottom of each stairway. For each pad, the top edges of the form boards should be level with each other.

Pour the concrete for the piers and pads. Before the concrete in the tubular forms sets, install steel post bases.

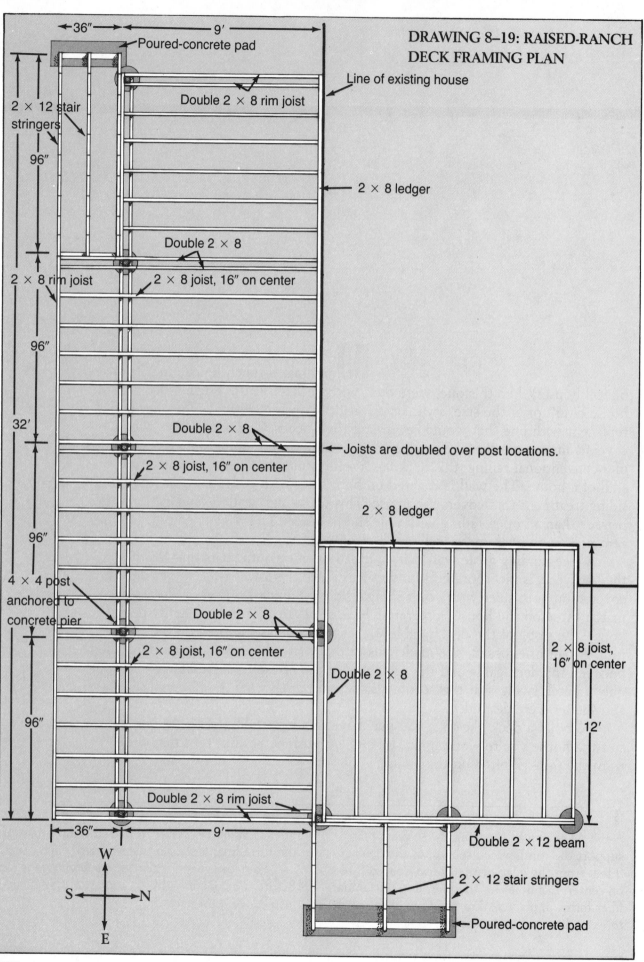

36″

9′

Poured-concrete pad

DRAWING 8–19: RAISED-RANCH DECK FRAMING PLAN

Line of existing house

Double 2 × 8 rim joist

2 × 12 stair stringers

96″

2 × 8 ledger

Double 2 × 8

2 × 8 rim joist

2 × 8 joist, 16″ on center

96″

Double 2 × 8

32′

2 × 8 joist, 16″ on center

Joists are doubled over post locations.

2 × 8 ledger

96″

4 × 4 post anchored to concrete pier

Double 2 × 8

2 × 8 joist, 16″ on center

Double 2 × 8

2 × 8 joist, 16″ on center

96″

Double 2 × 8

12′

Double 2 × 8 rim joist

36″

9′

Double 2 × 12 beam

W

S — N

E

2 × 12 stair stringers

Poured-concrete pad

Lumber Order

AMOUNT	MATERIAL	PART
Note: All Lumber Is Pressure Treated.		
2	2 × 8 × 16′	ledgers
2	2 × 8 × 12′	ledgers
8	4 × 4 × 6′	posts
4	2 × 12 × 16′	beams
2	2 × 12 × 12′	beam
7	2 × 8 × 10′	joists
32	2 × 8 × 12′	joists
2	2 × 8 × 16′	rim joists
1	2 × 8 × 12′	rim joist
1164 linear feet	2 × 6′	decking
3	1 × 4 × 16′	trim boards
2	1 × 4 × 12′	trim boards
5	2 × 4 × 8′	bottom plates for deck wall
2	2 × 4 × 12′	bottom plates for deck wall
1	2 × 4 × 10′	bottom plates for deck wall
4	2 × 6 × 16′	cap for deck and gable wall
1	2 × 6 × 12′	cap for deck wall
1	2 × 8 × 12′	wall plate
2	2 × 8 × 10′	header
4	2 × 8 × 12′	cross members
4	2 × 6 × 8′	gable-end rafters
1	2 × 8 × 12′	ridgeboard
2	1 × 6 × 12′	trim boards
8	2 × 6 × 8′	rafters
4	2 × 6 × 12′	bottom truss chords
3	2 × 12 × 10′	stair stringers, south stair
3	2 × 12 × 6′	stair stringers, east stair
1	2 × 4 × 10′	ledgers for stair stringers
1	2 × 4 × 10′	cleats for stair stringers
7	2 × 6 × 12′	treads and risers for south stair
6	2 × 6 × 12′	treads for east stair
3	2 × 8 × 12′	risers for east stair
1	4 × 4 × 4′	newel post for south stair railing
2	2 × 4 × 10′	top and bottom rails for south stair
16	2 × 2 × 24″	balusters
7	4 × 8′	lattice panels

(continued)

Lumber Order—*Continued*

AMOUNT	MATERIAL	PART
Note: All Untreated Dimension Lumber		
8	2 × 4 × 8'	top plates
12	½ × 4 × 8' CDX plywood	sheathing
16	2 × 4 × 10'	studs
5	2 × 4 × 8'	gable wall framing
8 boxes	18" cedar	shingles

Hardware

8 pcs. 8-in.-dia. tubular fiber forms

8 steel post bases

20 pcs. 8 × ⅜-in.-dia. machine bolts, with nuts and washers, for beams

30 single joist hangers

6 double joist hangers

26 pcs. 5½ × ⅜-in.-dia. lag screws with washers, for anchoring deck wall

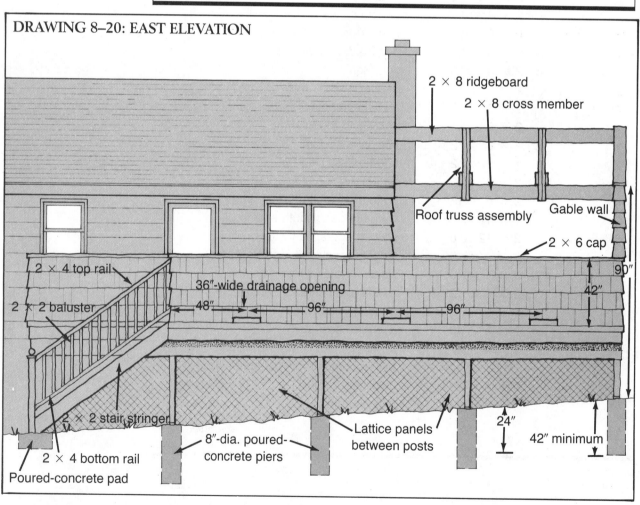

DRAWING 8–20: EAST ELEVATION

2 × 8 ridgeboard

2 × 8 cross member

Roof truss assembly

Gable wall

2 × 6 cap

90"

42"

36"-wide drainage opening

2 × 4 top rail

2 × 2 baluster

48"

96"

96"

2 × 2 stair stringer

Lattice panels between posts

8"-dia. poured-concrete piers

24"

42" minimum

2 × 4 bottom rail

Poured-concrete pad

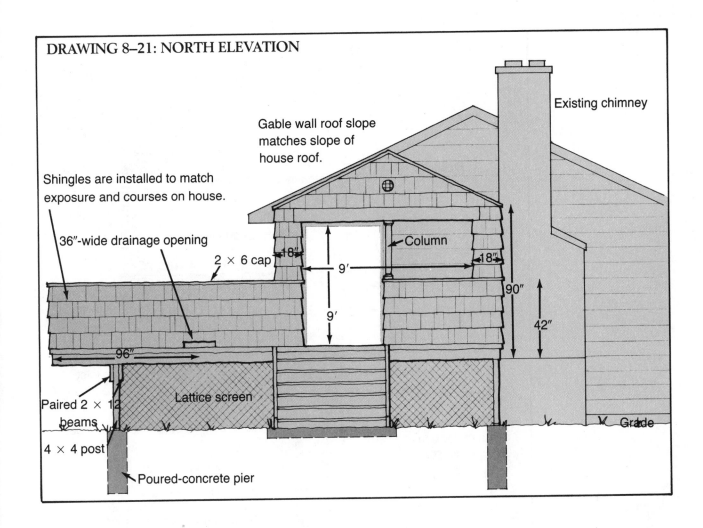

DRAWING 8–21: NORTH ELEVATION

Existing chimney

Gable wall roof slope matches slope of house roof.

Shingles are installed to match exposure and courses on house.

36"-wide drainage opening

2 × 6 cap

Column

18"

18"

9'

9'

90"

42"

96"

Lattice screen

Paired 2 × 12 beams

4 × 4 post

Poured-concrete pier

Grade

2 **Install 2 × 8 ledger boards.** On a wood-frame house like this one, it's best to remove the siding from the house wall where ledgers and decking boards will fit. This will enable you to screw the ledgers directly against the exterior sheathing, as shown in Drawing 8–22. Lag screws should extend through the siding and into the rim joists of the house. For details on attaching ledger boards to other types of walls, see chapter 5.

Allow the ledger on the south side of the house to extend beyond the corner of the house out to the perimeter pier, as shown in Drawing 8–19. Use a temporary post to keep the ledger extension level. Eventually, as you are installing the joists, you will double this ledger extension with a 12-foot 2 × 8.

Flash the ledgers, making sure to tuck flashing up underneath the exterior siding.

3 **Set the posts.** Cut the posts to length and fasten them to the post base connectors on the tops of the piers. Secure each post plumb with two temporary braces installed at right angles to each other, as shown in Photo 5–4 on page 62.

The tops of all posts should be aligned with each other and level with the bottom edge of the ledger. The ledger extension should have enough give to allow you to fit the two posts beneath it.

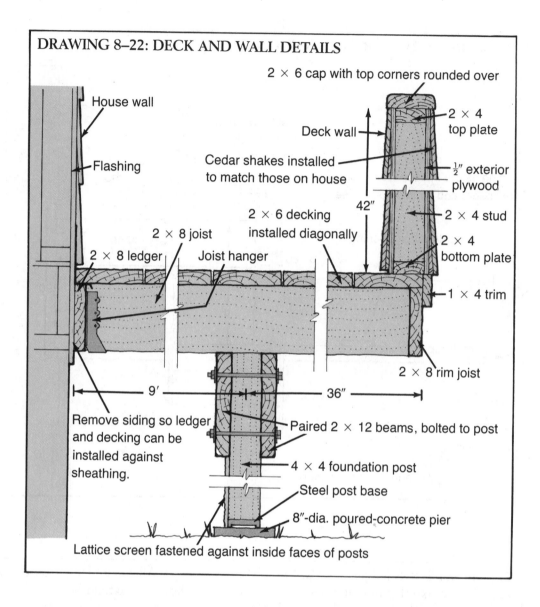

DRAWING 8–22: DECK AND WALL DETAILS

2 × 6 cap with top corners rounded over

House wall

Deck wall

2 × 4 top plate

Flashing

Cedar shakes installed to match those on house

$\frac{1}{2}$" exterior plywood

2 × 6 decking installed diagonally

42"

2 × 4 stud

2 × 8 joist

Joist hanger

2 × 4 bottom plate

2 × 8 ledger

1 × 4 trim

2 × 8 rim joist

9'

36"

Remove siding so ledger and decking can be installed against sheathing.

Paired 2 × 12 beams, bolted to post

4 × 4 foundation post

Steel post base

8"-dia. poured-concrete pier

Lattice screen fastened against inside faces of posts

4 **Frame the deck.** Install the pairs of 2 × 12 beams first, one on each side of the posts, as shown in Drawing 8–22. Also install the double 2 × 12 beam that runs between the ledger extension and the northernmost end of the deck. You can use two 20d nails to secure each 2 × 12 against a post, but for a stronger connection, through-bolt the beams to the posts, using a pair of 8-inch-long, $\frac{3}{8}$-inch-diameter machine bolts at each post.

Cut 2 × 8 joists to length and fasten them against ledgers and on top of beams, as shown in Drawing 8–22. Space the joists 16 inches on center and double them up over every post. Use single joist hangers to secure the single joists to the ledgers and double joist hangers to secure the doubled joists, and toenail the joists to the tops of the beams. The joists tying into the ledger extension can be secured by face-nailing through the extension. Then double the extension.

Cut rim joists to length and nail them to the ends of the joists. The top edge of the rim joists should be flush with the top edges of the joists.

5   **Lay the decking.** The 2 × 6 decking boards are installed diagonally. Cut one end of each decking board at a 45-degree angle to fit against the house. Let the boards run long, so they extend beyond the edges of the rim joists. When all decking boards are down, snap chalk lines to follow in trimming them. When trimmed, the ends of the decking boards should be even with the outside face of the rim joists.

Finish off the decking with 1 × 4 trim to conceal the ends of the decking boards. The top edge of the trim board should be flush with the top of the deck.

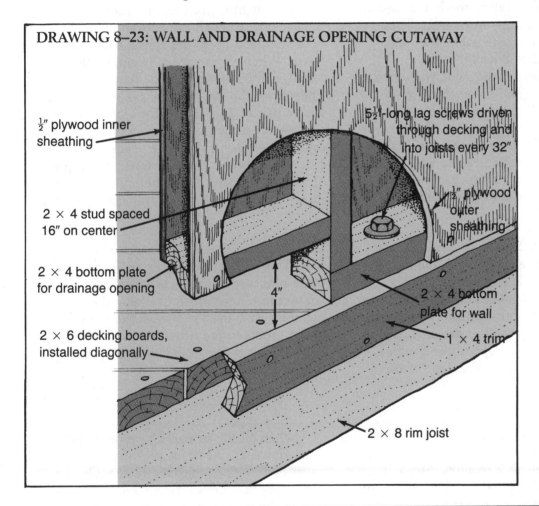

DRAWING 8–23: WALL AND DRAINAGE OPENING CUTAWAY

½" plywood inner sheathing

5½"-long lag screws driven through decking and into joists every 32"

½" plywood outer sheathing

2 × 4 stud spaced 16" on center

2 × 4 bottom plate for drainage opening

4"

2 × 4 bottom plate for wall

2 × 6 decking boards, installed diagonally

1 × 4 trim

2 × 8 rim joist

6   **Frame the deck's low walls.** Use pressure-treated 2 × 4s for the bottom plates. The top plates and studs can be untreated construction lumber. Frame each wall section and sheathe the inside face with ½-inch CDX plywood. Do this before you erect the walls, using the deck as a work surface. Drawing 8–23 shows how to frame the drainage openings along the bottom of the wall. Sheathe the outside face of each wall section with ½-inch plywood, then tilt it up into position and nail it to the deck. For extra rigidity, drive 5½-inch-long lag screws through the bottom plate and decking boards into the deck joists. Install screws 32 inches on center (one screw in every other joist).

Cap the deck wall with a 2 × 6, centering it over the wall's top plate. Miter the cap pieces where they meet at corners and in other locations on the wall. When all cap pieces are in place, use a router and ⅜-inch roundover bit to round the top edges of the cap.

7   **Frame the freestanding gable wall.** Fasten 2 × 4 studs and blocking on top of the lower wall, as shown in the Framing Elevation, Drawing 8–24. Before framing the gable-end rafters, install a horizontal 2 × 8 plate against the house wall. Plate level should match the level of the double 2 × 8 cross members that will connect the freestanding gable wall to the house. Install the paired 2 × 8 cross members next. These should be framed into the gable wall and toenailed into the 2 × 8 wall plate.

Make the header for the gable wall opening by sandwiching a length of ½-inch plywood between a pair of 2 × 6s, as shown in the Framing Cutaway, Drawing 8–24. Choose your straightest 2 × 6s to make the header. Make the two gable-end rafters the same way, using paired 2 × 6s. The pitch of the gable-end rafters and the pitch of the roof trusses should match the pitch of the house roof. In this case, roof pitch is 6-in-12, or about 26½ degrees.

Then, install a 2 × 8 ridgeboard between the top of the gable wall and the house wall. This framing will stiffen the gable wall and also support the open roof trusses.

Run wiring for the gable wall light (and any other lighting fixtures or outlets) beneath the decking, through the bottom plate of the deck wall, and up to the appropriate outlet boxes. When all wiring has been installed and tested, nail up all remaining plywood sheathing. Then cover the top edges of gable-end rafters with a pair of 2 × 6 cap pieces, routing the caps and centering them as you did the wall caps. Cover each side of the header with a 1 × 6 trim board. To shed water, the top edge of each trim board should be rounded over, as shown in the Framing Cutaway, Drawing 8–24.

8   **Complete the exposed roof framework.** Install 2 × 6 rafters, 2 × 3 struts, and 2 × 6 bottom chords, as shown in Drawing 8–25. Note that the width of the struts is actually, not nominally, 3 inches. Make the struts by ripping down 2 × 4 stock. The slope of the double 2 × 6 rafters should match the slope of the roof. This will determine the angles used to make bird's-mouth cutouts and plumb cuts. Allow the rafter tails to overhang the cross members by 6 inches. Toenail the top ends of the rafters to the ridgeboard and install 2 × 4 struts between the bottom edge of the ridgeboard and the 2 × 6 chords.

9   **Build the stairways.** Cut and install the stair stringers first. The 3-foot-wide stairway on the south side of the deck requires three cut stringers. The broad stairway on the east side of the deck is built with a central cut stringer and two solid stringers, which use cleats to support the ends of the treads. All stringers are cut from 2 × 12 stock. The unit rise height is 7 inches and the unit run is 9 inches. As shown in Drawing 8–26, 2 × 4 ledgers are used to secure the stringers to the beams and to concrete pads.

When all the stringers have been installed, screw down 2 × 6 treads and risers. You'll need a pair of 2 × 6s to make each step. On the narrow south stairway, fasten a 4 × 4 newel post to the outer stringer, using two machine bolts. (See ''Making a Decorative Post'' on page 96 for details on cutting the top of the newel.) Then cut and install top and bottom rails between the post and the deck's south wall. Next, screw the 2 × 2 balusters between rails, spacing them 6 inches on center.

10   **Install the lattice panels.** Cut the bottom of each panel section to follow the contour of the ground, and nail sections to the back edges of the 4 × 4 posts that support the deck.

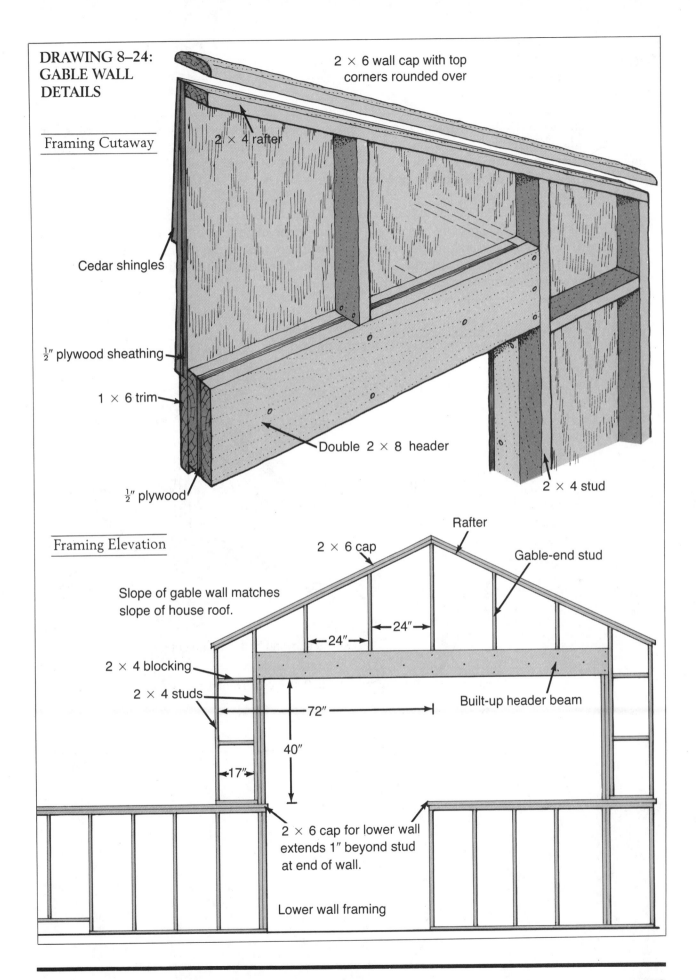

DRAWING 8–24:
GABLE WALL
DETAILS

2 × 6 wall cap with top corners rounded over

Framing Cutaway

2 × 4 rafter

Cedar shingles

½″ plywood sheathing

1 × 6 trim

Double 2 × 8 header

½″ plywood

2 × 4 stud

Framing Elevation

Rafter

2 × 6 cap

Gable-end stud

Slope of gable wall matches slope of house roof.

24″   24″

2 × 4 blocking

Built-up header beam

2 × 4 studs

72″

40″

17″

2 × 6 cap for lower wall extends 1″ beyond stud at end of wall.

Lower wall framing

179

11   **Finish the deck.** Before covering the walls with cedar shingles, it's a good idea to stain the deck and deck trim. On this deck, decking boards and the low wall cap received a gray semi-transparent stain. The remaining trim pieces, including the open roof trusses, were covered with white solid-color stain.

12   **Install shingles.** To properly integrate this deck with the house, cedar shingles must be installed at the same elevation as those on the house; they also need to be installed with the same exposure to the weather. The bottom or butt edges of the doubled starter course should be kept about ¼ inch above the decked surface.

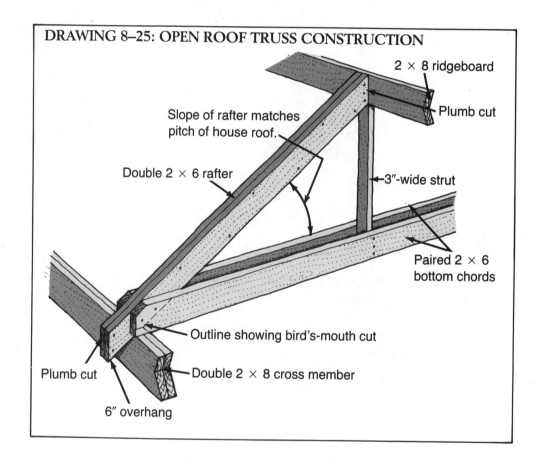

DRAWING 8–25: OPEN ROOF TRUSS CONSTRUCTION

2 × 8 ridgeboard

Plumb cut

Slope of rafter matches pitch of house roof.

Double 2 × 6 rafter

3"-wide strut

Paired 2 × 6 bottom chords

Outline showing bird's-mouth cut

Plumb cut

Double 2 × 8 cross member

6" overhang

DRAWING 8–26: FRAMING DETAILS FOR SOUTH STAIRWAY

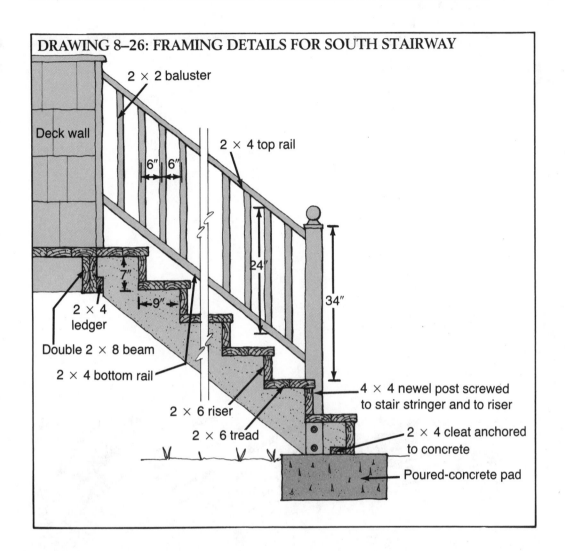

2 × 2 baluster

Deck wall

6″ 6″

2 × 4 top rail

24″

34″

7″

9″

2 × 4 ledger

Double 2 × 8 beam

2 × 4 bottom rail

2 × 6 riser

2 × 6 tread

4 × 4 newel post screwed to stair stringer and to riser

2 × 4 cleat anchored to concrete

Poured-concrete pad

PROJECT $\boxed{10}$

DECK TRELLIS

Shade is an important design factor in any deck project. Without it, a deck offers no respite from the heat or from the brightness and glare of the sun. When natural shading from trees isn't available, a trellis is an excellent feature to incorporate in a deck design. With its grid of overlapping members, a trellis will cast a pleasing geometry of sun and shadow on the deck surface or on the walls of the house. In addition to providing shade, a trellis can serve as an arbor for grapes, ivy, and other climbing plants. A trellis also offers a great opportunity for enhancing a deck's appearance with well-crafted joinery.

Usually a trellis is built over only part of the deck. This leaves some areas of the deck open so that the option of full sunlight remains. The trellis shown here, made from redwood, is nicely integrated into the deck design. At the deck perimeter, two of the 4 × 8 trellis posts support deck framing and sections of a custom-made fence. One of the support posts is put to yet another use. The builder used it as an opportunity to create an octagonal table. Plans for this optional table are provided in "Building a Table around a Post" on page 190.

For appearance and function, a trellis relies on at least two layers of overlapping members. The members in each layer are spaced at regular intervals, as shown in Drawing 8–27. Closer intervals and larger members will create a denser grid for greater shading effect. Overhangs or cantilevers at each level, or layer, of the trellis give it lightness and grace. The design shown here could easily be adapted to fit different decks.

Building the Trellis

1 **Install trellis posts and deck foundation posts.** First, lay out locations of trellis posts and all other posts that will become part of the deck foundation. As shown in Drawing 8–27, trellis posts should be spaced 10 feet on center. Dig holes for concrete piers, then use wood or fiber forms to elevate the top of each pier 1 to 2 inches above grade level. Fill pier holes with poured concrete.

Where codes allow, platform-type, cast aluminum post bases can be used as bases for trellis posts. You'll need two 4 × 4 bases under each 4 × 8 base. After fastening these post bases to the bottoms of trellis posts, position each post plumb on its pier and mark a cutoff line on the post 7 feet above the planned level of the deck. Trim the tops of the trellis posts at their cutoff lines, making sure the cut is square. Then position each post on its pier, using temporary diagonal braces to secure all posts in plumb position until deck framing is attached. The 4 × 4 posts for the deck foundation and fence can be installed the same way.

2 **Install ledgers, deck joists, and rim joists.** For installation details at post locations, see Drawing 8–28. After installing the ledger board against the house, the first joists to install are those that fit against the posts. Install the inner rim joists next; then the remaining joists. Drive nails through rim joists and into the ends of joists. Finish up the framing by nailing outer rim joists to inner rim joists.

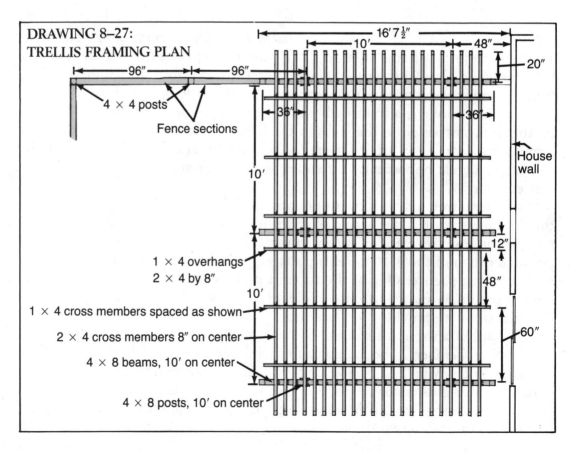

DRAWING 8–27:
TRELLIS FRAMING PLAN

16′ 7½″
10′
48″
20″
96″
96″
4 × 4 posts
Fence sections
36″
36″
House wall
10′
12″
1 × 4 overhangs
2 × 4 by 8″
48″
10′
1 × 4 cross members spaced as shown
2 × 4 cross members 8″ on center
60″
4 × 8 beams, 10′ on center
4 × 8 posts, 10′ on center

3   **Nail down decking boards.** As shown in Drawing 8–28, the inner edge of the perimeter decking board should butt against the outside face of the post. The board's outer edge will overhang the outer rim joist by 2½ inches. Nail this board down over both rim joists. Then notch the next decking board to fit around the edges of the post. Install the remaining decking boards, notching them where necessary to fit around trellis and fence posts.

Lumber Order

Note: All Redwood Dimension Lumber

AMOUNT	MATERIAL	PART
6	4 × 8 × 10′	posts
3	4 × 8 × 18′	beams
12	⁵⁄₄ × 6 × 8′	post trim pieces
12	1 × 3 × 8′	post trim pieces
6	1 × 4 × 16′	cross members
48	2 × 4 × 12′	cross members

Hardware

12 pcs. 4 × 4 cast aluminum post bases (2 bases for each 4 × 8 post)

DRAWING 8–28: DECK FRAMING DETAILS

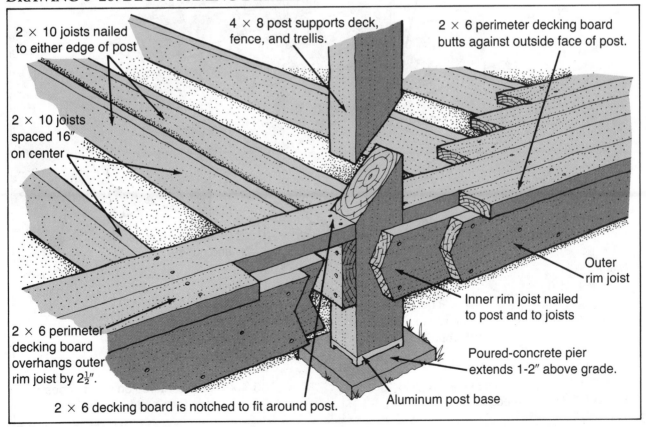

2 × 10 joists nailed to either edge of post

4 × 8 post supports deck, fence, and trellis.

2 × 6 perimeter decking board butts against outside face of post.

2 × 10 joists spaced 16″ on center

Outer rim joist

Inner rim joist nailed to post and to joists

2 × 6 perimeter decking board overhangs outer rim joist by 2½″.

Poured-concrete pier extends 1-2″ above grade.

2 × 6 decking board is notched to fit around post.

Aluminum post base

4   **Cut and embellish 4 × 8 beams.** As shown in Drawing 8–29, the 4 × 8 trellis beams extend 3 feet beyond the trellis posts. For decoration, they are chamfered on the ends and grooved 8 inches from the chamfered end, as shown in Drawing 8–29. To make these embellishments, use pipe clamps or wood cleats to gang the beams together, making sure ends and top surfaces are flush. Set your circular saw for a 45-degree cut and use a straightedge to guide the chamfer cut through one side of all four beams. If necessary, use a plane or belt sander to smooth saw marks.

Now, with the beams still ganged, use a straightedge-guided router to make 1-inch-wide, ¾-inch-deep dadoes across all the beams. With a ¾-inch straight bit, you'll have to make the dadoes' width in two passes. To avoid overloading the router and overheating the bit, it's a good idea to mill the dado to a ⅜-inch depth first; then adjust bit depth to ¾ inch and complete the dado. This means each dado will require four passes. Unclamp the beams, gang them together with another side up, and repeat the chamfering and routing process for all four sides of each beam.

If you don't have a router, set your circular saw for ¾ inches deep and use your straightedge to make two saw cuts defining the width of the dadoes. Make these cuts across each ganged side and then make a series of kerf cuts between the first two cuts. Use a chisel to knock out the kerfed waste.

DRAWING 8–29: TRELLIS CONSTRUCTION DETAILS

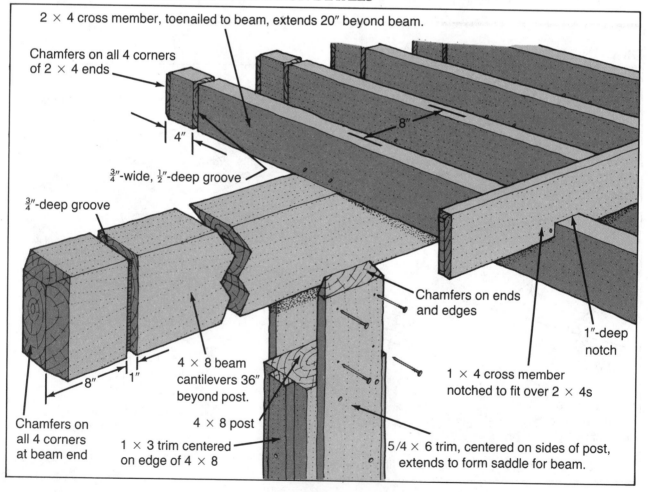

2 × 4 cross member, toenailed to beam, extends 20″ beyond beam.

Chamfers on all 4 corners of 2 × 4 ends

4″

8″

¾″-wide, ½″-deep groove

¾″-deep groove

Chamfers on ends and edges

1″-deep notch

8″   1″

4 × 8 beam cantilevers 36″ beyond post.

Chamfers on all 4 corners at beam end

4 × 8 post

1 × 3 trim centered on edge of 4 × 8

1 × 4 cross member notched to fit over 2 × 4s

5/4 × 6 trim, centered on sides of post, extends to form saddle for beam.

When the dado is finished along the beam edges that face up, turn the beams on their sides, keeping them butted together and with their ends flush. Repeat the dadoing operation until dadoes extend all the way around the beams.

5   Install beams and post trim boards. Carefully lift each beam into position and secure each post-to-beam connection by toenailing through beam sides into the top of the post.

Each trellis post gets a pair of $\frac{5}{4} \times 6$ trim boards that extend 7½ inches above the top of the post, forming a saddle that locks the beam in place. Cut these boards to final length. Chamfer the top ends and edges with a circular saw, smoothing the cut edges with a hand plane. Nail the boards to the posts and beams, as shown in Drawing 8–29.

Now cut 1×3 trim boards and fasten them to the edges of the posts. The top of each 1×3 butts against the bottom of the beam. On trellis posts that also support the fence, the 1×3 ends where the top of the fence begins.

6   Prepare 2 × 4 cross members. Each cross member in this trellis design is 11 feet, 8¾ inches long. One end of each cross member cantilevers 20 inches beyond an outer beam, while the other end rests on the center beam, butting against another cross member, as shown in Drawing 8–29.

Cut all 2×4s to final length and gang them together on the deck, with edges facing up and ends square and flush with each other. Decorative dadoes need to be cut around each cross member, and this can be done with the stock clamped or braced together, as when dadoing the beams. On the cross members, dadoes are ¾-inch wide, ½-inch deep, and located 4 inches from the cantilevered ends. Mill the dadoes using a ¾-inch straight bit. Guide the router base against a straightedge to make each pass. Repeat the dadoing operation along all four sides and edges of the cross members, keeping them ganged together with their ends flush.

While the cross members are ganged for each dado, use a block plane to make a small chamfer on each cross member on the edge closest to the dado.

7   Position the 2 × 4 cross members. This trellis is built with 2×4 cross members spaced 8 inches on center. Use a closer spacing (and more cross members) for greater shading effect, a wider spacing (and fewer cross members) to let in more sunlight. These cross members are secured by toenailing them to beams, but it's best to hold off on toenailing until the 1×4 cross members are installed. For now, simply position the 2×4s atop the beams.

8   Cut, notch, and install the 1 × 4 cross members. Each of these 1×4s extends 8 inches beyond the outer 2×4 cross members, as shown in Drawing 8–27. The 1×4s are notched to fit over the top edges of the 2×4s, as shown in Drawing 8–29. Cut notches with all six 1×4 cross members clamped together on the deck. Make sure that the ends of the 1×4s are flush with each other, then lay out notch locations using a tape measure and square. The notch width should match the thickness of the 2×4 cross members.

You can use a router and straight bit to cut notches in the 1×4 cross members, following the same procedures used when dadoing beams and 2×4 cross members. The notches can be cut more quickly, since they only need to be made on the edges that will face down. The notch width should match the thickness of the 2×4 cross members. The notch depth should be 1 inch. Mill to this depth in several passes, with bit depth adjusted first to ⅜ inch, then to ¾ inch, and finally to 1 inch.

When the notches are complete, unclamp the 1 × 4s and fit them, one at a time, over the 2 × 4 cross members. Space them as shown in Drawing 8–27.

Secure the 1 × 4s to the 2 × 4s by driving 16d nails through the top edges of the 1 × 4s and into the top edges of 2 × 4s. It's only necessary to nail every fourth joint, but pilot holes for the nails should be drilled in 1 × 4s to prevent splitting. Finally, toenail 2 × 4s to beams.

Building the Fence

Lumber Order

AMOUNT	MATERIAL	PART
2	4 × 4 × 6'	posts
36	⁵⁄₄ × 3 × 8'	slats
4	⁵⁄₄ × 6 × 10'	top and bottom rails

Note: This construction sequence is for a single fence section. Use the same techniques to build the entire fence. Fence height for this deck is 52½ inches above the deck surface, but you can choose a different height (and slat length) to suit your needs.

1   **Cut slats to length.** Slats for this fence are 48 inches long, which corresponds to a 38-inch distance between top and bottom rails.

Slats require an angle cut along their top ends to promote drainage. The bottom ends can be cut off square.

2   **Install slats against posts.** On this deck, fence posts are installed in the same way as the perimeter trellis posts. Each fence section contains a pair of slats that are fastened against the post edges. These slats help to anchor the rails. In each post slat, drill pilot holes for 20d nails through the narrow side of each post slat, as

shown in Drawing 8–30, spacing the holes 10 inches apart. Then nail the post slats to the posts, taking care to center the slat on the side of the post, as shown in Drawing 8–30. The bottom (square-cut end) of the slat should be 3½ inches from the deck surface.

3   **Install one top rail and one bottom rail.** Rail length should equal the distance between posts. Position the bottom rail against the post slats, its bottom edge flush with the bottoms of

the slats. Fasten the rail to each slat with a pair of 6d nails. For a stronger joint, use a pair of 2-inch buglehead screws. Then, using 8d nails, toenail the rail to each post.

In the same manner, install a single top rail on the same side of the slats as the bottom rail. The top edge of the top rail should be 52½ inches from the deck surface (unless you've elected to change fence height).

4   **Tack slats to top and bottom rails.** This fence is built with about 1 inch of space between slats, but you can use a different spacing if more or less privacy is desired. Position each slat using a spacer block. With the block wedged between slats at the top rail, drive a single 4d nail through the new slat and into the top rail. Then place the spacer block between slats at the bottom rail and secure the slat with another 4d nail. These nails simply hold the slats in place until the remaining rails are installed. Work from the posts toward the center of the fence section. Adjust the position of the last five or six slats so the spacing appears as uniform as possible.

5   **Install remaining top and bottom rails.** Nail or screw each rail to post slats and to posts, as before. Then strengthen the entire fence section by driving 9d nails through rails, slats, and into opposing rails.

DRAWING 8–30: FENCE CONSTRUCTION DETAILS

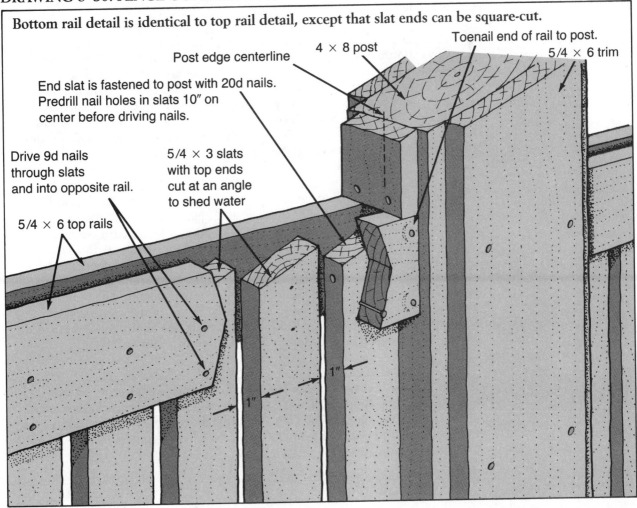

Bottom rail detail is identical to top rail detail, except that slat ends can be square-cut.

Post edge centerline

4 × 8 post

Toenail end of rail to post.

5/4 × 6 trim

End slat is fastened to post with 20d nails. Predrill nail holes in slats 10" on center before driving nails.

Drive 9d nails through slats and into opposite rail.

5/4 × 3 slats with top ends cut at an angle to shed water

5/4 × 6 top rails

1"

1"

1"

BUILDING A TABLE AROUND A POST

Lumber Order

Amount	Material	Part
1	2 × 6 × 4'	supports for cross members
2	2 × 4 × 8'	4 cross members
1	2 × 4 × 6'	4 end pieces
2	2 × 4 × 4'	2 diagonal braces
1	2 × 4 × 8'	4 angled members
36 linear ft.	2 × 6	decking

A post that extends through the deck presents a good opportunity for making a built-in table. The built-in table shown here has an octagonal surface that surrounds a trellis post. Because it is comprised of lots of little pieces, the table can be built from spare lengths of 2 × 4 stock and leftover decking boards.

1 **Cut and install 2 × 6 supports.** As shown in Drawing 8–31, each support is 16 inches long and has two 1½ × 3½-inch notches to receive a pair of 2 × 4 cross members. Make sure that the two supports are level with each other and centered on the post sides. To put the table surface 32 inches above the finished deck, the top edge of each 2 × 6 should be 30½ inches from the deck surface. Fasten each support to the post with three or four 3-inch galvanized buglehead screws.

2 **Cut lap joints in cross members.** Cut all four cross members 48 inches long. Gang these 2 × 4s, clamping them with the wide sides against each other. Make sure that edges and ends are flush. Lay out locations of lap joints, as shown in Drawing 8–32. Then adjust your circular saw for a depth of cut of 1¾ inches or half the width of the cross members. Make repeated passes inside the layout lines until thin strips of waste remain between saw kerfs. Then clean up the bottom of the notches with a chisel. Unclamp the cross members and test-fit the lap joints. If necessary, go over joints with a chisel to fine-tune the fit. For more on this joint-making technique, see Photos 4–12 through 4–14 on pages 46 and 47.

3 **Position the first two cross members on the 2 × 6 supports.** These members fit in the supports' notches and they should be centered with lap joint notches facing up. Hold cross members in place by partially driving 3-inch-long buglehead screws through cross members and into notches in the supports.

DRAWING 8–31:
TABLETOP EXPLODED VIEW

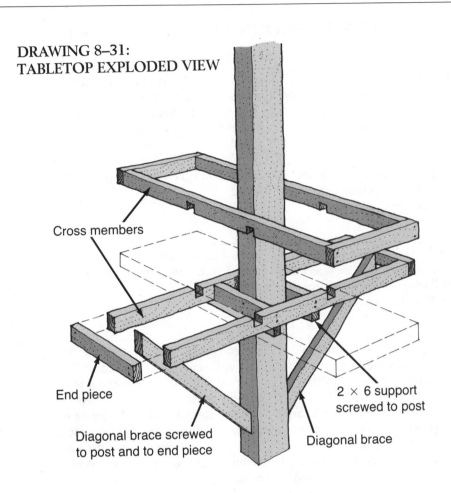

Cross members

End piece

Diagonal brace screwed
to post and to end piece

2 × 6 support
screwed to post

Diagonal brace

DRAWING 8–32: SUPPORT AND CROSS MEMBER DETAILS

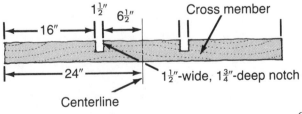

$1\frac{1}{2}''$

$3\frac{1}{2}''$

2 × 6 support

16''

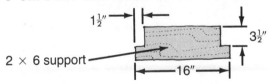

$1\frac{1}{2}''$ $6\frac{1}{2}''$

Cross member

16''

24''

$1\frac{1}{2}''$-wide, $1\frac{3}{4}''$-deep notch

Centerline

(continued)

BUILDING A TABLE AROUND A POST—*Continued*

4 **Install remaining cross members.** If necessary, adjust the position of the first pair of cross members so that all lap joints fit firmly together. Finish driving screws into support notches and secure each lap joint with a single 3-inch screw driven from the top of the joint.

5 **Screw end pieces to cross members.** Use a pair of 3-inch buglehead screws for each joint, and predrill each screw hole to avoid splitting the wood.

6 **Cut and install angled members.** Measure the distance that each angled member will span between end pieces, then make 45-degree end-cuts accordingly. Fasten angled members in place with 3-inch screws driven in predrilled holes.

7 **Cut and install 2 × 6 tabletop decking.** For a fancy look, the 2 × 6s can be cut and fit concentric to the post as shown in Drawing 8–33. Blocking will need to be added to the frame to support some of the shorter concentric boards. To install the top this way, begin at the post and work outward. Each concentric course will consist of eight pieces that require angled cuts to fit together. To lay out each angle cut, place a length of 2 × 6 where it will used. Use a straight-edge to mark lines from the two closest outer corners of the frame to the two closest corners of the post. Secure tabletop members to frame members with galvanized 10d finishing nails.

DRAWING 8–33: TABLE FRAMING PLAN

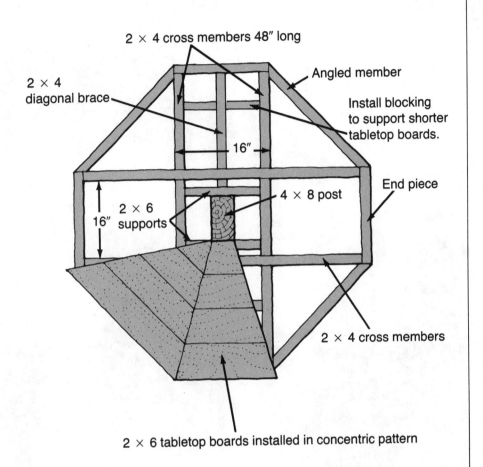

2 × 4 cross members 48" long

2 × 4
diagonal brace

Angled member

Install blocking
to support shorter
tabletop boards.

16"

16"

2 × 6
supports

4 × 8 post

End piece

2 × 4 cross members

2 × 6 tabletop boards installed in concentric pattern

PROJECT 11

STEEP-SITE DECK

In the San Francisco Bay Area, where this two-level deck was built, steep building sites are the rule, not the exception. Here, a deck often takes the place of a backyard. When this is the case, a deck isn't thought of as an addition, but as a necessary part of a new house. Of course, each steep site is unique, so this deck design would need to be adapted to fit specific site conditions. It also has to be integrated with the house design.

By extending deck framing inside the house, it's possible to create cantilevered sections of a deck that don't need to be supported outside the house by foundation posts. Each of this deck's two levels wraps around the angled form of the house, with cantilevered deck walkways on either side of a broad deck area, as shown in Drawings 8–34 and 8–35. The broad section of the deck at each level is supported by a pair of steel columns that extend from concrete piers.

The cable railing is another unusual feature on this deck. It consists of high-strength cable stretched horizontally between 4 × 4 posts. This railing is safe but nearly invisible, so it doesn't obscure dramatic views from the deck or from inside the house.

Like the foundation and framing for this house, the deck structure had to be approved by an engineer in order to comply with seismic and steep-site building codes. Some joists and beams extend through the exterior wall of the house, where they're anchored to the house framing. Because of this, the deck is much easier to build as part of a new house, rather than as an addition. House walls and floors can be framed at the same time as the deck, making it easier to integrate deck framing with house framing.

To build your own version of this deck, you'll need to adapt its design to your own site conditions and to the size and shape of your house. You may need only one level of this two-level design. But for a deck this complex, you should have an engineer approve your plans, whether or not this is required in your area. Note also that the Douglas fir dimension lumber used to frame this deck differs from the standard two-by framing lumber available in other parts of the country. For comparable structural value using standard dimension lumber (and possibly a different wood species), you'll have to consult a structural engineer.

The construction sequence for the lower deck is described here. Building the upper deck calls for the same sequence of operations, and the work should be easier because the completed lower deck can be used as a staging area.

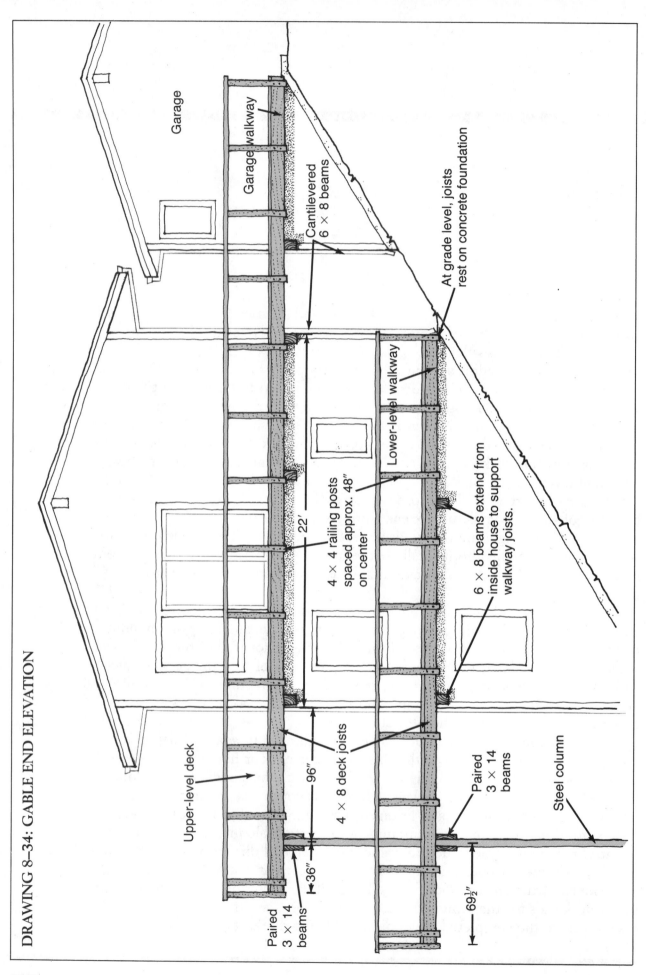

DRAWING 8–34: GABLE END ELEVATION

Garage

Garage walkway

Cantilevered 6 × 8 beams

At grade level, joists rest on concrete foundation

Lower-level walkway

22'

4 × 4 railing posts spaced approx. 48" on center

6 × 8 beams extend from inside house to support walkway joists.

Upper-level deck

96"

4 × 8 deck joists

36"

Paired 3 × 14 beams

Paired 3 × 14 beams

Steel column

$69\frac{1}{2}$"

Lumber Order

AMOUNT	MATERIAL	PART
2	3 × 14 × 22′ treated	beams
2	6 × 8 × 9′ treated	beams for gable-end walkway
7	4 × 8 × 16′ treated	joists for cantilevered walkway
7	2 × 4 × 14′ treated	joist build-up
2	½ × 4 × 8′ plywood	joist build-up
1	4 × 8 × 18′ treated	rim joist
1	4 × 8 × 20′ treated	rim joist for broad section of deck
8	4 × 8 × 14′ treated	joists for broad section of deck
2	4 × 8 × 12′ treated	joists for broad section of deck
1	4 × 8 × 16′ treated	joist for broad section of deck
3	4 × 8 × 24′ treated	joists for gable-end walkway
90 linear ft.	2 × 10 redwood	perimeter trim boards
25	4 × 4 × 4′ redwood	railing posts
1	2 × 4 × 22′ redwood	railing cap
1	2 × 4 × 18′ redwood	railing cap
1	2 × 4 × 14′ redwood	railing cap
2	1 × 3 × 20′ redwood	railing trim
2	1 × 3 × 22′ redwood	railing trim
2	1 × 3 × 18′ redwood	railing trim
2	1 × 3 × 14′ redwood	railing trim
4	1 × 3 × 20′ redwood	railing trim
490 linear ft.	2 × 6 redwood	decking boards

(continued)

Lumber Order—*Continued*

Hardware

2 pcs. 4 × 4 steel columns, length as needed

8 pcs. 3 × ½-in.-dia. anchor bolts

6 pcs. 12 × ¾-in.-dia. machine bolts, with washers and nuts

27 heavy-duty angle brackets (square)

5 heavy-duty angle brackets (135 degrees)

176 pcs. 3 × ½-in.-dia. lag screws, with washers

12 steel strap ties, with lag screws

6 steel tie plates

50 pcs. 7½ × ½-in.-dia. lag screws, with washers

630 ft. high strength, stainless steel cable, with anchoring and tensioning fixtures

Note: The lumber and hardware orders are for the lower level deck only. Materials for the upper deck will be the same except for the following:

1 additional 6 × 8 × 9′ beam for gable-end walkway

490 linear ft. 2 × 6 redwood decking.

Instead of 10 pcs. 4 × 8 × 14′ joists:

3 pcs. 4 × 8 × 14′ joists

7 pcs. 4 × 8 × 12′ joists

---

1 **Form and pour the concrete foundation.** Concrete piers should extend to stable soil or bedrock, depending on local conditions. The two piers for this deck had to be reinforced with steel reinforcing bars specified by an engineer. The piers are connected to each other and to the house foundation by grade beams—reinforced concrete beams that are poured in square forms made on site from plywood and dimension lumber. These beams can be poured at the same time the piers are poured, and effectively anchor the piers to the mass of the house foundation. Grade beams may not be necessary on gentler slopes or in more stable soil.

2 **Install the two steel columns.** Square in section, each column has a flange on its base that can be anchored to the top of the concrete pier with four ½-inch-diameter anchor bolts. The columns extend a full two stories to support the beams for both deck levels, as shown in Drawing 8–36. Plumb the columns and brace them by extending two-bys from the columns to the foundation wall or wall framing of the house.

3 **Bolt the lower pair of 3 × 14 beams to the columns.** The size and weight of each beam, combined with the height of the columns, make this work especially difficult. Beams can be hoisted into position by a crane, or scaffolding can be used, along with plenty of help. The beams have to be clamped firmly in place against the columns while ¾-inch-diameter holes for

DRAWING 8–35: LOWER-LEVEL FRAMING PLAN

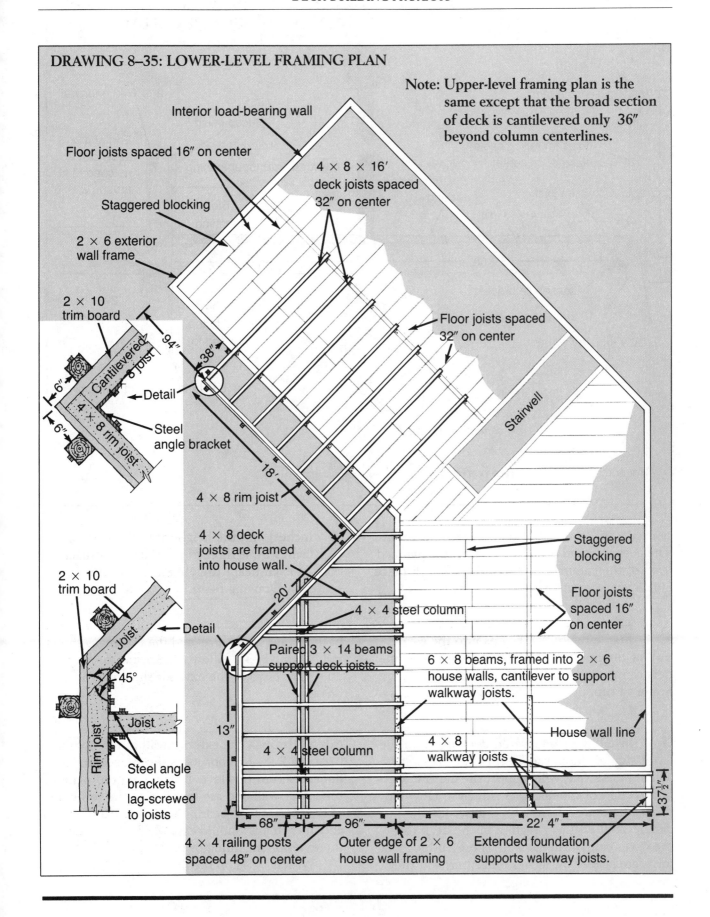

Note: Upper-level framing plan is the same except that the broad section of deck is cantilevered only 36″ beyond column centerlines.

Interior load-bearing wall

Floor joists spaced 16″ on center

Staggered blocking

2 × 6 exterior wall frame

2 × 10 trim board

4 × 8 × 16′ deck joists spaced 32″ on center

Floor joists spaced 32″ on center

Cantilevered 4 × 8 joist

4 × 8 rim joist

94″

38″

Detail

Steel angle bracket

18′

4 × 8 rim joist

4 × 8 deck joists are framed into house wall.

20′

2 × 10 trim board

Joist

Detail

45°

Joist

Rim joist

Steel angle brackets lag-screwed to joists

13″

Paired 3 × 14 beams support deck joists.

4 × 4 steel column

4 × 4 steel column

4 × 4 railing posts spaced 48″ on center

68″

Outer edge of 2 × 6 house wall framing

96″

Stairwell

Staggered blocking

Floor joists spaced 16″ on center

6 × 8 beams, framed into 2 × 6 house walls, cantilever to support walkway joists.

House wall line

4 × 8 walkway joists

Extended foundation supports walkway joists.

22′ 4″

37½″

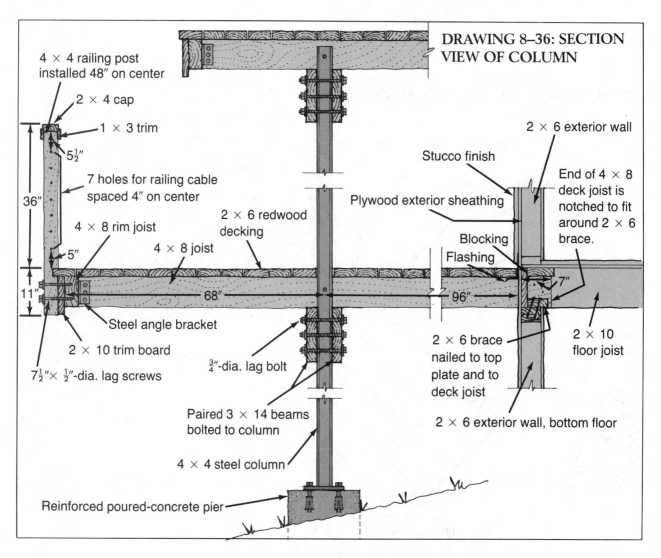

4 × 4 railing post installed 48" on center

2 × 4 cap

1 × 3 trim

5½"

7 holes for railing cable spaced 4" on center

36"

4 × 8 rim joist

5"

2 × 6 redwood decking

4 × 8 joist

2 × 6 exterior wall

Stucco finish

Plywood exterior sheathing

End of 4 × 8 deck joist is notched to fit around 2 × 6 brace.

Blocking

Flashing

11"

68"

96"

7"

Steel angle bracket

2 × 10 trim board

¾"-dia. lag bolt

2 × 6 brace nailed to top plate and to deck joist

2 × 10 floor joist

7½" × ½"-dia. lag screws

Paired 3 × 14 beams bolted to column

2 × 6 exterior wall, bottom floor

4 × 4 steel column

Reinforced poured-concrete pier

---

bolts are drilled through the beams and columns. The beams should be 9 inches below the planned level of the completed lower deck. This distance equals the sum of the decking thickness

(1½ inches) and the height of the 4 × 8 joists (7½ inches). Use three ¾-inch-diameter machine bolts at each beam-to-column connection, as shown in Drawing 8–36.

4 **Frame the 6 × 8 beams into the east wall of the house.** These two 9-foot-long members cantilever beyond the exterior wall of the house to support the deck walkway that leads

back toward grade level and the garage, as shown in Drawing 8–35. Allow each beam to extend 36 inches beyond the exterior sheathing of the house.

5 **Install the cantilevered deck joists on the eaves side of the house.** Begin with the cantilevered joists that will support the narrow walkway section of the deck. As shown in Drawing 8–35, there are seven 4 × 8 joists for the cantilevered walkway section of the deck (on the eaves side of the house). These 16-foot-long joists are spaced 32 inches on center, and they

extend through the exterior wall of the house, between 2 × 10 floor joists. Both deck and floor joists for this level bear on the top plate of the lower wall and are fastened to the top plate of an interior load-bearing wall. The cantilevered end of each joist should extend 33 inches beyond the exterior sheathing of the house.

With 2 × 4s on the flat and strips of ½-inch

plywood, build up the top edges of these first seven deck joists inside the house so that they'll be level with the top edges of the 2 × 10 floor joists. This will allow deck joists to help support the house floor.

6   **Attach the 4 × 8 rim joist to the ends of the cantilevered joists.** Use a pair of heavy-duty steel angle brackets at the end of each joist. Fasten the angle brackets to the joists and the rim joist with 3-inch-long, ½-inch-diameter lag screws (six per bracket and two brackets per joist).

7   **Install the 4 × 8 joists for the broad section of the deck.** These joists are also framed into the house, but they extend only 1½ inches beyond the top plate of the lower wall. Outside the house, these 4 × 8s bear on the twin 3 × 14 beams that are fastened to the columns. The first of these members to cut and install is the 20-foot-long 4 × 8 rim joist that forms the angled section of the deck where the walkway meets the broad deck area. This long 4 × 8 should meet the house wall and the walkway's rim joist at a right angle. Cut the outside end of the joist at a 45-degree angle, and notch the house end to fit around 2 × 6 brace, as shown in Drawing 8–36. Then position the joist on top of the 3 × 14 beams and the house wall's top plate. Secure the house end of the joist with blocking; then connect it to the walkway rim joist, using lag screws and angle brackets. Toenail the joist to both 3 × 14 beams where it crosses them.

Next, install the remaining joists for the broad section of the deck. As shown in Drawing 8–35, there are five shorter 4 × 8 joists, which meet the 20-foot-long 4 × 8 at a 45-degree angle. Two of these joists should be bolted to opposite sides of the steel column using a pair of 12-inch-long, ¾-inch-diameter machine bolts.

There are four joists for the broad section of the deck that are 14 feet long. These meet the long joist at right angles and extend into the wall, where their notched ends hold 2 × 6 blocking. As shown in Drawing 8-36, the blocking is nailed to the top plate of the wall and to the deck joists, locking the deck and house structures together. Beyond the house wall, use a pair of steel angle brackets with lag screws to fasten each joist to the adjoining rim joist.

Install the remaining three deck joists for the broad section of the deck. These members are each 13 feet, 7¼ inches long. Instead of being framed into the house wall, each of these joists is supported at one end by the 6 × 8 beam that cantilevers from the house corner. The end of each joist should rest along the centerline of the 6 × 8, leaving room on this beam for the ends of the walkway joists.

Install the rim joist to complete the framing for the broad section of the deck. This 4 × 8 should be close to 13 feet long, and requires a 45-degree-angle end cut to fit against the long joist at the angled corner of the deck (see the detail in Drawing 8–35). Use steel angle brackets and 3-inch-long lag screws to connect the rim joist to the ends of the joists.

8   **Install the 4 × 8 joists supporting the gable-end walkway.** These joists should be 22 feet, 1¾ inches long, but be sure to double-check the measurement before cutting them to length. All three joists rest on the cantilevered 6 × 8 beams that extend from the gable wall, and on the poured-concrete extension of the house wall at the grade-level corner of the house. Use steel strap ties and lag screws to fasten these joists to the beams that they rest on. Use tie plates and nails to join these three long joists to the shorter deck joists they butt against.

9   **Tack down a temporary floor.** Use exterior plywood sheets at least ⅝ inch thick. This sheathing will act as a work surface until it's time to lay down the deck.

10   **Nail 2 × 10 trim boards against the rim joists.** The top edges of the trim boards should be flush with the top edges of the rim joists.

11   **Close any openings where deck joists penetrate the walls of the house.** Start off by nailing plywood sheathing over blocking to cover openings between framing members. Then seal airspaces around these joists and beams with an expanding foam sealant. When the second-story walls have been framed, install flashing to direct water away from penetration points where joists or beams meet the house. The flashing should be nailed directly to the exterior sheathing and bent over the top edges of deck framing members where they meet the wall. These steps are important on this project because the deck framing is integrated with the house framing. Good flashing will prevent water damage to the deck and house.

12   **Install the railing posts.** First, cut the 4 × 4 posts to a final length of 45½ inches. Then drill ¼-inch-diameter holes for cable railings. Each post gets seven holes drilled along its centerline spaced 4 inches on center, as shown in Drawing 8–36. The center for the highest hole should be 5½ inches from the top of the post.

Holes for fastening the posts to the deck can also be drilled at this time. Each post gets a pair of ½-inch-diameter holes, centered on the outside face of the post and spaced 6 inches apart. Start the bottom hole 2 inches from the bottom of the post.

Fasten the posts to the deck, using 7½-inch-long, ½-inch-diameter lag screws. As shown in Photo 8–4, the cable railing design calls for a pair of corner posts, rather than a single corner post. Locate each post 6 inches away from the corner. Otherwise, space posts 4 feet on center or closer, if one side of the deck needs to be divided into equal sections. Post locations are shown in Drawing 8–35.

13   **Install railing cap and trim pieces.** This railing gets a 2 × 4 cap, screwed into the tops of the posts. Miter the cap pieces where they meet at the corners. After the cap has been installed, nail 1 × 3 trim on both sides of it. As shown in Drawing 8–36, the top edge of the trim should be ¾ inch below the top face of the cap to create a pleasing reveal. Miter trim pieces at the corners.

14   **Install the 2 × 6 decking boards.** On the eaves-side walkway and on the broad section of the deck, the deck boards run parallel to the house walls. On the gable-side walkway, they are perpendicular to the wall. Install the boards closest to the house first and work outward toward the outer edge of the deck. The perimeter decking boards should overhang the 2 × 10 trim boards by about 1½ inches. Deck boards should also be notched to fit around railing posts.

15   **Install the cable railing.** Each of the seven cable courses, or levels, requires a 90-foot-long cable. Using the manufacturer's hardware, secure one end of the cable to the post located at the end of the eaves-side walkway. Run the cable through the remaining 24 posts and stretch it tight before anchoring it to the post at the end of the gable-side walkway. Special turn-buckles and other tensioning hardware are available from the manufacturer (see Sources on page 238). Repeat these installation procedures for each cable course.

16   **Complete the upper deck.** To do so, repeat the operations detailed in steps 3 through 15. Note, however, that the gable-side walkway is longer on the upper deck and extends to the garage, where it is supported by an additional cantilevered 6 × 8 beam. Also, the broad section of the upper deck extends only 3 feet from the center of each column.

Photo 8–4: The cable railing runs through holes drilled in 4 × 4 posts. A pair of posts is required at corners. The cap detail consists of two 1 × 3 side pieces that are nailed to posts and to a 2 × 4 cap piece.

PROJECT $\boxed{12}$

ENTRY DECK TO STONE HOUSE

This deck serves as the main entry to a stone barn that has been converted into a house. One stairway leads up to the parking area; the other connects the deck with a play area that's part of the barnyard-turned-backyard. Thanks to its broad, T-shaped plan, this deck does more than just offer a pathway from car to house. There's room to sit down and relax, too. The deck is built around a tree and around the remains of a stone foundation that once supported a shed. As the deck was designed, both the tree and the old foundation were seen as assets that should become part of the entry. By building around the tree and the stone foundation, the new deck really looks as if it belongs with the old structure. Sometimes it takes a little extra work to integrate a deck with existing features like trees and stone walls, but the results justify the effort.

1 **Fasten the ledger board to the house.** With temporary braces or a helper (use both, if possible), prop the 2 × 10 ledger against the wall with its top edge level and 3 inches below the doorway. Drill through the board and into the wall so that masonry anchors can be installed. Ledgers aren't easily fastened to old stone masonry. It will be easier to drill into mortar than into stone, but old, wide mortar joints can crumble. Try to drill into narrow mortar joints so that the anchors will be wedged between stones. The ledger can be removed to finish drilling out the wall and to install anchors. To cope with irregularities in the wall surface, thick steel washers can be placed over the anchor bolts between ledger and wall, as shown in Drawing 5–7, page 67. When fastening the ledger to the wall, try to keep the face of the board plumb. Using 3-inch buglehead screws, fasten a 2 × 4 secondary ledger to the 2 × 10 ledger. Make the bottom edges of both ledgers flush.

2 **Form and pour the concrete piers, pads, and walls.** As shown in Drawing 8–37, two piers are required to support a post-and-beam framework beneath the long joists. Each stairway requires a concrete pad. The pad for the upper stairway must be formed on top of the stone wall. Here, place form boards carefully, with their top edges level and aligned so that the side of the pad where the stringers will fit will be perpendicular to the long deck joists. To prevent concrete from leaking out between forms and stones, fill these voids with clean gravel.

The ends of the long deck joists bear on stud walls that are framed against existing stone walls, as shown in Drawing 8–38. The stud walls are built on concrete foundation walls that

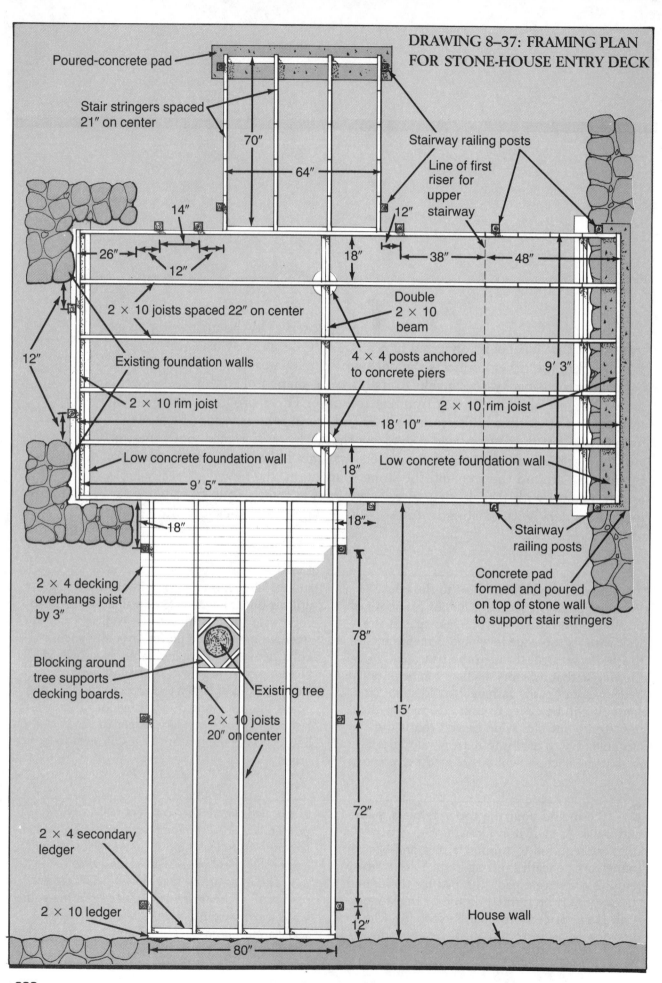

DRAWING 8–37: FRAMING PLAN
FOR STONE-HOUSE ENTRY DECK

Poured-concrete pad

Stair stringers spaced
21″ on center

70″

64″

14″

26″

12″

18″

Stairway railing posts

Line of first
riser for
upper
stairway

12″

38″

48″

2 × 10 joists spaced 22″ on center

Double
2 × 10
beam

12″

Existing foundation walls

4 × 4 posts anchored
to concrete piers

9′ 3″

2 × 10 rim joist

2 × 10 rim joist

18′ 10″

Low concrete foundation wall

18″

Low concrete foundation wall

9′ 5″

18″

18″

Stairway
railing posts

2 × 4 decking
overhangs joist
by 3″

Concrete pad
formed and poured
on top of stone wall
to support stair stringers

Blocking around
tree supports
decking boards.

Existing tree

78″

2 × 10 joists
20″ on center

15′

2 × 4 secondary
ledger

72″

2 × 10 ledger

12″

House wall

80″

Lumber Order

Note: All Lumber Is Pressure Treated.

AMOUNT	MATERIAL	PART
1	2 × 10 × 8'	ledger
1	2 × 4 × 8'	secondary ledger
6	2 × 4 × 10'	top and bottom plates for 2 foundation walls
7	2 × 4 × 12'	studs for 2 foundation walls
2	2 × 10 × 10'	rim joists
2	2 × 10 × 10'	double 2 × 10 beam
2	4 × 4 × 6'	foundation posts
6	2 × 10 × 20'	joists
5	2 × 10 × 16'	joists
960 linear ft.	2 × 4	decking
4	2 × 12 × 8'	stair stringers for lower stairway
6	2 × 12 × 6'	stair stringers for upper stairway
1	2 × 4 × 6'	bottom stair cleat
1	2 × 4 × 10'	top stair cleat
16	2 × 4 × 10'	stair treads for upper stairway
20	2 × 4 × 6'	stair treads for lower stairway
5	4 × 4 × 12'	railing posts
1	4 × 4 × 8'	railing posts
80 linear ft.	2 × 4	bottom rails
80 linear ft.	2 × 6	top rails
80 linear ft.	2 × 6	railing cap pieces
116	2 × 2 × 24"	balusters

Hardware

2 steel post bases

8 J-bolt anchors, with washers and nuts

40 pcs. 5½ × ⅜-in.-dia. carriage bolts, with nuts and washers

are formed and poured against the stone walls. This type of foundation helps to consolidate the old stonework, and is a good choice where wall surfaces are so irregular that ledgers can't be installed. To form the concrete walls, dig down to the base of each stone wall, or to the frost line, whichever comes first. With a hose, wash away as much dirt as possible from between the stones. Then place the forms, keeping top edges level and several inches above grade.

If foundation walls extend 3 feet below grade, just under 2 cubic yards of concrete will be required for piers, pads, and walls. Instead of mixing this volume of concrete yourself, you can save time by ordering ready-mixed concrete from a local supplier after all forms are in place. Once the forms have been filled with concrete, place steel post bases for 4 × 4 posts

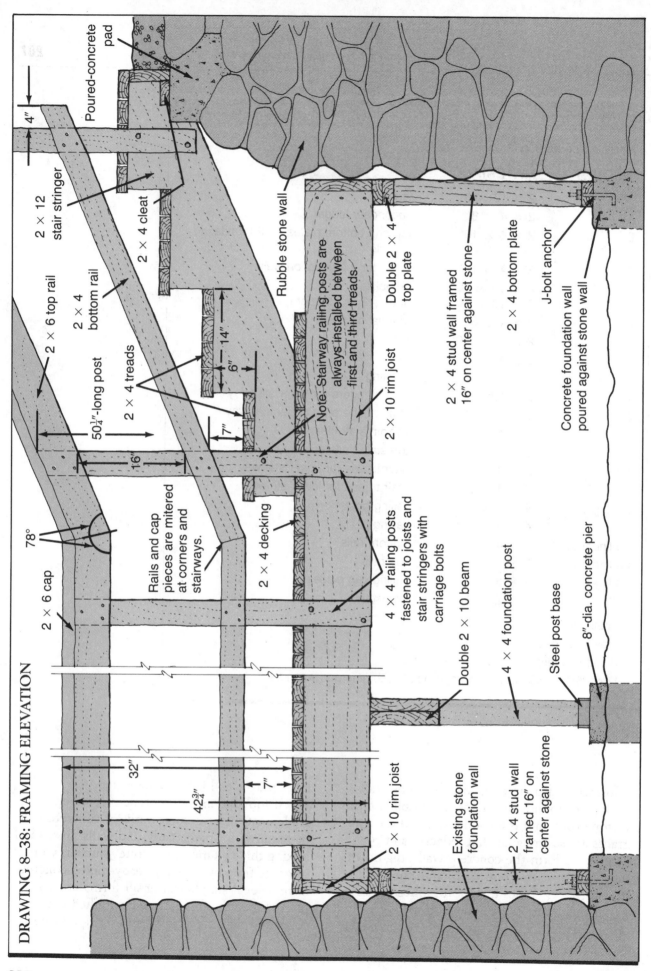

DRAWING 8–38: FRAMING ELEVATION

Poured-concrete pad

4"

2 × 12 stair stringer

2 × 4 cleat

2 × 6 top rail

2 × 4 bottom rail

Rubble stone wall

50¼"-long post

2 × 4 treads

14"

6"

Note: Stairway railing posts are always installed between first and third treads.

Double 2 × 4 top plate

2 × 10 rim joist

2 × 4 stud wall framed 16" on center against stone

2 × 4 bottom plate

J-bolt anchor

Concrete foundation wall poured against stone wall

7"

16"

78°

Rails and cap pieces are mitered at corners and stairways.

2 × 4 decking

4 × 4 railing posts fastened to joists and stair stringers with carriage bolts

2 × 6 cap

Double 2 × 10 beam

4 × 4 foundation post

Steel post base

8"-dia. concrete pier

32"

42¾"

7"

2 × 10 rim joist

Existing stone foundation wall

2 × 4 stud wall framed 16" on center against stone

in the top of each pier. Also, place four J-bolt anchors in the tops of each foundation post. These anchors will be used to secure the bottom plates of both walls. They can also be used to fasten 2 × 4 cleats to stairway pads. Space J-bolts 24 inches on center, and make sure that bolts are aligned along the centerline of the wall or cleat.

3 **Frame the two 2 × 4 foundation walls.** First, drill out the 2 × 4 bottom plate for each wall so that it will fit over protruding J-bolts. Slip washers over bolt ends and tighten nuts to lock each bottom plate in place. Then cut wall studs to length. Calculate stud length based on the level of the ledger board you fastened beneath the doorway. The top of each wall (including its double 2 × 4 top plate) should be level with the bottom edge of the ledger.

To frame up a wall after studs have been cut to length, face-nail the lower 2 × 4 top plate to the top ends of the studs, spacing studs 16 inches on center. This work can be done on the flat. If necessary, adjust stud spacing slightly to avoid putting studs over anchor bolts. Next, toenail the bottoms of the studs to the bottom plate. If necessary, use diagonal braces to hold the wall plumb until joists are installed.

Nail a 2 × 10 rim joist to each upper top plate before nailing this two-piece assembly to the lower top plate, as shown in Drawing 8–38.

4 **Install the post-and-beam framework between the two stud walls.** Make the beam by nailing together a pair of 2 × 10s. Cut posts to length so that in the finished assembly the top of the beam will be level with the top face of the stud walls' top plates. Secure the posts in the steel post bases. Toenail the beam to the post.

5 **Install long joists.** For this deck, these six joists measure about 18 feet, 7 inches long. Spacing the joists 24 inches on center would have provided adequate support, but 22-inch centers were used because they more evenly divide the space between existing foundation walls. Toenail joist ends to rim joists and to wall top plates. To force the rim joist against a joist while toenailing, you can use a pry bar wedged between the rim joist and the stone wall. Toenail all joists to the double 2 × 10 beam.

6 **Install joists between the house and long section of deck.** As shown in Drawing 8–37, these five joists are spaced 20 inches on center, a nonstandard interval that allows the joists to fall on either side of the tree trunk.

Since the ledger may not be perfectly parallel with the long joists, it's best to measure and cut each of these joists individually. Notch the house end of each joist to fit around the 2 × 4 secondary ledger. Secure the opposite ends of the joists by face-nailing through the long joist.

When the joists are in place, cut and nail blocking around the tree trunk. First install a couple of 2 × 10 boards at right angles to the joists, then cut and nail angled blocking in place, as shown in Drawing 8-37. All framing members, including joists, should be 4 to 7 inches from the trunk. This will provide ample support for decking boards, while allowing room for the tree to grow.

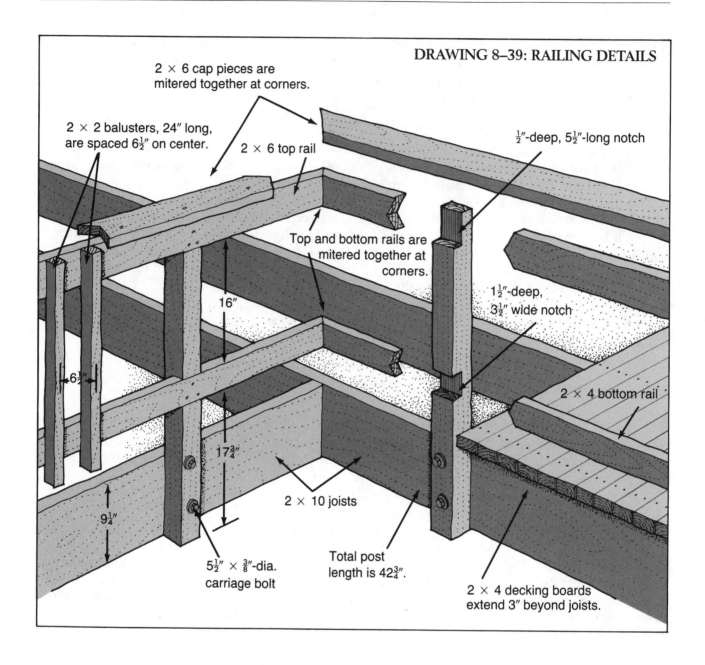

DRAWING 8–39: RAILING DETAILS

2 × 6 cap pieces are mitered together at corners.

2 × 2 balusters, 24″ long, are spaced 6½″ on center.

2 × 6 top rail

½″-deep, 5½″-long notch

Top and bottom rails are mitered together at corners.

1½″-deep, 3½″ wide notch

16″

6½″

2 × 4 bottom rail

17¾″

9¼″

5½″ × ⅜″-dia. carriage bolt

2 × 10 joists

Total post length is 42¾″.

2 × 4 decking boards extend 3″ beyond joists.

7   **Install decking.** The treated 2 × 4 decking boards for this deck are laid perpendicular to joists. If possible, use only 8-foot-long boards for the narrow section of the deck, and 10-foot-long boards for the rest of the deck. This will avoid butt joints between decking boards. Start decking against the house, and work toward the tree. Cut the decking boards for a 3-inch overhang on each end, as shown in Drawing 8–39. When you come to a railing post location, cut

that decking board flush with the outside face of the rim joist. Post locations are given in Drawing 8–37.

Using a coping saw or a portable jigsaw, cut decking boards to fit around the tree trunk. To allow for growth and to prevent the tree from rubbing against wood, allow about 1 inch of space between the decking and the trunk. Depending on the tree, you'll probably need to cut the boards back farther in a couple of years.

8   **Cut and install stair stringers.** The upper stairway requires six stringers, while the lower stairway needs four stringers. All stringers are cut from 2 × 12 boards and are positioned over joists. Basic stringer layout is shown in Drawing 8–38. Note that the lower stair has five steps, while the upper stair has four. With a unit run of 14 inches and a unit rise of 6 inches, both stairways have steps that are broader than normal, which encourages a more leisurely approach to the deck. See "Stairs, Railings, and Built-in Benches" on page 84.

Notch the upper stair stringers to fit against the concrete pad and around a 2 × 4 cleat that is fastened to the pad. Toenail the lower ends of these stringers to decking boards. The lower stair stringers are installed in similar fashion, except that the pad and cleat are at the bottom of the stairway instead of at the top. To secure the top ends of these stringers, nail through the rim joist and into the end of each stringer. To strengthen this connection, install blocking between stringers.

9   **Install 2 × 4 stair treads.** Like decking boards, treads extend 3 inches beyond stringers at stairway sides. But at top and bottom steps where railing posts will be installed, the second

2 × 4 tread should be cut so that its ends are flush with the outside face of the stringer, as shown in Drawing 8–38.

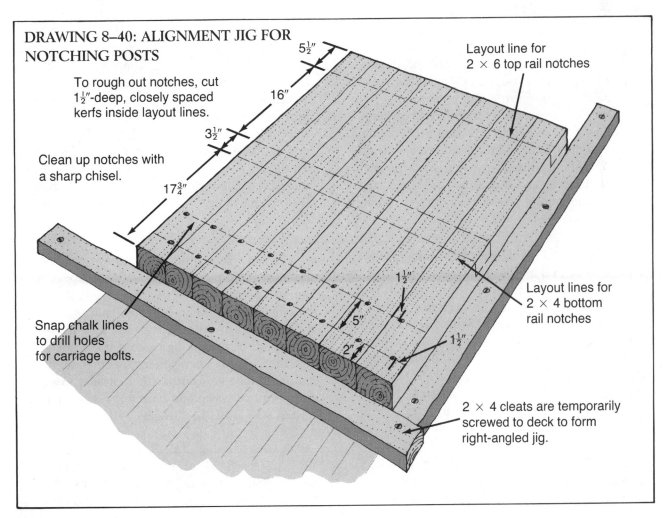

DRAWING 8–40: ALIGNMENT JIG FOR NOTCHING POSTS

To rough out notches, cut 1½"-deep, closely spaced kerfs inside layout lines.

Clean up notches with a sharp chisel.

Snap chalk lines to drill holes for carriage bolts.

5½"

16"

3½"

17¾"

Layout line for 2 × 6 top rail notches

1½"

5"

2"

1½"

Layout lines for 2 × 4 bottom rail notches

2 × 4 cleats are temporarily screwed to deck to form right-angled jig.

10 **Cut and notch railing posts.** As shown in Drawing 8–39, all posts are notched to hold a 2 × 6 top rail and a 2 × 4 bottom rail. Notch depth and width should match the thickness and width of the 2 × 4 and 2 × 6 railing stock.

To save time, notches in deck posts can be laid out and cut with seven or eight posts ganged together in a simple jig. Drawing 8–40 shows how to set up this jig on the deck. Choose a pair of 2 × 4 cleats with straight edges to make a right-angled frame for holding the 4 × 4 posts. Cut the posts to a finished length of 42¾ inches. Fit seven or eight posts tightly together in the jig. With a tape measure and straightedge, lay out notches, as shown in the drawing. Note that holes for carriage bolts can also be marked at this time. Adjust your circular saw's depth of cut to 1½ inches (the thickness of the rails), then cut a series of closely spaced kerfs inside the notch layout lines. With a hammer and chisel, remove waste pieces from the notches, then pare the notches flat and square. This final shaping can be done by removing posts from the jig and working on them individually. For an illustrated step-by-step sequence of notching a post, see Photos 4–12 through 4–14 on pages 46 and 47.

11 **Install deck railing posts.** The bottom end of each post should be flush with the bottom edge of the joist that it joins. Use a pair of 5½-inch-long, ⅜-inch-diameter carriage bolts for each post-joist connection.

12 **Install top and bottom rails on deck railing posts.** In this railing design, there are no corner posts. Instead, top and bottom rails from adjacent sides are mitered together at corners of the deck, as shown in Drawing 8–39. To lay out miter cuts, clamp the top and bottom rails from one side into their notches, allowing each rail to extend several inches beyond the corner. Then fit the joining pair of rails in their notches, and butt their ends against the adjacent rails. This will establish the exact location of the corner so that you can lay out the miter cuts. Some cutting and test-fitting may be necessary to get the joints just right. Allow all rails to run long at stairways so that they can be mitered after stair posts are installed. After cutting the rails, screw them into their notches. Use two 2½-inch galvanized buglehead screws per notch.

13 **Cut and install stairway railing posts.** Like the deck railing posts, these are notched to hold a 2 × 6 top rail and a 2 × 4 bottom rail. But the tops of the posts and the notches must be cut at a 24-degree angle, which approximates the slope of a stairway with a unit rise of 6 and a unit run of 14. Also, the two stairway posts at the bottom of the upper stair need to be 50¼ inches long, so that they can be fastened to the rim joist as well as to the stair stringers. Lay out angled notches and top cuts using the information in Drawing 8–38. These notches can also be roughed out with all eight stairway posts ganged together, but post ends won't be flush with each other, as was the case in step 8. So instead of using a jig to hold these posts together, simply clamp them together with pipe clamps. Make kerf cuts with a circular saw, then remove waste and pare notches smooth. Fasten stair posts to stringers with carriage bolts.

14 **Cut and install top and bottom rails for stairway railings.** These rails will meet top and bottom deck rails with miter joints, as shown in Drawing 8–38. Miter cuts for joining members should measure 78 degrees. It's best to lay out these cuts by positioning each pair of joining rails so that they overlap. Using a bevel gauge adjusted to 78 degrees, you can then mark miter cuts on both pieces at their intersection point. Again, a cut-and-fit strategy will yield the tightest joints. To hold these mitered joints together, toe one or two 2½-inch buglehead screws into each joint. Screw rails in their notches.

15 Cut and install cap pieces and balusters. Like the rails, cap pieces need to be mitered together at corners and at each juncture where deck rails meet stair rails. Position each cap piece so that its outside edge extends 1½ inches beyond the outside face of the top rail. Cut and fit the cap pieces together and screw them to the top rail and to each other using 2½-inch galvanized buglehead screws. Where horizontal cap pieces meet stair cap pieces, bevel the top end of each stair cap piece to fit against its horizontal cap (see Photo 8–5). You may need to do a little work with a chisel and block plane to smooth out this change in direction and elevation.

Once the caps are in place, balusters can be installed. Space these 24-inch-long 2 × 2s 6½ inches on center. Fasten them to the outside faces of deck and stair rails. Butt the top end of each baluster against the bottom face of the railing cap. On stairways, the top of each baluster requires a 24-degree bevel-cut to fit snugly under the cap. Drive a single 2½-inch galvanized buglehead screw through the baluster at each rail connection.

Photo 8–5: Shaping the cap rail on the deck to meet the slope of the cap rail on the stairs gives this deck a more finished appearance.

CHAPTER **9**

MAINTENANCE AND REPAIR

Good materials and sound construction are crucial, but they are only part of the formula for a long-lasting deck. To survive the ravages of weather and to look good doing it, a deck also needs regular maintenance and even occasional repairs. Without this attention, outdoor wood can decay and deteriorate after just a few years of exposure.

Deck maintenance involves quite a few choices. There are cleaning and restorative solutions as well as different finishes that contain preservatives, water repellents, and other protective elements. In addition to protecting your deck, you might elect to give it a different look using a semi-transparent exterior stain. To understand how these various preparations work, we first need to know a little about the natural forces that act on wood, causing it to change in appearance or even causing deterioration and decay.

HOW WOOD WEATHERS, WEARS, AND DECAYS

There are a number of natural forces that contribute to the weathering and decay of outdoor wood. Sun-

Photo courtesy of Kop-Coat, Inc.

Photo 9–1: Outdoor wood that isn't treated with a protective finish won't last as long as it could.

light, or more specifically, the ultraviolet radiation (UV) in sunlight, is the most universal weathering factor. This invisible ultraviolet radiation acts on the surface of the wood, breaking down wood cells as well as natural extractive compounds. The loss of colored extractives and other cellular material leaves the wood surface gray or silver-gray. UV degradation only takes place within about 1/100 inch of the wood surface, so the damage is aesthetic rather than structural. In fact, many people do not consider the graying of wood to be an aesthetic disadvantage; they find it attractive.

If you're interested in retarding or counteracting the graying effect of the sun, there are several deck finishing options to consider. There are special outdoor finishes for decks that contain *UV absorbers, UV blockers,* or *UV inhibitors.* Absorbers and blockers are particles, dissolved or suspended in a finish, that either absorb or reflect UV light to minimize its effect on the wood. UV inhibitors work in a different way. These compounds (also used in fabric dyes and plastics) actually disrupt the normal chemical action caused by UV light, thus short-circuiting UV degradation.

While sunlight is the most prevalent weathering force, water does far more damage to decks. It can work with the sun, washing away UV-degraded material to expose fresh wood to UV weathering. But more significantly, wood swells when it's wet and shrinks as it dries out. Cycling through wet and dry conditions really takes a toll on decking boards and other horizontal surfaces. Following a rainy spell, the underside of a decking board can retain moisture while the sun-drenched surface of the board becomes dry. This differential in moisture content stresses the board and can cause significant warping, cracking and splitting. Boards that aren't securely fastened can pull loose or gradually cause nail heads to pop free of the wood surface. And even minor cracks, called checks, can bring water into the center of the board. This causes greater swelling and eventually enlarges the crack. Freeze/thaw cycles accelerate this process.

And then there is mechanical wear caused by foot traffic. Keeping a deck free of dirt and sand will slow the abrasion of finish and wood. When mechanical wear does show up in a well-trodden spot, worn boards can be replaced with new ones.

Wood-destructive organisms of-ten work in conjunction with weather conditions to cause decay in outdoor wood. Wood that remains damp for prolonged periods of time, with limited exposure to direct sunlight, can easily become host to various types of mold and mildew. Apart from staining the wood, these growths aren't a problem by themselves, since they are confined to the wood surface. But mold and mildew tend to retain moisture, and continually moist wood becomes an attractive host for micro-organisms that feed on cellulose. Decay occurs as these organisms eat their way through the wood, leaving behind a pulpy shell with little structural strength.

Wood-destructive insects include termites, carpenter ants, and carpenter bees. These insects also favor wood that is wet or damp. Insect infestation can be difficult to detect in wood. Termites usually build earthen tubes or tunnels to connect ground colonies

Photo 9–2: Instead of soaking into the wood, water will bead on decking that has been treated with a sealer or water repellent.

with wood. Carpenter bees can enter and exit a wood colony through a single hole.

CHOOSING THE RIGHT WOOD TREATMENT

The good news is that wood decay and insect attack can almost always be prevented and weathering can be controlled, thanks to different wood treatments. In evaluating different treatment strategies for decks and outdoor wood, it's important to note that manufacturers are reformulating their finishes to remove benzene and other volatile solvents that have been associated with ozone depletion and deteriorating air quality. Clean-air legislation has made some finishes illegal in different parts of the United States. The coatings industry is responding by developing water-based finishes and other environmentally safe preparations.

Selecting a finish for your deck can be confusing. Not only are there different types of finish to consider, but different brands of each type. Prices can vary widely for any type of finish, and ambitious claims by various manufacturers add further layers of confusion. The information ahead should help you choose the right finish for your deck and help in selecting not only the type of finish but key ingredients as well.

Before delving into specifics, there's a simple rule to follow when choosing and using any kind of finish: Read the label. Take a careful look at safety precautions and first-aid instructions given by the manufacturer. Be suspicious of containers that look like they've been in stock for a long time. This older finish might contain pentachlorophenol, a wood preservative that has been banned from general use because of its toxicity to humans and animals. Details relating to formulation, storage, recommended uses, surface preparation, coverage, and compatibility with other finishes are important, too.

Clear Finishes

Also called natural finishes or clear penetrating finishes, clear finishes protect the wood while allowing its natural grain and color to show. Unlike varnishes and paints, which are film-forming finishes, clear finishes for decks penetrate into the pores of the wood. Some clear finishes can be followed by applications of stain or paint, while other clear finishes must be used alone.

A good clear finish for outdoor wood will contain a wood preservative in the form of a fungicide or combination fungicide/insecticide. Most clear exterior finishes will also contain a water repellent in the form of paraffin or other wax. The wax is dissolved in a solvent base that evaporates following application. The wax remains in the pores of the wood, creating a barrier to water penetration. Instead of soaking into the wood surface, water beads on wood that has been treated with a water repellent (see Photo 9–2 on the opposite page). By limiting moisture penetration, a water-repellent treatment makes the wood on a deck more stable.

Many varnishes and paints are formulated with linseed oil, tung oil, or alkyds (also called alkyd resins), resins that act as sealers and film-forming agents. Some clear penetrating finishes for outdoor wood also include one or more of these resins, but in much lower concentrations. A limited amount of resin can help to seal the wood and accent its grain (as regular varnish does) without forming a varnish-type film on the wood surface.

DIP TREATMENT

Short of pressure treatment, the most thorough way to apply finish is to dip-treat the wood after it's been cut to size, but before it's nailed down. Dip treatment, where wood is immersed in a bath of finish for several minutes and then allowed to air-dry, maximizes finish coverage and penetration. Clear, water-repellent finishes and sealers (with or without a preservative) are best-suited for dip treatment. Even pressure-treated wood will gain extra stability following dip treatment in a water-repellent finish.

The problem with dip treatment is, of course, that it can only be done before the lumber is nailed in place. And it is time-consuming, since some sort of trough must be used to hold the finish and the wood. As a result, you may want to dip-treat selectively. While it might not be practical to dip-treat long posts or decking boards, you might consider dip treatment for balusters and short railing posts—smaller parts of the deck that can benefit from the extra stability and complete coverage that dip treatment affords.

An easy way to make a dip-treatment trough is to place a seamless plastic sheet in a wood frame, as shown in Photo 9–3, on the opposite page. The frame should rest on a flat surface, such as a concrete walk or a piece of plywood. Use a heavy-duty sheet (at least 6 mil thickness) and make sure that its edges are well away from the edges of the frame. To save your hands, wear rubber gloves when moving wood around in the trough. Excess finish that remains in the trough can be reused. To filter out wood fibers and other debris, pour the finish through cheesecloth into a container that can be tightly sealed.

The least expensive clear finishes for outdoor wood are usually no more than a water repellent dissolved in a solvent solution. This inexpensive finish is especially good for pressure-treated wood, which is already saturated with a rot-preventing wood preservative. Once the pressure-treated wood begins to dry out, however, you might want to consider a clear finish that contains a resin-type sealer as well as a water repellent.

Each added ingredient increases the performance of the finish, and also makes it more costly. You can expect to find a resin-type sealer and either a UV inhibitor, UV blocker, or UV absorber in more expensive finishes. There are even clear finishes formulated especially for pressure-treated southern pine, or for redwood and cedar (see "Species-Specific Formulations" on page 221). If time allows, it's a good idea to decide on the brand you want to use, and then shop around for a good price. Paint stores, hardware stores, and home centers put finishes on sale at least several times a year.

Penetrating clear finishes are among the easiest finishes to apply. Basically, you want to give the wood all the finish it can absorb, so application should be generous (see "Dip Treatment," above). Horizontal surfaces such as decking boards can be coated with a roller or spray equipment can be used. For posts, railings, and stair stringers, brush application is

Photo 9–3: Dip treatment can be a good alternative for balusters and short railing posts that will benefit from complete coverage with water-repellent finish.

best. The important thing is to saturate the wood. Finish that isn't absorbed and remains on the wood surface after 10 to 20 minutes should be wiped off with a clean rag (see "Safety Note," below).

When applying finish, give extra attention to exposed end grain, especially at the tops of posts and balusters and at the ends of decking boards. End grain is extremely absorbent, so a cursory application of finish won't do

SAFETY NOTE

Remember to take precautions against spontaneous combustion when working with finishes. Rags that have been used to apply finish or wipe away excess finish can burst into flame because of the heat that is generated as the finish evaporates. Rags can be buried to prevent spontaneous combustion; or you can soak them in water and then seal them in an airtight plastic bag. If rags will be reused, store them in an airtight container.

much to seal or protect this part of a board or post. It's good practice to go over exposed end grain several times, using a brush to work the finish into the wood.

Frequency of application for a clear finish depends on weather and wear conditions and also on the finish itself. It's easy to tell when a water-repellent finish needs to be renewed: Instead of forming beads on the wood surface, water will soak into the wood. Treatment once a year usually is sufficient. A more complex finish (with resin, wood preservative, and water repellent) has a better chance of building up in the wood so that after two or three years of annual treatment, it's possible to skip a year between treatments. On many decks there are high-traffic areas, sun-drenched surfaces, or mildew-prone sections that require more frequent spot-treatments.

Semi-Transparent Stains

Semi-transparent stains are pigmented penetrating finishes that are widely used on all kinds of exterior wood siding, from roughsawn plywood to clapboards and shingles. They have also proven to be very effective on decks. The term *semi-transparent* accurately describes the effect this finish has on a wood surface. The resin or oil in the finish penetrates into the pores of the wood, acting as a sealer. Enough pigment remains on the wood surface to change the color or tone of the wood without covering the grain pattern or creating a surface film. A wide selection of colors and wood tones is available.

Semi-transparent stains for exterior use usually have a natural oil or alkyd base, though latex formulations are also available. Pigment particles in a semi-transparent stain act as UV absorbers or UV blockers, while the oil or alkyd resins act as penetrating sealers. Some semi-transparent stains will also contain a water repellent and/or a wood preservative. These stains provide the most comprehensive protection for decks.

Although semi-transparent stains are classified as penetrating finishes, they are heavier-bodied than clear finishes. Thorough and frequent mixing is required to achieve consistency of color. And when you choose the stain for your deck, be sure to buy more than enough stain for the entire job. Manufacturers sometimes discontinue or alter their selection of tints, so buying only a few cans at a time could cause a problem. Semi-transparent stains should be applied by brush or roller. Brush application does the best job of working the finish into the wood. Once in the wood, a stain finish will lighten due to wear and sunlight, but most decks can last two years between treatments. It's also possible to make repeated applications (following the interval specified by the manufacturer) to darken or even switch the stain color.

Solid-Color Stains

This type of finish is really more like a paint than a stain. Heavily laden with pigment, solid-color stains will provide good UV protection but offer little in the way of water repellency or durability. Developed primarily for use on exterior siding, these stains aren't recommended for horizontal surfaces; in fact they can be worn down fairly quickly by foot traffic. A solid-color stain would be a good choice for the posts and balusters of a deck's railing. Acrylic latex-based solid-color stains have been shown to perform better than other latex-based or oil-based solid-color stains.

Paints

Paint offers the best protection against UV degradation and mechanical wear, but it's not a good deck finish, especially on horizontal surfaces. The thin film of paint that covers the wood surface inevitably cracks and chips as the wood in a deck expands and contracts with changes in temperature and humidity. Once cracks form in a painted finish, water can make its way into the wood, where it becomes trapped due to paint's limited permeability. Extra moisture beneath the finish usually causes severe cracking and peeling as the adhesive bond between paint and wood is broken down. The wood can only be repainted after sections of cracked and peeled paint are removed. This type of surface preparation is difficult and time-consuming.

Porches, exterior siding, and exterior trim are good candidates for a painted finish. In these situations, the wood is either protected or in a vertical position to ensure minimum water penetration. If you must have paint on your deck, confine it to vertical members like posts and balusters. Exterior paints formulated with acrylic latex resins have the highest durability.

Species-Specific Formulations

The tight, clear grain of redwood or cedar differs greatly from the open, porous grain of southern pine. Finish-

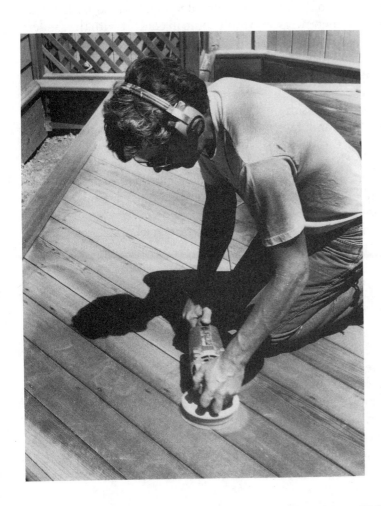

Photo 9–4: Stains and surface weathering can be removed from cedar or redwood decking using a disk sander.

ing characteristics for these woods are correspondingly different. Recognizing this, several companies have developed species-specific finishes. Heavier-bodied finishes have been formulated specifically for sealing and staining pressure-treated southern pine. There are also several brands of finish (clear and stain) designed for use on redwood and cedar. Manufacturers of these and other finishes are listed in Sources on page 238.

Surface Preparation

While specifics relating to application techniques, coverage, and drying time will vary from one brand of finish to the next, good surface preparation is a universal rule in using any type of finish. Wood that is moist or dirty won't allow finish to penetrate or dry as it should. Wood that has been freshly pressure-treated can also be unsuitable for some finishes. It may not be fully dry, oozing either sap, preservative solution, or both. If this is the case, you'll be able to see and feel moisture on the surface of the wood. Residual preservative can show up as an oily film or as a powder on the wood surface. Air drying, combined with exposure to sunlight and rain (or a washdown with a garden hose), makes pressure-treated lumber more receptive to finishes.

At least several days of clear, dry weather should precede any application of finish on a deck. There are several ways to remove stains, dirt, and mold from wood surfaces. Sanding the wood will expose a clean, unweathered wood surface that should take finish evenly. Redwood and cedar gain the greatest benefit from a light sanding. Avoid sanding pressure-treated wood, since this will produce toxic sawdust.

The best tool to use in sanding a deck is a heavy-duty disk sander fitted with a circular foam pad that holds adhesive-backed sandpaper disks. The flexibility and resiliency of the foam pad help you to avoid gouging the wood. Sandpaper disks are pressure-sensitive and can simply be peeled free when they wear out. If you don't have this type of sander, tool-rental agencies usually carry them, along with a selection of sanding disks. A fine-grit sanding disk will usually work best on redwood and cedar.

If you elect to sand all or part of your deck, take time out beforehand to check decking boards and other parts of the deck. You'll probably find a few nails or screws that have worked loose. Now is the time to drive these fasteners deep enough so their heads won't come in contact with the sander.

As an alternative to sanding wood in preparation for finish, it's possible to treat wood with a special deck cleaner or deck restorative. Though formulated for wood, these preparations work much like laundry detergents and bleaches. Like laundry products, deck cleaners and restoratives come in concentrated form, usually as a powder that must be dissolved in water.

Most deck-cleaning preparations are alkaline, like laundry detergent. After applying a cleaner by brush, spray, or roller, use a stiff brush to scrub down the wood surface, loosening dirt and weathered wood. Then hose the wood clean. The water rinse removes surface debris and neutralizes the cleaning solution.

Like laundry bleach, restoratives are acidic, containing oxalic acid or sodium percarbonate. When flooded onto the wood surface, these bleaches lighten the wood, affecting areas darkened by weathering as well as areas (on redwood and cedar) that are naturally dark because of colored extractive compounds.

Deck cleaners and restoratives can be used separately or in combination (the cleaning process should be done first). Both treatments will remove surface mold and mildew, but for long-term protection against these organisms, you'll need to apply a preservative finish. Following treatment with a cleaner or restorative, be sure to give the deck ample time to dry out before applying finish.

CHAPTER 10

OUTDOOR WIRING

Outdoor wiring is an inevitable part of most deck projects. After all, you shouldn't have to wander off your deck to plug in a radio. And a few well-placed lights can make a deck inviting after sundown, at the same time promoting safety and security. By incorporating a timer or photosensitive switch in your deck's lighting scheme, you can even program your lights to operate when you're away from home.

A deck's lighting and wiring scheme should be planned at an early stage, at the same time decisions are being made about framing details for the deck. This way you can plan to hide wiring runs beneath decking boards and against joists or beams. Lights and receptacles can be assigned to specific locations on and around the deck.

Consult your local building inspector or electrical inspector about the outdoor receptacles and lights you plan to add. He or she will make you aware of local code requirements. In some areas, all electrical work must be done by a licensed electrician. But in most municipalities, you can do a good part of any outdoor wiring job yourself even if you're short on experience. For

Photo courtesy of TerraDek

example, you can select locations for added receptacles and lights and then install appropriate outlet boxes just where you want them. You can also run conduit between boxes or bury cable if you need to reach a location away from the house. Finally, you can wire receptacles and lights yourself, calling in an electrician just to hook up the new wiring to the service panel or to an existing interior circuit. The electrician can inspect the work you've already done, correcting mistakes if necessary.

Whenever you do electrical work, be sure to follow basic safety procedures. Always make sure that the power is off on the particular circuit you're working on. In addition to turning off the breaker or removing the fuse at the service panel, use a voltage tester to confirm that wiring is "dead" before you do any work on it. When installing lights, timers, and other special equipment, follow the manufacturer's instructions closely. Use materials and techniques that comply with the National Electrical Code (NEC) (see Sources on page 238). If your planned electrical work is extensive or if you want basic background information on home wiring, consult a book that is devoted to home wiring. Finally, if you run into trouble, call in a licensed electrician.

GROUND FAULT PROTECTION

To comply with the NEC, all outdoor circuits that control receptacles must have ground fault protection. Ground fault circuit interrupters, commonly known as GFCIs or GFIs, can be installed in the form of a circuit breaker or in the form of a receptacle

Photo 10–1: Ground fault interrupters (GFIs) should be used on outdoor circuits to protect against shock. A GFI circuit breaker (left) can be installed at the service panel to protect the entire circuit. A GFI receptacle (right) provides point-of-use protection.

(see Photo 10–1 on page 225). These safety devices measure the current that travels through an electrical circuit, shutting off immediately if any leakage current is detected.

A GFI circuit breaker will provide ground fault protection for every switch, receptacle, light, or electrical device on the circuit it controls. A GFI receptacle provides ground fault protection at the receptacle and at every electrical fixture farther along on the circuit. All GFI devices have test and reset buttons. The test button should be depressed periodically to make sure that the GFI is working properly. By pressing the reset button, the circuit is restored.

OUTDOOR CABLE, CONDUIT, AND BOXES

Electrical components approved for exterior use are designed to remain safe and functional when exposed to the weather. There are two types of outlet boxes approved for outdoor use. Made from sheet metal, with shields to deflect water, drip-tight boxes can be used outdoors in protected situations. In most cases where outdoor receptacles are going to be added, you're better off using watertight outlet

Photo 10–2: Gasketed, spring-loaded covers protect this outdoor receptacle from moisture. Wiring between outlets runs in conduit, and conduit connections are always made on the underside of the outlet box.

boxes. Made from rust-resistant metal (like aluminum, galvanized steel, or bronze) or plastic, these boxes have thick walls and threaded entry holes. Outlet box covers are gasketed and the receptacles themselves have spring-loaded covers with gaskets. Watertight boxes can safely be located where they'll get soaked by rain or sprayed by a garden hose or lawn sprinkler (see Photo 10–2 on the opposite page).

There's also special cable (type UF) that can be run underground for use on outdoor circuits. The NEC requires that UF cable be buried at least 1 foot deep, but check your local code; it could be different. Exterior wiring that runs above ground usually has to be protected by an approved metal or plastic conduit—hollow tubing that is connected to exterior outlet boxes with special fittings.

Outdoor receptacles should be located in spots that are convenient but well-protected. Never locate a receptacle outlet box near a horizontal surface that may collect water. Boxes can be mounted against the exterior siding, or recessed into the siding. They also can be fastened against the foundation wall of the house or against the deck's foundation or railing posts.

EXTENDING OR ADDING A CIRCUIT

To add outdoor receptacles, lights, or both, you can either extend an existing circuit or, if you have space at the service panel, create a new circuit. In general, extending an existing circuit is adequate if you are just adding lights and not receptacles, because the lights won't draw much power. But for receptacles that might be used for appliances such as an electric lawn-mower or rotary trimmer, it's usually better to wire a new circuit to avoid overloading the circuit.

This isn't a strict rule, however. For example, if you have an underused basement circuit with just a few outlets on it, it might have plenty of capacity for a few outdoor receptacles. Generally, there should be no more than a total of eight outlets (receptacles and/or lights) on a 15-amp circuit. No more than ten outlets should be installed on a 20-amp circuit. Use these guidelines to determine whether your planned outdoor wiring requires a new circuit. If you need to bring power outdoors for electric heaters, pumps, and other equipment for hot tubs or spas, heed the manufacturer's recommendations; these appliances often require circuits of their own.

If you just need one outdoor receptacle for your deck, you might consider tapping into an interior receptacle that's located in an exterior wall, as shown in Drawing 10–1 on page 228. Ideally, the interior receptacle should be the last outlet box on the circuit. An end-of-run outlet box will be connected to the rest of the circuit with only one cable, so there will be plenty of room inside the box for added wiring. Remember, when extending a circuit, new wiring should be of the same gauge as the wiring on the rest of the circuit. Most household circuits are either 15 amp, which uses 14/2 cable, or 20 amp, which uses 12/2 cable. When you ask for 12/2 cable at a wiring supply store, you'll see that the cable actually contains three wires—a black insulated conductor, a white insulated conductor, and a bare ground wire.

To add more than one outdoor receptacle, it's usually best to run your new wiring through the basement or crawl space, connecting either with an existing circuit or with the service panel. New wiring is easy to install in basements, utility rooms, and other

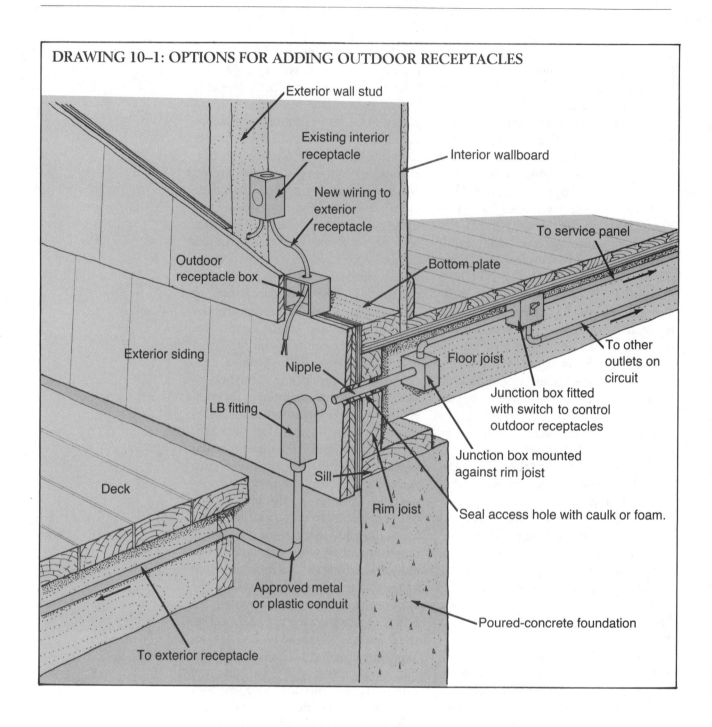

DRAWING 10–1: OPTIONS FOR ADDING OUTDOOR RECEPTACLES

Exterior wall stud

Existing interior receptacle

Interior wallboard

New wiring to exterior receptacle

To service panel

Outdoor receptacle box

Bottom plate

Exterior siding

Nipple

Floor joist

LB fitting

Junction box fitted with switch to control outdoor receptacles

Deck

Sill

Junction box mounted against rim joist

Rim joist

To other outlets on circuit

Seal access hole with caulk or foam.

Approved metal or plastic conduit

Poured-concrete foundation

To exterior receptacle

spaces where framing remains exposed. Also, many basement circuits are underused, so you can extend them without overloading. Another advantage is that you can easily install a switch to shut off outdoor receptacles for safety and security.

Drawing 10–1, above, shows how

a junction box is used to contain the connections between interior and exterior cable when running outdoor wiring from a basement or crawl space. Drawing 10–2, on the opposite page, shows how to make the wiring connections. A nipple fitting, connected to the back of the junction box, shields

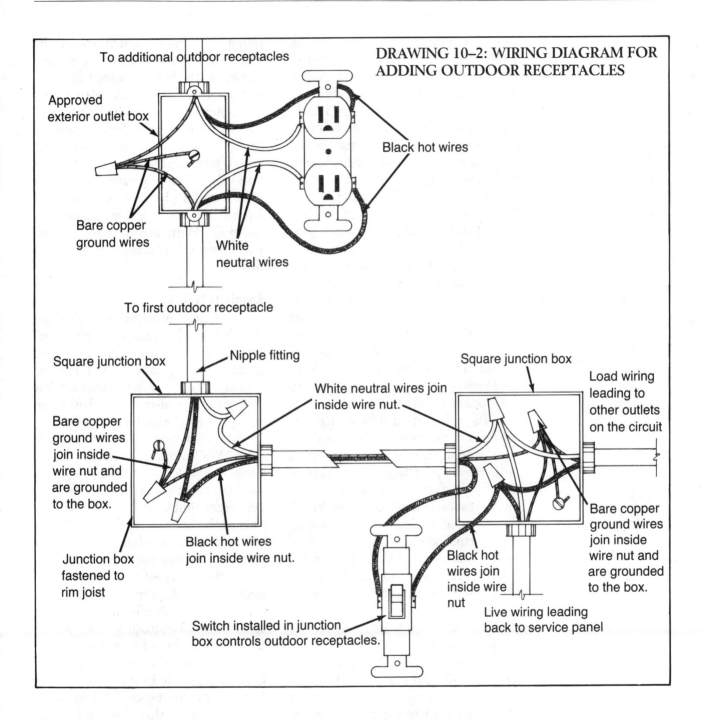

DRAWING 10–2: WIRING DIAGRAM FOR ADDING OUTDOOR RECEPTACLES

To additional outdoor receptacles

Approved exterior outlet box

Black hot wires

Bare copper ground wires

White neutral wires

To first outdoor receptacle

Nipple fitting

Square junction box

White neutral wires join inside wire nut.

Square junction box

Load wiring leading to other outlets on the circuit

Bare copper ground wires join inside wire nut and are grounded to the box.

Junction box fastened to rim joist

Black hot wires join inside wire nut.

Bare copper ground wires join inside wire nut and are grounded to the box.

Black hot wires join inside wire nut

Live wiring leading back to service panel

Switch installed in junction box controls outdoor receptacles.

the cable as it passes through the rim joist, sheathing, and siding. If possible, install the nipple at a slight slope, with the low end outside the house. This way, water won't tend to run into the opening. Outside the house, use an LB fitting between the end of the nipple fitting and exterior-rated conduit. Seal the opening for the nipple fitting with caulk or expanding foam sealant.

SPOTLIGHTS AND FLOODLIGHTS

Designing a lighting scheme for your deck is challenging and creative. At the brightest extreme, spotlights and floodlights can be used where high levels of illumination are desired, either for security or to create a dramatic "nightscape" of light and shadow. Spotlights are designed to direct a fairly narrow, intense beam of light, while floodlights do just the opposite, casting a broad wash of light. Both types of lights can be used interchangeably in the same socket.

There are quite a few effects possible with these high-intensity lights, but use them judiciously. In general, outside lighting needs less wattage than inside lighting. Too much light will create a harsh nighttime environment, destroying the ambiance and privacy that a deck can offer. Expense is another consideration. Lights that run on 115/125-volt current will have very high operating costs compared to low-voltage lights.

To try out different lighting schemes in the location of your deck, do a little nighttime experimentation with the help of family members or friends. Use flashlights to set up different light sources and intensities. You'll discover that it's best to avoid placing a powerful light directly in a line of view for someone on the deck or in the house. Spotlights and floodlights do their best work at a distance or in semi-concealed locations. Ideally, you should be able to see the light, but not the light source.

By mounting a floodlight up in a tree and directing it downward, a moonlight effect is achieved, with shadows of branches, limbs, and leaves cast onto the deck surface. For an up-lighting effect, place a spotlight near the base of a tree and point it upward to highlight the shape and texture of the trunk and major branches.

Wiring a spotlight or floodlight is no more difficult than wiring a receptacle. The main difference is that lights require a switch, which should be placed in a convenient location, usually inside the house. Instead of a conventional switch you may elect to use a dimmer so you can adjust the intensity of outdoor light. Incorporating a timer at the switch location will enable you to turn lights on and off at preset intervals. A less expensive alternative is to install a photosensitive screw-in fixture between the light socket and the bulb. With this accessory, lights will come on at dusk and go off at dawn.

Specialty Lights

In many instances, spotlights and floodlights will create too bright an effect on or around a deck. There are quite a few options if your lighting scheme needs to be more subdued. For example, a wall-mounted lamp can provide a moderate level of light near an exterior doorway that opens onto a deck. Wall-mounted outdoor lamps come in a wide variety of styles. Most models accept conventional incandescent light bulbs, and an easy way to change the intensity of the light is simply to switch to a light bulb with a different wattage rating.

If there is a roof overhang near the deck, you might consider installing a recessed, or flush-mount light in the soffit area. Unobtrusive when not in use, at night these fixtures will cast a warm cone of light onto the deck. Because of possible heat buildup in the light fixture, most recessed lights must be installed so that the light dome doesn't contact insulation or other material. If you're considering recessed lights, make sure to specify that they will be used in an outdoor location and follow the manufacturer's installation instructions carefully.

Another kind of recessed light fixture is designed to be installed in the riser of a stairway. If a deck will be used frequently after the sun goes down, specialty lights like these will add safety, convenience, and elegance.

Low-Voltage Lights

Low-voltage outdoor lights are especially well-suited to decks. These lights draw power through a transformer which is plugged into a conventional receptacle, as shown in Photo 10–3, below. The transformer reduces standard household current (115/125 volts) to about 12 volts. Since low-voltage lights aren't nearly as bright as standard lights, there's less concern with glare and overlighting. These lights can be placed right where they're needed. They're also safer and more economical to operate than conventional lights. And you don't need a permit to install 12-volt wiring. The components for a low-voltage system are expensive, however. Some of this expense is offset by low installation costs, since low-voltage cable doesn't need to be buried or run in conduit, which is the case for standard 115/125-volt cable.

Because low-voltage lights rely on relatively small bulbs, the light fixtures themselves can be quite small. There are even fixtures designed specifically for installation on balusters (see Photo 10–4, on page 232). At home centers, hardware stores, and lumber outlets, you'll find low-voltage lights for use on posts and stairways (see Photo 10–5, on page 233), as well as "spiked" light fixtures that can be driven into the ground to direct a wash of light on pathways or plants (see Sources on page 238). If you feel like innovating, automobile lights can be adapted for

Photo courtesy of TerraDek

Photo 10–3: Low-voltage lighting systems get their power from a transformer that is plugged into a 115–120 volt receptacle.

use in low-voltage outdoor systems (see "A Do-It-Yourself Low-Voltage Fixture" on page 234).

Most low-voltage outdoor lights are sold in kit form and include a transformer, several lights, wire, and connection fittings. While splices and connections in 115/125-volt wiring require junction or outlet boxes, low-voltage wiring connections can be done quickly with compact snap fittings (see Photo 10–4 below). The plastic-sheathed cable between fix-tures can be stapled against the deck. This makes it easy to relocate lights.

There are some limitations in using low-voltage lights, but they can be circumvented by careful planning. The total wattage of lights that run off a transformer shouldn't exceed 80 percent of the transformer's power rating. For example, a transformer rated at 72 watts should only handle a total of five 11-watt lights. If more lights are needed, they should run off a separate transformer.

Photo courtesy of TerraDek

Photo 10–4: This small baluster light is typical of the compact, easy-to-install fixtures that are available for low-voltage outdoor lighting.

Photo 10–5: Redwood sides make it possible to mount this low-voltage light on the edge of a deck or at the end of a stair. tread.

Cable length is another factor in designing a low-voltage lighting scheme. The longer the cable runs from a single transformer, the greater the power loss, which means dimmer lights. In most cases, noticeable power loss can be avoided by limiting cable length to about 100 feet. This means that low-voltage lights should be fairly close to their transformer. In situations where the lights will be some distance from the house, it's a good idea to add a 115/125-volt receptacle near the lighting location, where the transformer can be plugged in.

A DO-IT-YOURSELF LOW-VOLTAGE FIXTURE

With a little ingenuity and some off-the-shelf items from an auto supply store, you can make very nice outdoor lights for a deck, walkway, or patio. The light fixture shown here was made from a generic auto license plate light and a scrap piece of ¾-inch-thick rough-sawn cedar. The sloping cedar hood hides the light fixture, sheds water, and directs a wash of light downward.

Photo 10–6: Scraps of cedar and a license plate light create outdoor lighting.

To make the unit, the first step is to attach the auto light fixture to a wall or post. At the same time, run low-voltage cable from a transformer to the fixture. Ground one of the cable's wires to the fixture by attaching it to a mounting screw. The other wire should supply current to the bulb.

Once the light has been secured, you can make the wood shade. Drawing 10–3, on the opposite page, shows a cutting diagram and a view of the assembled shade. Fasten a cleat to the inside face of each side so that the cleats can be screwed to the wall. Lag screws or buglehead screws can be used, and one screw per cleat should provide adequate holding power. Note: You can direct a limited amount of light upward by allowing a slight airspace between the top of the hood and the wall. Don't worry about moisture damaging the fixture; license plate lights are designed to get rained on.

DRAWING 10–3: A DO-IT-YOURSELF LOW-VOLTAGE FIXTURE

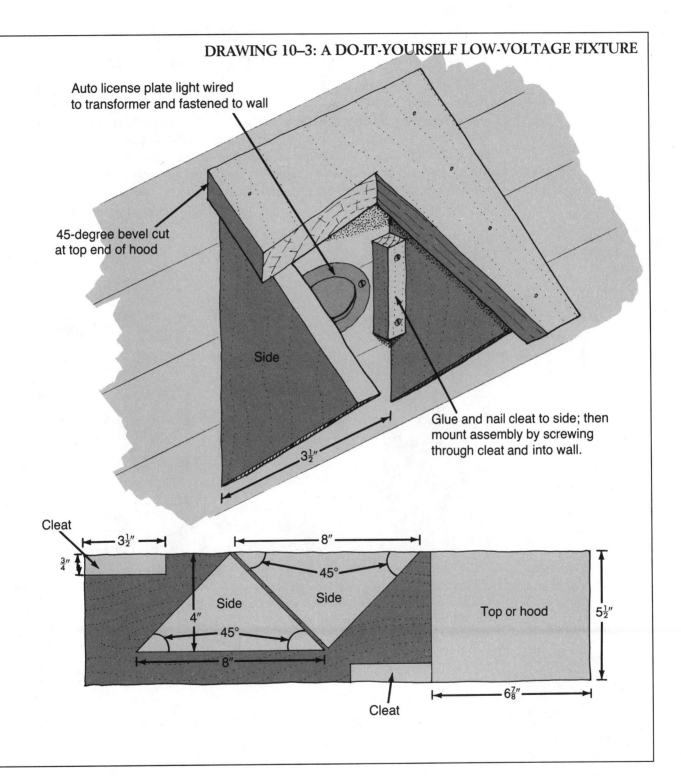

Auto license plate light wired
to transformer and fastened to wall

45-degree bevel cut
at top end of hood

Side

$3\frac{1}{2}''$

Glue and nail cleat to side; then
mount assembly by screwing
through cleat and into wall.

Cleat

$3\frac{1}{2}''$

$\frac{3}{4}''$

8″

45°

Side

Side

4″

45°

8″

Cleat

Top or hood

$5\frac{1}{2}''$

$6\frac{7}{8}''$

A DO-IT-YOURSELF POST-TOP LIGHT

Railing posts are good candidates for built-in light fixtures. A light atop a post is up high and out of the way, and it can illuminate a wide area. Here's a post-top light you can make with some frosted acrylic, a low-voltage back-up light fixture that you can buy at any auto parts store, and a 30-inch-long 1 × 6 cedar or redwood board. The light shown here fits a 4 × 4 post. You can adapt this design to fit atop a 6 × 6 post. Remember, low-voltage lights require a transformer, along with special low-voltage wire.

DRAWING 10-4: POST-TOP LIGHT

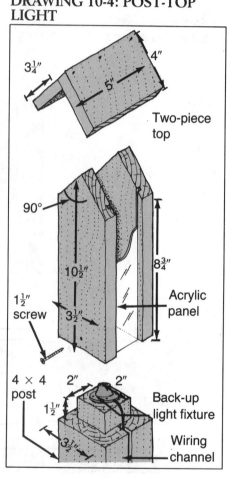

Photo 10–7: Post lights are simple to make and blend beautifully with decks.

1 **Pare down the post top.** Draw a horizontal line around all four sides of the post 1½ inches from its top. Set the circular saw for a ¾-inch-deep cut and cut a kerf, following the layout line around the post. Cut a series of closely spaced horizontal kerfs above the first kerf. Then use a chisel to remove the waste and square up this 1½-inch-high, 2-inch-square section.

2 **Install the fixture.** Set the circular saw for a ¼-inch-deep cut and make two passes to create a ¼-inch-wide wiring channel down one side of the post. Install the fixture on the post and run the wire down the channel.

3 **Cut and groove the sides.** From 1 × 6 stock, cut two pieces 10½ inches long and 3½ inches wide. Using a miter box or table saw, make 45-degree angle cuts to form a peak on one end of each side piece.

Each side gets two grooves to hold the acrylic panels. To make the grooves, adjust the blade height on your table saw to ¼-inch. Set the rip fence 3⅛ inches from the blade. One pass on each side will make a groove wide enough to hold the panels.

4 **Install the sides.** Screw each side to the small square at the top of the post, using a single 1½-inch galvanized buglehead screw. When attaching the sides, make sure that side edges are in line with post edges and parallel with each other.

5 **Cut and install the acrylic panels.** On the table saw, cut the panels to 2⅜ × 8¾-inch size. Slide them into their grooves. You may have to back off one of the screws to get the panels in.

6 **Cut and assemble the top.** Cut a piece of 1 × 6 to about 8 inches long and rip it to 5 inches wide. Then cut it into a 4-inch-long piece and a 3¼-inch-long piece. Assemble the top with three 4d galvanized finishing nails through the face of the long piece into the edge of the short piece. Center the top on the sides and nail it to the sides with 4d galvanized finishing nails.

SOURCES

BORATE-TREATED WOOD

U.S. Borax and Chemical Corp.
P.O. Box 75128
Los Angeles, CA 90010-1294
(213) 251-5400

BUILDING CODES

Boca Basic Building Code
Building Officials and Code
Administrators International, Inc.
4051 W. Flossmoor Rd.
Country Club Hills, IL 60478
(708) 799-2300

Cabo One- and Two-Family Dwelling Code
Council of American Building
Officials
5203 Leesburg Pike
Suite 708
Falls Church, VA 22041
(703) 931-4533

Southern Building Code (SBC)
Southern Building Code
Congress International
900 Montclair Rd.
Birmingham, AL 35213
(205) 591-1853

Uniform Building Code (UBC)
International Conference of
Building Officials
5360 S. Workman Mill Rd.
Whittier, CA 90601
(213) 699-0541

EXOTIC WOOD FOR DECKS

BRE Lumber
10741 Carter Rd.
Traverse City, MI 49684
(616) 946-0043

Exotic Decks, Inc.
5005 Veterans Memorial Hwy.
Holbrook, NY 11741
(516) 563-4000

FINISHES (INCLUDING SEALERS, STAINS, AND CLEANING AND BLEACHING SOLUTIONS)

Akzo Coatings, Inc.
1845 Maxwell St.
Troy, MI 48084
1-800-833-7288
Offers Sikkens wood finishes.

Chapman Chemical Co.
416 E. Brooks Rd.
P.O. Box 9158
Memphis, TN 38109
(901) 396-5151

The Darworth Co.
50 Tower Ln.
Avon, CT 06001
1-800-624-7767
Offers the product Cuprinol.

Duckback Products Co., Inc.
P.O. Box 1038
Chico, CA 95927
(916) 343-3261

Hickson Corp.
Perimeter Rd., 400 Center
1100 Johnson Ferry Rd. NE
Atlanta, GA 30342
(404) 843-2227
Offers Wolman deck stains.

Penofin Performance Coatings, Inc.
P.O. Box 1569
Ukiah, CA 95482
(707) 462-3023 (in CA)
1-800-468-8820

FRAMING CONNECTORS

Collier Industries
P.O. Box 203
Colliers, WV 26035
(304) 748-1600 (in WV)
1-800-438-8326

Simpson Strong-Tie Co., Inc.
1450 Doolittle Dr.
P.O. Box 1568
San Leandro, CA 94577
(415) 562-7775

United Steel Products Co.
703 Rogers Dr.
Box 80
Montgomery, MN 56069
(612) 364-7333 (in MN)
1-800-328-5934
FAX (612) 364-8762
Offers the product Kant-Sag.

LATTICE AND LATTICE MOLDING

Cross Industries
3174 Marjan Dr.
Atlanta, GA 30340
(404) 451-4531
Offers PVC lattice.

OUTDOOR LIGHTING EQUIPMENT

American Lighting Association
435 N. Michigan, Suite 1717
Chicago, IL 60611
(312) 644-0828

Craftlite-Hadco
100 Craftway
P.O. Box 128
Littlestown, PA 17340
(717) 359-7131

Intermatic, Inc.
Intermatic Plaza
Spring Grove, IL 60081
(815) 675-2321

Lightolier
100 Lighting Way
Secaucus, NJ 07096
(201) 864-3000

Nightscaping Loran, Inc.
1705 E. Colton Ave.
Redlands, CA 92373
1-800-544-4840

TerraDek Light Systems
(Division of Minnfac, Inc.)
5155 East River Rd., Suite 414
Minneapolis, MN 55421
1-800-456-1800
FAX (612) 571-4927

TORO Home Improvement Division
5300 Shoreline Blvd.
Mound, MN 55364-1630
(612) 472-8300

REDWOOD

California Redwood Association
405 Enfrente Dr.
Suite 200
Novato, CA 94949
(415) 382-0662

STAINLESS STEEL NAILS AND SCREWS

Manasquan Premium Fasteners
P.O. Box 669
Allenwood, NJ 08720-0669
(201) 528-6809

Swan Secure Products, Inc.
1701 Parkman Ave.
Baltimore, MD 21230
(301) 646-2800

TRANSITS AND OPTICAL LEVELS

David White
11711 River Ln.
P.O. Box 1007
Germantown, WI 53022
(414) 251-8100

TREATED WOOD

Osmose Wood Preserving, Inc.
P.O. Drawer O
Griffin, GA 30224
1-800-522-9663

Southern Forest Products Association
P.O. Box 52468
New Orleans, LA 70152
(504) 443-4464

TURNED RAILINGS, POSTS, AND BALUSTERS

Bruce Post Co., Inc.
P.O. Box 332
Chestertown, MD 21620
(301) 778-6181

Gerber Industries
1 Gerber Industrial Dr.
P.O. Box 600
St. Peters, MO 63376-0600
(314) 278-5710

Pacific Coast Wire Rope
and Fittings, Inc.
2603 Union St.
Oakland, CA 94607
1-800-888-2418
Offers stainless steel cable for cable
railings.

Weyerhauser Co.
CH1C28
Tacoma, WA 98477
(206) 924-2345

WATER LEVELS

Versa-level
Price Brothers Tool Co.
P.O. Box 1133
Novato, CA 94948-1133
(415) 897-3153

INDEX

Page references in *italic* indicate illustrations.